Stage Directing

A Director's Itinerary

To my partner, Kamon,
and my talented, dedicated colleagues at SCAD

Stage Directing
A Director's Itinerary

By Michael Wainstein

Focus Publishing
Newburyport

Stage Directing A Director's Itinerary
© 2012 Michael Wainstein

Focus Publishing/R. Pullins Company
PO Box 369
Newburyport, MA 01950
www.pullins.com

ISBN 13: 978-1-58510-395-9

Printed in the United States of America.

10 9 8 7 6 5 4 3 2 1

0212V

Table of Contents

Acknowledgments and Photo Credits

We wish to thank Laurence Ballard, Sharon Ott, Dawn Testa, The Savannah College of Art and Design, Dean Peter Weishar, my two brilliant teachers Mira Felner and Michael Hankins whose inspiration has lasted a lifetime, Vivian Majkowski, Kathryn Brown, my family, and every actor, designer and playwright I've ever worked with and from whom I have learned so much.

We would also like to acknowledge and thank those whose work is featured in the photographs throughout this book. We are especially grateful for the cooperation and generosity of Robin Stone and Kelsey Emry of Roger Williams University, who provided us with photographs throughout the entire process of their production of *The Glass Menagerie*. Listed below are the photographs in the order in which they appear. They include some or all of the following: the title and author of the production, individuals whose work is featured, the theatre, location, date of performance, and the photographer.

p. 1　　Director's preparation for *The Glass Menagerie* (Williams); director, Robin Stone. Roger Williams University, Bristol, Rhode Island: 2011. Photograph by Kelsey Emry.

p. 49　　*Hair* (Rado, Ragni, and MacDermot); director, Michael Wainstein; scenic design, Schuyler Burk; costume design, Dawn Testa; lighting design, Colin Scott, Savannah College of Art and Design, Lucas Theatre, Savannah, GA: 2011. Photograph by John McKinnon.

p. 55　　Auditions for *The Glass Menagerie* (Williams); Rebecca Murphy auditioning for Amanda; director, Robin Stone. Roger Williams University, Bristol, Rhode Island: 2011. Photograph by Kelsey Emry.

p. 70　　*Once Upon a Mattress* (Rogers and Barer); Shawna Hamic as Winifred; director, Michael Wainstein; scenic design, Jason Bolen; costume design, Susie Rettig. Naples Dinner Theatre: 2005.

p. 85　　Rehearsals for *The Glass Menagerie* (Williams); Karson Baird reading for Tom; Natalie Brough reading for Laura; director, Robin Stone. Roger Williams University, Bristol, Rhode Island: 2011. Photograph by Kelsey Emry.

p. 119　　*Fahrenheit 451* (Bradbury); featuring David Bonham, D'Antwuan Roper, Daniel Molina, and B. Todd Johnson; director, Sharon Ott; scenic design, Hal Tine; lighting design, Ruth Hutson; costume design, Dawn Testa. The Savannah College of Art and Design, Savannah, Georgia: 2010. Photograph by John McKinnon.

Preface

In this book, I have endeavored to create a step-by-step guide for the student director. There are already many books that offer an experienced director's point of view on the art of dramatic interpretation or the craft of working with actors. Although these perspectives can be valuable, they are secondary. For what use is a groundbreaking dramatic interpretation if a faulty rehearsal schedule, poor casting notice, or mismanaged budget sinks the production before the curtains even open?

Everything a director needs to know about successfully navigating these practical concerns is provided in this book. Because of the great responsibility that comes with being a director—from upholding the playwright's work, to ensuring the actors deliver convincing performances, to satisfying an audience and guaranteeing a profitable production—being detailed and organized are essential. For this reason, keeping a Director's Production Notebook (DPN) is important for the student director. It allows the director to organize his or her notes, budgets, analysis, research, schedules, designs, cast information, blocking, etc. in one easy-to-reference place.

Throughout *Stage Directing: A Director's Itinerary*, you will find sample worksheets and schedules, director's checklists, examples, and references that lead you through the practical concerns of directing. At the end of chapters, the *In Your DPN* sections will help you organize your own director's production notebook. Tried-and-true exercises for both the classroom and the rehearsal room are provided throughout the text. For student directors, directing terms located in the glossary at the back of the book appear in bold face when first used in the text. Finally, perspectives from experienced directors, which build on the student director's foundational knowledge, are provided in the sections *From Experience* and *Suggested Reading*.

Mastering the practical side of directing is intrinsic to unlocking the creative potential of this craft. I often think of the director as a captain of a ship, staffed by a crew of diverse artists and artisans with varying temperaments, guided by the playwright's map. When one masters the project of organizing the crew, rationing the provisions, and reading the map, just think of the places one can sail, the new places one can discover, the mystery of what lies beyond the horizon!

After twenty-seven years as a director, I am no less in awe of those mysteries than I was when I began my first rehearsal of Edward Albee's *The Death of Bessie Smith* in 1984. Faced with the intensity of the story, and the intricacy of Albee's tight one-act script, I had little idea how to begin. But there was something in the story that touched me. What drove me to stage that show is what drives the directorial process; the desire to journey into that unknown, and come back with a story to tell.

This is the book I wish I'd had back then to direct the Albee play. Because as daunting as those mysteries may seem at times, there are clear steps every director must take in order to ensure that the mystery, the moments of clarity, the inspiration, all lead to a satisfying and artistically sound final product. This book provides those clear steps, for both musicals and non-musicals, with specific directions, rehearsal exercises, problem-solving techniques, and strategies for communicating with designers and actors, that will allow you to imagine and then create a theatrical masterwork.

This book offers, in chronological order, an itinerary to follow that takes the director from first inspiration to opening night. Part I explores the history of the director and addresses the process of reading and selecting a play or musical. It includes play analysis, concept development, and budgeting. Bringing the written word to the three-dimensional stage is the subject of Part II, which includes design and casting. Part III deals with staging rehearsals, and it includes scheduling, table work, and blocking. Part IV explores rehearsal in the context of musical theatre. Finally, Parts V and VI guide the director through rehearsals to opening night.

Nearly two hundred productions later, I still find myself wrestling with this ever-mysterious art. Yet I have found that by faithfully adhering to the process detailed in this book, the director can successfully see the ship to the completion of its journey. Along the way, you will experience the mystery, the joy, and the challenge of creating a work of art. This book will be the sound structure that you will use as you direct, and that you can come back to when you encounter challenges.

As I have found, a director is constantly discovering and refining his or her own process. Follow my itinerary, but discover your own way. Good luck.

PART I: FIRST THINGS FIRST

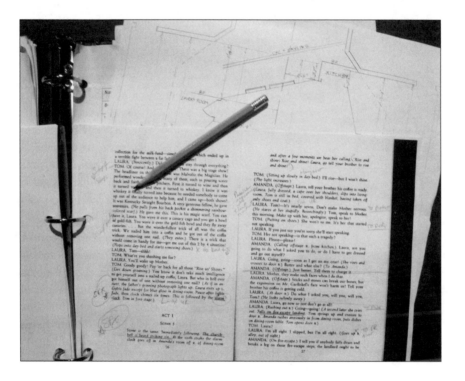

Chapter 1
The Director:
Past and Present

What Is a Director?

The director is the leader in the process of creating a production of a play. A director is both chief and arbiter of all aspects of the creative process and is ultimately responsible for its success or failure. When a play is great, a critic often praises the actors and designers; but when it's a flop, fingers always point at the director.

The Evolution of the Modern Stage Director

The stage director appeared as part of the creative process only recently in theatre history. For thousands of years, throughout the Greek and Roman periods, playwrights staged their own works, often appearing in them as well; a tricky task even for the most seasoned of directors. The acting style was very stylized and young actors learned as apprentices. A member of the chorus organized the movement, but the writer was ultimately responsible for the visual appearance of the play. A wealthy "benefactor," such as a government official or wealthy patron, would fund the productions.

The formal process of directing began evolving with medieval religious plays. Huge productions that involved large crowds, processions, and pageantry required someone to take control and organize the movement. This person oversaw the building of the large scenic elements, the casting of local performers, and the organizing of rehearsals, and also served as the public face of the event.

The idea of a "theatre professional" is relatively new as well. Until the late nineteenth century, actors and writers were either avocational, only earning a small stipend for their work, or members of a company that shared in the box office revenues, barely earning a living. Actors were not thought well of, and no parent wanted their child to pursue the lowly profession.

With the rise of the actor/manager in the mid-eighteenth century, the role of the modern director began to take shape. This experienced member of the acting troupe assumed the duties of casting, season selection, and artistic direction. The most famous of these was David Garrick.

Garrick, who managed the Theatre Royal Drury Lane in London from 1747 to 1776, introduced a variety of innovations that included adding importance to production design and introducing a realistic acting style. Although he was referred to as a producer, his control over each production was similar to that of a modern director. His interest in realism required actors to spend a great deal of time rehearsing in order to realize the deep emotional life that Garrick expected.

In the mid-nineteenth century, the great actor W. C. Macready put more emphasis on rehearsal and pointed the way towards realism with his acting style and artistic approach. Yet it was not until George II, Duke of Saxe Meiningen, founded his company in Germany in 1874 that the first "modern" direction was established. The director of the company, Ludwig Chronegk, developed a style of ensemble playing that influenced the future development of theatrical production and paved the way for Constantin Stanislavsky.

Stanislavsky took ensemble acting to a new level, creating a performance style in which actors totally immersed themselves in their characters. He often spent months and sometimes years developing and rehearsing shows, perfecting his acting technique and directing style. This style, along with both the belief that the character "lived" and a departure from overtly oratorical performance, planted the seeds of modern realism.

No sooner did realism become the primary acting style than anti-realism emerged. Some directors saw that realism was not essential to telling dramatic stories and that non-realistic interpretations could be more powerful. Because the scenic elements of anti-realistic theatre were central to the vision, the director became deeply involved with the conceptualization of the designs.

Throughout the early part of the twentieth century, directors like Elia Kazan, Harold Clurman, and Tyrone Guthrie further refined the role of the director through their work on landmark productions with theatre companies like the Guthrie and Group Theatres. The director's role as leader of the collaborative process of play production took on the modern characteristics we recognize today.

During the late 1950s and 1960s, the avant-garde theatre movement led by such visionary directors as Peter Brook in France and Julian Beck of Living Theatre in New York gave the director absolute autonomy from rules and theatrical standards. Directors became able to partner with playwrights in making strong theatrical statements in unique and often surprising ways.

A director starts with the playwright's words, and those words are the seed from which all theatre blooms. Yet, lest one understate the effect of the director, remember that the director has the power to mold a playwright's words in accordance with his or her own personal vision. In the last 125 years, the role of the director has evolved into one of central importance. Today, the playwright and director are partners, and this partnership of words and vision is the central force behind play production

What Does a Director Do?

The director's primary purpose is to serve the playwright by creating a production of the play that conveys its main ideas in a stimulating, exciting, and dramatic way. The following is a brief list of the primary tasks of the director in the process of play production.

Interpreting the Script Through analysis and research, the director conceives the production, transferring the work from page to stage.

During analysis a director considers:

- Playwright's intentions
- Main action or super-objective
- Dramatic action
- Structure
- Functions of and conflicts between main characters
- Overall tone and atmosphere
- Period
- Style of acting
- Language
- Technical requirements

Generating the "Concept" The director first identifies ideas in the play, and then decides on a defining idea (the concept) that will guide all decisions thereafter. Sometimes called the "master metaphor" or "directorial concept," this idea becomes the central factor influencing the work of the director and artistic team. This concept influences decisions about visual images, playing style, atmosphere, and every aspect of how the story is told.

Generating the concept is a critical step, because once the director sets sail in a sea of compromise and collaboration, the initial vision can become confused and distorted if it is not closely adhered to by the director. Therefore, the concept must be clear, grounded in the playwright's words, and understood and agreed to by the artistic team.

Collaborating with Designers Once the concept is defined, the director and designers begin their collaboration, creating the visual world of the play. This intricate process involves many meetings, or in today's world, many emails with attachments. From initial meeting to final design presentation, the director must stay true to his or her vision while collaborating in an open way with the design team. The final outcomes of these meetings are decisions synthesized from the input of all artists involved.

Casting Actors Through the process of auditions, the director selects the cast of a show. Casting can make or break a production. Successful directors hire the right actors. The director determines the casting needs, the character's qualities, both internal and external, then, through auditions, finds the best actors possible to fill those roles.

Rehearsal: Table Work and Blocking Rehearsal is a process of collaboration with actors to create the vocal, physical, emotional, and psychological interpretation of the play. Depending on the situation, this process can last for a few days to a few months. In rehearsal, the director "directs" two components: the development of each character's psychology and the blocking (also called staging) of the actors' physical movements.

Unifying the Production Throughout the process of creating a show, all artists involved make compromises. With so many collaborators, keeping the ensemble unified is a director's responsibility. Staying true to the defined "directorial concept" keeps the group moving in the same direction. The director has to look at both the minutia and the larger picture while remaining open to different points of view in the unified march to the finish.

Cheerleading It is important that the director encourage members of the artistic team to stay focused and on track. Putting on a play can be difficult, even painful at times. It is surely not for the faint of heart! Sometimes directing means cheering up a disheartened designer whose budget gets cut, or an actor struggling to find their character, or an utterly exhausted stage manager. Once the show opens, the pain is usually forgotten. The director keeps an eye on the prize and makes sure that everyone on the team moves forward despite the occasional desire to give up and go home. Understanding how to motivate each individual is an important tool to develop as a director.

Ultimate Decision-Making The buck stops with the director. The director is responsible for everything! Therefore, the director must be willing to make the tough decisions necessary to ensure a product as close to the original conception as possible.

Skills Required

Ability to Communicate Clearly A good director communicates complex ideas in a simple and clear way. The theatre is full of drama—and not all of it is onstage. With so many "artistic" personalities working closely in a tension-filled environment, clarity is essential. Nothing is worse than a designer who is left out of the loop when a major change happens in the blocking, or if an actor doesn't understand what the director expects. Without clear communication, a director may fail to realize his or her vision.

Understanding Diverse Artistic Personalities The artistic team and cast are composed of unique individuals who will likely approach their work in various ways. Some may be divas, some intense and uncommunicative, some flamboyant, and some quiet and reserved. Understanding each relationship requires patience and sensitivity. Although it may be easy for directors to get caught up in the offstage drama, they must remain above it.

Strong Knowledge of Acting and Design Processes In order to speak intelligently, a director should understand the processes of acting and design. Without at least a simple understanding of the design process, a director can't possibly get the best results from their design team. Likewise, in order to direct actors, the director must speak the language of actors. This will enable a fluent and effective relationship. Speaking the language of each individual artist provides a sense of security and comfort.

Ability to Make Decisions Directors can't afford to be indecisive, but at the same time, they must listen and consider all angles before making decisions. Total harmony is not an unachievable ideal; with so many artists working together, there are always divergent options. When making a decision, the director should always consider what is in the best interest of the production.

Imagination Without an active and unbridled imagination, a director is little more than a traffic cop. Remember, a director's job is to transform a play from a two-dimensional page to three-dimensional stage. Reading the play, envisioning its stage life, and ultimately realizing that vision requires courage, passion and imagination.

Experience By living a rich and full life, a director is able to utilize all the benefits such experience affords. If someone wishes a career as a director, then in the words of Auntie Mame: "Live!" Seek out as many experiences as possible, and learning from these experiences will create a treasure trove which the director can draw upon.

Energy It takes a lot of energy to direct a play. The work is never done, the product can always be better, and the compromises constantly threaten your sense of well-being and impending success. A director must have drive and an insatiable desire to do the best work possible.

Goal and Process-Oriented Personality Directing is a marriage of process and product. The process of creating the play can be thrilling and consuming, but the director must also never lose sight of the ultimate goal. It is this ability to marry process and product that makes a great director.

Additional Skills

- Good organizational skills (if you lack that, a good stage manager can cover for you)
- Strong dramaturgical skills
- Sense of history
- Ease with authority
- Comfortable being a leader

Final Thoughts

There is nothing more exciting than directing a play. The collaborative atmosphere, in which talented artists all work together towards the same goal, is unique to this profession. To be a great director, you have to be egotistical while being sensitive, firm while being flexible. You have to know everything and be willing to admit you know very little. You have to love the process. But above all, you must respect the playwright's work.

Student Exercise 1.1

What kind of director do you want to be? What skills do you possess that will make you a strong director? What motivates you to want to direct? What kind of theatre excites you?

Read *Directors on Directing*. Which of the directors interviewed sounds like the kind of director you'd like to be? Write a short journal paper, identifying what attracts you to the director and why.

Hold onto this paper. Re-evaluate the answer as you go through your career, noting how your reactions change.

Suggested Reading

Cole, Toby and Helen K. Chinoy. *Directors on Directing: A Source Book of the Modern Theatre*. New York: Macmillan Publishing, 1963.

Chapter 2
Choosing a Play and Securing a Performance License

A director's first steps are choosing and securing the rights to perform a play. Applying for a performance license is often handled by a production manager, but understanding the process is important when you produce your own projects.

What Play Will I Direct?

If you have been hired for a specific project, you will not choose the play. However, in many circumstances, especially in a college or community theatre setting, the director will drive the specific project and therefore choose the play to direct. A director must consider talent available, budget, audience tastes, suitability, stage configuration, rehearsal time available, and personal taste.

Considerations when Choosing a Play

Personal Taste Directors are sometimes hired to direct plays they don't particularly care for, driven by the need to put food on the table and pay bills. However, when directors have the luxury of choosing a piece, they ought to choose one for which they have a passion.

If you are interested in period pieces, read several before making a decision. If you there is a play you have wanted to direct for some time, suggest it, but only after making sure the following issues are taken into consideration.

Available Talent A director must consider the availability of talent when selecting a play. For example, if requested to submit a musical theatre project for a community theatre that has primarily women in its talent pool, *1776*, which has twenty-seven men and two women in the cast, would be a bad choice. The director can't depend on a miracle that will draw dozens of men to audition that have the requisite talent. Claire Booth Luce's *The Women* might be a better choice, or Robert Harling's *Steel Magnolias*.

The second consideration is the skill level of the talent available. If you are directing first-year college students, a restoration comedy might be a disaster. On the other hand, restoration might be the perfect challenge for third- or fourth-year students who have had style classes. If the community theatre doesn't have any musical talent, pick a non-musical. Shape your project around the talent pool, not the other way around.

Budget Even though a limited budget shouldn't rule out any project, it must be taken into consideration. Many directors do lavish musicals on a shoestring, but it depends on the "length" of that shoestring. If you have $50, you can't do *Guys and Dolls*. The royalties alone will break the bank. But if you have $2500 and a small house, a creative design team, and actors that work for free, you might be able to do a scaled-down version of a big musical. (See the royalty section later in this chapter for guidance on considering costs.)

Low budgets force directors to be creative. This can be a good thing. Most off-off Broadway directors work with next to nothing, yet have created masterpieces. Find clever solutions if you want to do a large project, but be realistic.

Audience and Suitability Don't do *Waiting for Godot* in a summer stock theatre used to musicals! You must consider your audience. Even in a college environment where the production's fiscal success is not as important as its artistic success, you want people to see your project. If the theatre is driven by ticket sales, choose a show that will attract an audience. If avant-garde theatre is supported, then be adventurous. Push the envelope, but know that the audience will follow you only so far.

Stage Configuration Ninety-nine percent of available plays and musicals can be done in any configuration. However, you might not want to do certain plays in the round or three-quarter. As you select the play, imagine the piece on the stage of the theatre. Ask yourself if this is a play you really want to direct in the available configuration.

Rehearsal Time If you don't have a lot of time to rehearse the show, consider the skill level of your actors. If they are inexperienced, don't pick a complex show. Pick a show you can do well given the allotted time and the available actors. Challenge yourself and your actors, but be realistic.

Making It Legal

Because plays are protected under copyright law, regardless of where you plan to perform a play, unless it is part of the **public domain**, *you must obtain a license to* *produce the play or musical.* In most cases, you must also pay a fee if it is a **public performance**.

> **Public domain:** plays are protected by copyrights, which usually have a legal life of 50–100 years. Once the copyright has expired, the rights pass into the public domain, allowing anyone to produce the works without paying a royalty.
>
> **Public performance:** a play is considered public when it is performed "at a place open to the public or at any place where a substantial number of persons outside of a normal circle of a family and its social acquaintances is gathered."[1]

Most plays written prior to the early twentieth century are in the public domain and do not require licenses to perform (e.g. Shakespeare, Restoration, Greek and Roman). However, if a play has been translated from another language, the translation might be copyright-protected. For example, Richard Wilber's wonderful translations of Moliere require licenses to perform.

The rights to produce plays and musicals are held by various publishing houses. The largest are Samuel French and Dramatists Play Service for plays, and Music Theatre International, Rodgers and Hammerstein Musical Library, Tams Witmark and Samuel French for musicals.

Finding the publisher of a play or musical is your first step to securing rights. A great website to begin your search is Stage Agent. To find a play's publisher, follow these steps:

1. Go to the Stage Agent website. (www.stageagent.com)
2. Scroll down to the middle of the main page, to "Stage Agent Resources."
3. Type in the name of the play.
4. Select the play from the drop down list.
5. Go to the play's page.
6. See the name next to "Licensing."
7. Follow the link or search the name on Google to open the publisher's site.
8. Find the play on the publisher's site and proceed from there.

Unfortunately, Stage Agent does not list the agent for every play or musical. If you can't find the publisher on Stage Agent, search individual publishers' websites (starting with large companies listed below). The publishers listed at the end of this chapter hold the rights for almost every play and musical.

Applying for a License

Although most publishers require the same information, read each application

---

1   Crooks, W. Edward. "When do I need a license to play music and where do I get it?" Hahn, Loesser, and Parks, LLC, accessed August 1, 2011. http://www.hahnloeser.com/references/705.pdf

carefully because there may be differences. If you are selling tickets, the publisher will calculate the cost of the license based on the anticipated gross income. In addition, they will add a fee for music rental or script purchase. (An exception is Tams Witmark, whose initial costs are higher in lieu of a rental fee). Generally, the publisher makes its money on the score rental and script sales, passing on most of the income to the creators as royalty payments. This makes musicals more expensive because the book writer, lyricist, composer, and orchestrator all get a cut.

Most applications require the following information:

- Details and contact information of the producing company
- Primary contact name and phone
- Theatre name and address (where the play will be produced)
- Website address of producing company
- Performance dates
- Number of total performances
- Number of seats in theatre
- Ticket prices (and breakdown of anticipated sales by price category)
- Previous productions produced by company or school
- Designation as professional or amateur production (most sites have separate applications for each with different fee schedules).

Keep in mind the following when applying:

Apply in Advance There are many considerations when applying for the rights to present a show. If the show is touring or still on Broadway, you might be denied the rights. By applying in advance, you will have the option to choose another title if the one you want is restricted. If there are several companies in your area and you want a popular title, chances are you are not the only company seeking a license. If you want to be assured the exclusive right to perform the play in your area, call the publisher and ask how you can lock in the rights to a title. Some publishers allow you to do that for a fee.

Stipulate Range of Prices Because you might be charging different prices per show (e.g., matinees may be cheaper than evening shows) and per customer (e.g., student and senior discounts, group discounts), make sure to find a way to indicate the range of prices and projected percentage of sales at each price point. Include complimentary tickets, or "comps." This will save you money.

Make Sure the Right Person Signs the Contract If you are presenting a play at a school, there might be a person who is officially responsible for financial commitments such as royalty contracts. The person who signs is responsible for the payment of the royalties.

Read and Understand the Contract It is very important to read the entire contract and understand everything stated in that contract. It is a legal, binding document and you must adhere to all stipulations therein. If you are not legally-minded, find someone who is. Don't sign something you don't fully comprehend. If anything confuses you, call the publisher and ask them for clarification. Check dates, prices, all charges, and other details to insure accuracy.

Pay Attention to Cancellation Clauses Since you are applying well in advance, you want to know the conditions for cancellation should your plans change. But more importantly, ask the publisher under what conditions could they revoke your license and what notice are they required to give you. Cancellation goes both ways.

Don't Accept the First Fee Schedule if You Think it's Unfair When you receive your quote, if you feel it is unfair, you can contact the publisher and work with them to reduce the rate. A rule of thumb is to expect to pay 10–13% of the gross potential income for musicals, and less for plays. Generally, amateur productions of plays will have very low royalty rates, but percentages don't vary between amateur and professional productions of musicals.

Don't Claim Your Production is Professional Unless You Have To A professional production is one that employs union actors or paid actors. Generally, royalties for amateur productions of non-musicals will be far less than for professional productions. If you can get away with being an "amateur" production, do it. Educational and community theatre productions are considered "amateur" productions.

Negotiate Deposits In the case of musicals, scores are usually sent one to two months before the production opens, and not until the initial deposit is paid. Depending on the publisher, you might have to pay a small deposit or as much as full royalties (in the case of Tams-Whitmark Music Library) before receiving scripts or the play's opening. You can negotiate these terms as well, especially if you have a relationship with individual publishers. In the case of plays, you will buy the scripts from the publisher and royalties will be due sometime on or before opening night.

Weekly Statements and Payments Some publishers base royalties on a percentage of actual sales. These companies require weekly box office reports to be sent along with royalty payment due (in excess of deposit already paid). It is your responsibility to generate these reports and make the payments within a week or so. Report numbers honestly!

Handle Rented Materials Carefully If you rent materials, you will be required to pay a refundable deposit. If materials are not returned, or returned in bad condition, you may lose your deposit and/or be charged. Make sure the stage manager carefully monitors the rented materials so you don't get stuck with a big bill at the end. If the scripts have been purchased, you can give them to the actors; there is no need to return the scripts to the publisher. The producer can decide if the actors can keep their own scripts after the show closes.

Shipping The publisher will charge you for shipping the materials to you, and you will have to pay for the return shipping. Return the materials on time. Often there is a charge for late return.

Licenses Can be Denied If a national tour of a show is coming within a certain mileage radius of your performance venue, or if another theatre already has secured rights to a title, or if the show is not available because the Broadway production is still running, you might be denied the license. If this happens, you can call the publisher and ask for an explanation. Sometimes, if you pursue a title, the publisher can pull strings for you. In the case of a national tour a region might be blocked, but one call to the producer could free up the license for your company. Most new shows are not available until all national tours and regional productions are concluded. If a show is a huge hit, it can be blocked for years as in the case of *Les Miserables*. Most publishers have services that will inform you when rights become available. Sign up for the notification if you want to do the show in the future.

Theatrical Publishing Houses

The website Findaplay.com (http://www.playscripts.com/findaplay/) is a quick way to find a publisher of any play. Enter the play's title and then a quick search tool brings up the play and publisher with a link to the publisher's website.

Figure 2.1 and Figure 2.2 contain lists of publishers and their current websites. Website addresses can change—a Google search will lead you to the publisher's current web address.

Publishing House	Description	Website
R&H Theatricals	Primary Agents for the works of Rogers and Hammerstein. Catalogue includes Irving Berling, Elvis Presley, Andrew Lloyd Webber, T.S. Eliot, Sheldon Harnick, Adam Guettel, Jimmy Roberts, Joe DiPietro, et al.	http://www.rnh.com/show_home.asp Licensing: http://www.rnh.com/show_license_1.asp
Music Theatre International (MTI)	Primary agents for Sondheim, Bernstein, Jonathan Larson, Bock and Harnick, several Disney stage properties, and recent hits like *Avenue Q, Les Mis, Rent*, et al.	http://www.mtishows.com/ Licensing link: http://www.mtishows.com/content.asp?id=3_1_0
Tams-Witmark Music Library, Inc	Handles golden age and classic musical theatre properties, such as *Kiss Me, Kate* and *Hello, Dolly*, as well as all of the *Nunsense* spinoffs (but not the original *Nunsense*, which is handled by French).	http://www.tams-witmark.com/musical.html Licensing link: http://www.tams-witmark.com/contact.html
Samuel French, Inc	While the bulk of their properties are plays, they handle many well-known and obscure musicals, including *Chicago* and *La Cage Aux Folles*. Unlike the other publishers, most musical scripts are available for purchase and rental.	http://www.samuelfrench.com/store/index.php Licensing Information: http://www.samuelfrench.com/store/royalties.php
The Really Useful Group	Handles musicals penned by Andrew Lloyd Webber.	http://www.reallyuseful.com/shows Licensing Information: http://www.reallyuseful.com/licensing
Baker's Plays	Catalogue includes plays and musicals, obscure titles, children's titles.	http://www.bakersplays.com/store/index.php/cPath/10 Licensing link: http://www.bakersplays.com/store/royalties.php?osCsid=056a89c43c077ce33b78a335482ff9d3
Dramatist's Play Service	Handles plays and musicals including several lesser-known and popular off-Broadway shows such as *Bat Boy, Hedwig, Jacques Brel*, and *Hello, Again*, et al.	http://www.dramaticpublishing.com/index.html Licensing link: http://www.dramatists.com/text/npalinks.html
Dramatic Publishing Company	Catalogue includes plays and musicals.	http://www.dramaticpublishing.com/ licensing link: http://www.dramaticpublishing.com/licensing.php

Figure 2.1
Contact information of large publishing houses that hold rights to most musicals and plays

Publishing House	Description	Website
Pioneer Drama Service	Plays and over 130 lesser-known inexpensive musicals.	http://www.pioneerdrama.com/ Licensing Information: http://www.pioneerdrama.com/ContactUs.asp?ID=1
Broadway Play Publishing	Full-length American contemporary plays and the agent for Tony Kushner's *Angels in America*.	http://www.broadwayplaypubl.com/ Licensing Information: http://www.broadwayplaypubl.com/licensing.htm
Steele Springs	Specializes in small cast jukebox musicals.	http://www.steelespring.com/ (also for licensing)
Ted Swindley Productions	Handles *Always, Patsy Cline* and a few other titles.	http://www.tedswindleyproductions.com/

Figure 2.2
Smaller, specialty houses

Student Exercise 2.1

1. Choose a play you'd like to direct.
2. Find the publisher of the play.
3. Gather the information required to fill out the application.
4. Fill out an application online (don't send it).
5. Print out the application.

Try this for a few different titles.

Chapter 3
Budgeting

Understanding a Budget

In most large theatre companies, the production manager handles budgeting. However, when directors produce their own shows, they create their own budgets. Large or small, the principals are the same. List the potential income, calculate the expected expenses, and hope the bottom line is black and not red.

Income and Expenses

When creating a budget of any size, the expenses can't be more than projected income. Otherwise fundraising is required to make up the deficit. Most non-profit theatres do extensive fundraising because ticket sales only partially cover operating expenses.

To determine the production's chances of making money, calculate the **breakeven number**.

> **Breakeven number:** the percentage of the gross potential revenue needed to cover expenses.

For example, if your potential revenue is $1000 and your budget is $200, then your breakeven number is 20%. That means you have to sell 20% of your potential seats to break even financially. The lower the breakeven point, the better chance the production has of making money.

Income	Estimated	Actual
Ticket Sales		
___number of seats @ $___		
___number of seats @ $___		
___number of seats @ $___		
___number of comps		
Subtotal Ticket Revenue		
Donations		
Advertising Sales		
Total Income		
Expenses		
Materials		
Scenic materials		
Props		
Furniture Rental		
Costume materials, rentals, purchases		
Make-up and hair costs		
Lighting equipment rental		
Lighting soft-goods purchase like gobos, gels		
Sound equipment rental		
Subtotal Materials		
Advertising		
Printed materials costs (posters, fliers)		
Agency fees for preparing materials		
Subtotal Advertising		
Other		
Musicians		
Truck rental to transport materials		
Opening night party		
Script purchases		
Rights/royalty fee		
Music rental fee and shipping costs		
Subtotal Other		
Total Expenses		
Total Income		
Breakeven %		

Into the Woods
2000 Seat Theatre
3 Performances
Equity and Non-Equity Cast

Income	Estimated	Actual
Ticket Sales		
2,050 seats @ $55	110,000	
2,000 seats @ $35	70,000	
2,000 seats @ $25	50,000	
150 comps	0	
Subtotal Ticket Revenue	230,000	
Donations	10,000	
Advertising Sales	2,000	
Refreshment Sales	1,000	
Total Income	**243,000**	
Expenses		
Materials		
Scenic materials	8,000	
Props	1,000	
Furniture Rental	1,000	
Costume materials, rentals, purchases	5,000	
Make-up and hair costs	2,000	
Lighting equipment rental	1,000	
Lighting soft-goods purchase like gobos, gels	500	
Sound equipment rental	5,000	
Subtotal Materials	23,500	
Advertising		
Publicity placement buys	8,000	
Printed materials costs (posters, fliers)	1,200	
Agency fees for preparing materials	1,000	
Subtotal Advertising	10,200	

Personnel		
Director fee	5,000	
Musical director fee	3,500	
Choreographer fee	2,500	
Rehearsal pianist fee (2 weeks, $500/wk)	1,000	
Orchestra (rehearsal and tech week, 8 players)	7,200	
Stage manager	2,000	
Assistant stage manager	1,000	
Deck crew (4 people)	2,000	
Cast salaries	24,000	
Costume designer fee	2,000	
Lighting designer fee	2,000	
Set designer fee	4,000	
Prop designer fee	1,000	
Make-up and Hair crew costs	2,000	
Construction costs	5,000	
Subtotal Personnel	64,200	
Other		
Truck rental to transport materials	1,400	
Travel costs if artists come from out of town	5,000	
Opening night party	500	
Script purchases	300	
Rights/royalty fee	26,000	
Music rental fee	2,000	
Accommodation costs	8,000	
Per diem for equity artists	3,200	
Audition/casting expenses	1,000	
Telephone/postage/office supplies	200	
Subtotal Other	47,600	
Total Expenses	145,500	
Total Income	243,000	
Breakeven %	59.88%	

Figure 3.1 is a sample budget worksheet that lists all the income sources and expenses that may be associated with a production. Different productions will require different expenditures. For example, a musical will require a rehearsal pianist, whereas a play will not. A professional equity production will need to pay cast salaries, but a college theatre production most likely will not. Consider all possible expenses and sources of income applicable to your production, and keep track of them on a budget worksheet like this one.

Final Thoughts

Do the research with your designers and production manager to accurately assess the projected costs of materials. Wild guesses can create big problems down the line. Try to be as accurate as possible when budgeting expenses, and be realistic when projecting income.

Always overestimate expenses and underestimate income.

Figures 3.2 & 3.3
An example of an estimated budget of a major production

Chapter 4
Reading the Play

Once you have selected a play or have been hired to direct one, reading and becoming intimately familiar with the work is the next priority. Every director has a unique way of preparing a script for rehearsal, but below is a simple plan that includes three readings of the play.

First Reading: Read for Pleasure

The director has to know the play better than anyone else. To do this, the director must carefully read and re-read the play, reacting, imagining, analyzing. Yet the director must keep in mind that the ultimate goal in directing a play is to evoke a strong reaction from the audience. What reaction does the director wish to produce? In order to answer this question, directors must allow themselves to react to the play, by engaging in an initial, unfettered reading of the play.

The first read allows for the director's personal reaction that is the seed from which all further work grows.

Directors should first read all plays, even those with which they are familiar, for pleasure. The term "for pleasure" means exactly that. Read the play without analyzing, or developing ideas and concepts; abstain from visualizing the play—just let it wash over you. Is the play moving, stirring, thought-provoking, or simply entertaining? Keep in mind this is a passive reading. Your goal is to experience it as audience members will experience it when they see your production for the first time.

When finished, put the book down, and record your initial reaction to the play in a journal. Record the following:

- What exactly did you feel when you put down the play after reading the last page?
- What did you love about the play?
- What did you dislike?
- What did it make you think about?
- Was it entertaining? Thought provoking? Emotionally charged?

- What characters could you relate with?
- What are the obvious themes of the play?
- What did you relate to personally?
- Why do you think the author wrote the play?
- Anything else that occurs to you as a result of the reading.

This one page notation can serve the director for the entire duration of the production's genesis. By noting how the play felt after the first reading, the director will always have a strong initial reaction to refer back to.

Student Exercise 4.1

1. Pick up a book of Shakespeare sonnets or poetry.
2. Randomly choose a sonnet or poem.
3. Read it for pleasure.
4. Pick up a pen and note your reactions to the poem or sonnet.
5. Repeat with a short story or magazine article.
6. Repeat with a painting.
7. Repeat with a film.
8. Repeat with a play.
9. Get attuned to being aware of your initial reaction to a work of art.

Second Reading: Read for Vision

After the initial experience with the play, read it again for **vision**.

> **Vision:** the ability to think about or plan the future with imagination or wisdom.

The primary job of the director in the early stages is to develop a concept that will guide the further development of the production. The key to forming a concept is the ability to actively envision what your personal reaction "can become."

Vision is both physical and psychological. In the second read, think in both ways. Imagine what the design elements might look like, but don't worry about specifics. Don't think logically. Ignore limitations of technical resources or budget. Freely imagine without restraint. Later you will have to compromise; for now let your imagination be limitless.

Imagine the actors speaking the words, interacting, moving. Imagine the style of their movement, the flavor of their repartee, their laughter, their tears. As you imagine the design elements, let the psychological world of the play freely come alive in your imagination.

Great ideas often come as you read, so make notes. Just don't lose the flow of the text by writing too much.

At the conclusion of the second reading, be sure to record any ideas that you found exciting, interesting, or useful. Don't forget to continue writing, as ideas will continue to flourish over the next days or weeks.

Student Exercise 4.2

Return to the sonnet or poem. Do a "second read," actively imagining visual and psychological elements. Write them down. What feelings are aroused by the poem? What visual images are conjured? *Develop your imagination.*

Third Reading: Read for Analysis

The third reading, described in detail in the following chapter, is slow and detailed with pen and paper or computer close at hand. Unlike the first and second read, forego concerns of flow; study details. Jot down information as it is revealed, noting entrance and exit requirements, props and costume needs, scenic requirements, climaxes, pace, and action points.

The third reading may take hours or even days as it is a thorough examination of the text that must leave no stone unturned. New discoveries may be made later on, but the third reading for analysis is the chance for an undistracted exploration of plot, characters, dialogue, production values, back story, and themes, etc.

This slow, painstaking, and delightful exploration must not be rushed. Otherwise, the director may overlook the "diamonds" that make a production rich. How to mine the text to uncover these precious insights is the subject of the next chapter, Interpreting the Script.

Student Exercise 4.3

Read Tennessee Williams' *The Glass Menagerie*. Note your initial reaction to the play, and proceed to the next chapter to analyze the text.

Final Thoughts

Reading the play repeatedly is important because it allows the director to discover nuance and detail that might not have been noticed in the initial readings. Furthermore, each of the three types of reading yields its own particular benefit. Whereas reading for pleasure produces the unfettered personal reaction from which the play grows, reading for vision creatively opens possibilities for design and the psychological life of characters. Finally, reading for analysis distills the details that will become critical to unleash the imagination. Remaining faithful to the spirit of the play is the director's responsibility. Reading the play ensures that level of integrity.

Suggested Reading

Giddens, Eugene. *How to Read a Shakespearean Text*. New York: Cambridge University Press, 2011.

Hayman, Ronald. *How to Read a Play*. New York: Grove Press, 1999.

Chapter 5
Interpreting the Script

The Importance of Analysis

The process of interpreting or analyzing a script might not be the most exciting aspect of directing. However, when we realize that upon deeper investigation underlying meanings may become evident, the purpose of analysis becomes clear.

Aristotle was the first to define the structure of a drama. Instead of relating the play to its author and time, Aristotle held that the investigation of six elements existing in every well-written play would furnish all the information necessary to interpret the play: plot, character, ideas, language, music, and spectacle. These six elements, described in his Poetics, have remained the foundation of script analysis for over 2,300 years.

An easy way to remember the elements: A play is about people (character), in a situation (plot), who communicate with one another (dialogue), about something (ideas), in a certain way (music/rhythm), somewhere in time and space (spectacle).

Following Aristotle, playwriting may be understood as composing these elements into a unified coherent script. Analysis, then, may be seen as breaking the script back down to these elements, if only to see how they fit back together again. In a sense, this undoing and redoing of the playwright's work is part of an important dialogue between the director and playwright. This dialogue gives the director the information needed to translate intellectual information into dramatic action.

What is dramatic action? It's the emotional movement of the play, the decisions the characters make in the face of the conflict presented by the playwright, and finally, the journey the audience is taken on by the play itself. Dramatic action takes into account how the characters react to a situation and each other, as well as their journey and transformation. The audience wants to see the characters fight adversity, learn, grow as human beings and either succeed in the case of comedy, or fail in the case of tragedy.

Be aware that some plays may not fit neatly into the analytic categories we use. Even some of Shakespeare's plays do not easily fit into the traditional categories of comedy or tragedy. Yet keep in mind the importance of analysis, because only when you know the rules can you see when they are being broken.

Directors who ignore the rules risk producing plays that are more exercises in vanity than art. Like an authority figure, the playwright's intent, as encountered through the analysis of the play, must be respected and understood, even if it is ultimately the subject of criticism.

What follows in this chapter is an easy-to-follow outline for analysis, based on Aristotle's six elements. Each element is accompanied by a sample analysis worksheet that can be used or adapted for recording analysis in the Director's Production Notebook, or DPN. See the case study in Addendum 2 for an application of this format.

I. Spectacle

Most playwrights don't include descriptions of costumes, special effects, or theater design. Nevertheless, it is important to analyze the script for any clues that may help determine how the play might "look" onstage.

Genre

Plays are grouped together according to style, theme, and subject matter. Knowing the "genre" of the play allows the director to situate it within certain expectations. A romantic comedy might, for example, involve two people, who despite being unlikely lovers, end up a happy couple. Like other romantic comedies, the style is realistic with a breezy pace, and there must be romantic chemistry between the lovers. Physical styles and manners depend on the period of the play. (See Addendum 1 for a catalogue of theatrical genres.)

Given Circumstances

Given circumstances are "everything that is true about the situation," including time, place, specific location, climate, relationships, occupations, moral and ethical codes, and anything else that exerts outside influence on the characters and creates "The World of the Play." Consider the following categories, also listed on the Spectacle Analysis Worksheet (figure 5.1), when investigating given circumstances:

Time Consider the time the play was written, the time in which it is set, and the time that passes during the play.

Place or physical environment What is the immediate location (city, state, country)? How does the physical environment influence the characters and contribute to the overall meaning of the play?

Society What are the social groups that characterize the play? What is considered moral, ethical and normal behavior? Include considerations of class structure, social status, and racial, gender, and sexual identities. Also, what role does family play in structuring relationships and constituting selfhood?

Economics How does money figure into the story and what control does it have over the characters?

Culture What trends in art, theatre and literature are implicitly or explicitly revealed in the play, and how does their culture affect the lives of the characters.

Spirituality Identify the religious or spiritual aspects of the play and how they affect the characters or impact the story.

Spectacle Analysis Worksheet

Genre _____

Genre characteristics _____

Playing style _____ Dangers _____

Given Circumstances

Time _____

Place or physical environment _____

Society _____

Economics _____

Cultural _____

Spirituality _____

The World of the Play _____

Notes

_____
_____
_____
_____
_____
_____

Figure 5.1
Sample worksheet outlining analysis relating to spectacle

II. Character

Character is defined by the entire pattern of behavior that identifies a person. Outlining the characters in the play is important to do before rehearsal, as it will allow the director to guide the actors in their attempt to build these characters.

Identify and Define the Characters

First, identify the **protagonist** and **antagonist**, and then all major and minor characters.

Protagonist: the main character who drives the plot.

Antagonist: the character or thing that gets in the protagonist's way, and creates the central conflict of the play.

Character Analysis Worksheet

Name of Character _____

Name of Show _____ by _____

Outer World: Environment and physical traits

Age _____ Language _____ Time period _____

Social status _____ Education _____

Family history _____

Brief physical description _____

Any unusual physical or mental characteristics?

Kinesthetics (how he/she moves, i.e. lumbering, lithe)

Inner World: Psychological/Emotional

Super-Objective of Character _____

Scene by Scene analysis

Scene	Objective	Emotional state of being	Conflict	Resolution

Figure 5.2
Sample worksheet outlining analysis relating to character

For each character, define the following:

Given Circumstances: age, type, job, role in society, gender, physical or mental traits.

Qualities: the tactics the character uses to pursue those goals.

Conflict and relationships: who or what each character is in conflict with; tensions in situations; character vs. character, character vs. himself, character vs. environment, character vs. destiny or force of nature; character vs. ideas.

Conflict of objectives: obstacles encountered as characters pursue their **objectives.**

Willpower: the amount of intensity employed to achieve a goal.

Values: how a character views what is good or bad; what characters stand for or against.

Personality: how characters appear, think and feel; how they behave.

Complexity: how aware characters are of their situation.

Objectives and Super-objectives

Stanislavky's method of directing actors, known as his "system," includes defining what he called "objectives." According to his system, a play consists of actors who want, need, or must accomplish a specific goal. An actor's "objective" may be as simple as "to sweep the floor" or as daunting as "to avenge the death of one's father." Each scene may be said to have an objective, and the objective may not always be achieved. A table on the Character Analysis Worksheet (figure 5.2) demonstrates how a character's objectives can be recorded scene-by-scene.

A character's super-objective is the need that governs all other needs. According to Stanislavsky the play's super-objective, also called the play's "spine," evolves from the playwright's reason for writing the play, and is the main idea explored. Each character has a specific objective, or main goal in the play that directly relates back to the play's super-objective. By identifying the super-objective of the play, you have the "hat rack" on which all the hats hang.

To find the super-objective, consider what is needed to resolve the conflict. In *Hamlet*, the ghost reveals that Hamlet's father was murdered by Claudius, which then impels Hamlet to revenge his death, or "to make things right." The super-objective should be stated in the infinitive.

III. Plot

The plot is the collection of action points from the beginning to the end of the play. Aristotle said that plot is the first and greatest of things that belong to a drama. The plot is the action of the play, the story, what happens.

Action Points

Creating an outline of **action points**, organized by scene, allows the director to chart the progression of the plot in a detailed way. In the case of plays without designated scenes, use **French scenes**.

Figure 5.3
Sample worksheet outlining analysis relating to plot, page 1

Plot Analysis Worksheet page 1

Action Points

Scene	Characters present	Internal action	External action

Backstory

Backstory	Who	To whom	How	True/False	Impact

> **Action point:** a single element of action that advances the plot to the next action point.
>
> **French scene:** a new section of dialogue that begins with an entrance or exit of a character and ends with the next entrance or exit.

Each action point can be understood as containing two separate actions: those that exist physically on the stage and those that exist psychologically in the character's mind. Stanislavsky was instrumental in making this distinction, and we refer to them as the external and internal actions, respectively.

For each action point, identify the **external** and **internal actions**. Organize them in a chart like that on the Plot Analysis Worksheet shown in figure 5.3.

> **External action:** Stanislavski referred to this as "First Plan," and it consists of the blocking, movement, and location of characters on the stage.
>
> **Internal action:** what happens in the character's mental, spiritual and emotional life.

Example: Act 2, Scene 5, *Hamlet*, on the roof of Elsinore castle, late night

> Characters present: Hamlet, Ghost
>
> External action: Hamlet speaks with the ghost
>
> Internal action: Hamlet resolves to avenge his father's death

Backstory

Anything that is referred to in the play about events that occurred in the past is called backstory. **Exposition** is dialogue that reveals backstory and is either spoken by characters or indicated in playwright's notes. By creating a list of all backstory plot points and how they impact the play and the characters, directors can contextualize the action of the play and help actors better understand their characters' motivations.

Create a list of all backstory points. For each point, list the following:

1. Who reveals it?
2. To whom is it revealed?
3. How is it revealed?
4. Is the information true or false?
5. How does this information impact the plot and characters?

Dramatic Action Structure

The play can be seen as a physical structure, composed of major dramatic actions, conflicts, climaxes, and resolutions. The narrative is carried through this structure, bending at certain points, rising or falling at others. It is important for the director to identify these major moments that help define the play.

Given the long and varied history of drama, it would be difficult to describe one overarching plot structure that accurately describes the action of every play. Some contend that the action be framed in terms of three parts. This tripartite view of plot structure follows from Aristotle, who wrote in Poetics that a whole plot in a tragedy must contain a beginning, middle, and end. Often, classical drama is described in terms of a protasis, epitasis, and catastrophe.

Others—most notably Gustav Freytag, a nineteenth century German play-wright—have described the structure of dramatic action in terms of five parts. When these five parts are visually represented, they are often drawn as a map that represents the rise and fall of suspense experienced by the audience. As suspense rises in the lead up to the climax and subsequently falls afterwards, this "map" takes the shape of a pyramid, known as "Freytag's Pyramid."

Still others contend that the structure of dramatic action is best understood as a series of crises or climaxes that build to a final climax, which occurs near the very end of the play.

Figure 5.4
Sample worksheet outlining analysis relating to plot, page 2

Ultimately, when determining how action is structured in a play, everyone agrees that there is a conflict (usually initiated by an inciting action) that builds to a climax and is ultimately resolved. These are the structural components the director must identify. (For further information on understanding the structure of action, consult the suggested reading at the end of this chapter.)

Identify the major moments in the play:

Inciting Action The first major moment is the inciting incident, which is the event that sparks the rest of the action of the play. This is the moment where the major conflict comes alive. It is important the director clearly reveal the essential elements that spark the conflict in order to ensure that the story is properly developed.

Plot Analysis Worksheet page 2

Major Moments

Inciting action: _____
_____
_____

Climax: _____
_____
_____

Falling action: _____
_____
_____

Major Conflicts and Obstacles

Major conflict: _____
Obstacle(s): _____

Notes

_____
_____
_____
_____
_____
_____
_____
_____
_____

Climax The play's climax is the moment where the conflict reaches its highest intensity. After this, the play changes to a downward direction towards the resolution. Identifying the main climax gives the director important information about how to direct the play.

When directing a climactic moment, keep in mind:

- it is a scene of high intensity
- the stakes peak for each character
- pace is intensified
- atmosphere is emotionally charged
- important information is being revealed
- critical plot action is occurring

Falling Action The falling action is the moment the conflict is resolved. The nature of the resolution and the preceding climax determines how the director handles the falling action

Conflicts and Obstacles

It is important to identify the conflict introduced in the inciting action. This clash usually exists between two characters, although it can also take the form of man vs. nature, man vs. himself, man vs. God, etc. It is best to state conflicts in an X vs. X format. For example, in the case of *Hamlet*, the play's major conflict could be stated as either Hamlet vs. Claudius, or Hamlet vs. himself.

An obstacle can be seen as something that gets in the way of the protagonist in their quest to achieve their super-objective. In *Hamlet*, Claudius can be seen as the obstacle to Hamlet's desire to make things right. Hamlet himself can also be seen as the obstacle because he is unable to achieve his goal due to his misgivings and fear of acting immorally.

IV. Ideas

Identify Ideas

In philosophical terms, an idea can be understood as the inner form of the thing as opposed to its physical reality. In more practical terms, it can be seen as the meaning or significance behind a word, action, or image. The following are places to search for ideas:

The Title What does the title tell us about the play?

Discussions What major ideas are discussed in the dialogue?

Aphorisms A concise statement of principle or truth is known as an aphorism. Do characters use aphorisms in their dialogue? If so, when, how and why? What does that tell us about the character?

Allusions What references to people or things outside the play are made? What do they mean?

Imagery Is there any special significance of something's appearance? Identify figurative language such as metaphors and similes. What mental images are conjured by the words the characters speak?

Symbolism Does something in the play represent another thing? If so, what is the significance of the symbol?

Themes

When ideas reoccur throughout a play, they may be called thematic. Plays often have many minor **themes** and one or more major themes. Identifying themes is the first step to finding "a concept" for directing the play. (Developing a concept is the subject of Chapter 8.) Identify and list each theme and write a short description of how that theme is expressed in the play.

Idea Analysis Worksheet

Identify Ideas

Title _____

Discussions _____
_____

Aphorisms _____
_____

Allusions _____
_____

Imagery _____
_____

Symbolism _____
_____

Themes

Theme _____

How it is expressed _____
_____
_____

Theme _____

How it is expressed _____
_____
_____

Theme _____

How it is expressed _____
_____
_____

Figure 5.5 Sample worksheet outlining analysis relating to idea

> **Theme:** an idea that recurs in or pervades a work of art or literature.

V. Rhythm

The ancient Greek tragedies, about which Aristotle was writing, were forms of poetry. Understanding the verse of a drama thus included identifying its "music" or "song." Although modern drama is not necessarily considered "poetry," we can still identify a pattern of changing tactics, or *beats*; a rate at which events unfold, *tempo*; and a rising and falling of tensions, *rhythm*.

Beats

A play is broken down as follows:

1. **Act** the largest subdivision of the play usually defined by intermission and explicitly noted in the script.
2. **Scene** the subdivisions of the act. For example, in *The Glass Menagerie*, there are seven scenes in two acts. Like acts, they are often explicitly noted in the script.
3. **Major Beat** Although not explicitly noted, a major shift in the dramatic action of the scene indicates the start of a new 'beat.' A scene usually has 3-5 major beats.
4. **Minor Beat and Objective** Every time a character's objective changes, a new minor beat begins and is defined by that new objective. Several minor beats can add up to the objective of one major beat.

Figure 5.6
Sample worksheet outlining analysis relating to rhythm

Once the beat is identified, assign it an infinitive verb phrase (to + verb) for each character, describing their new or continuing objective and the tactic they employ to achieve that objective. For example, in Act I, scene 2 of *The Glass Menagerie*, Amanda's objective is "to confront." Remember, the objective is what the character wants in that "moment" of the beat. Characters with differing wants in a scene create the conflict, and how the characters struggle to resolve the conflict is the heart of dramatic action.

Finding the action verb that describes the beat objective helps the director define the action and gives the actor a key to unlock the behavior of the beat. Acting is doing. The beat objective is what the actor does. Two characters might be in a coffee shop talking about the weather, but there is always something dramatic happening. Perhaps one is trying to impress or seduce or ridicule the other.

Rhythm Analysis Worksheet

Beats

Script lines	Beat	Objective
	Major beat	Major objectives
	Minor beat	Minor objectives

Atmosphere

Mood • Rhythm • Pace and Tempo

Brief description _____

_____

_____

_____

_____

Scene by Scene

Scene	Atmosphere	Scene	Atmosphere

Write the beat information right in the text. If you want to write into the actual script, make sure it is one you own and not a rented script! If rented, make a copy and notate your copy. Note the new beat with a slash, and jot down the objectives in the margin.

Another way to notate beats is to cut the script into pages, and paste them in your production book. Then on the other side create a grid like the one in the Rhythm Analysis Worksheet (figure 5.6), and notate information in the grid.

Atmosphere

When analyzing the play, determine the following:

Pace and Tempo Pace is the speed of the action and tempo is the rate at which the events unfold. This is often determined not only by the play's content, but also its genre. For example, the pace of farce is fast, while the pace of realistic drama tends to be slower and more measured.

Rhythm Rhythm is a pattern of changing tensions in beats, units, scenes and acts—a pulsing sensation that occurs when the dramatic intensity rises and falls within each progression. By looking at the rising and falling of tensions in the play, one can feel the rhythm of the play.

Atmosphere The mood is a consistent external force outside the actors that is affected by time, locale, season, social conditions and situation. Sometimes characters' moods are so strong, they create the atmosphere of the play.

Write a brief description of the play's overall atmosphere, and then scene by scene, chart how it varies throughout the play.

Figure 5.7
Sample worksheet outlining analysis relating to dialogue

Dialogue Analysis Worksheet

Style of Dialogue

Description _____

_____

_____

_____

By Character

Character	Dialogue style	Character	Dialogue style

Identifying Subtext

Scene	Script lines	Subtext

VI. Dialogue

Dialogue comprises all spoken passages in the play. The quality and style of the dialogue provide important clues to character.

Dialogue Styles

Realistic: language that sounds natural to the character and period.

Abstract: the expression of ideas characterized by language separated from concrete action or a material basis.

Naturalistic: imitating everyday life in a way that heightens the sense of realism.

Formal or informal: a speech pattern that rigidly adheres to grammatical rules is formal; conversely, one that is relaxed and does not is informal.

Colloquial: a pattern of speech that can be characterized as conversational, marked by phrases and words used in everyday conversation specific to a particular region or country.

Dialect: defined by a specific regional or foreign dialect

Diction and Grammar

Characters are shaped by the way they speak. How would you characterize their diction? Their grammar usage? Do they use emotional words?

Identify Subtext

Because a play is not readily afforded the luxury of third-person narration like a novel, what a character is really thinking is often not explicitly stated. This unspoken dialogue is called subtext. Great playwrights, such as Chekhov, are masters of subtext. To identify it, consider the following questions: what are the true thoughts beneath the words a character speaks? What is the percentage of truth in what they say out loud? What is being concealed? It is important that the director identify the subtext because each actor must understand the real thought under the spoken words.

Final Thoughts

Once the director has completed analysis, it is important to return to the play as a unified, coherent whole. Formulating the "main idea" of the play is part of this reassembling of elements.

Formulate the Main Idea

Create a subjective statement that expresses, in a short sentence, what the play is about. Based on the super-objective, the director creates this statement to express their point of view. The director can use this main idea to communicate to the artistic team and actors what the director wants the production to say.

Student Exercise 5.1: Beat Exercise

Select a scene from the play, and break it down into beats and objectives. Give each beat a name, and each character in the beat a "to + verb" statement of their beat objectives.

Student Exercise 5.2: Using a Film

Analyze a film you have seen recently. Determine the super-objective. What do you think the director's main idea was in conceptualizing the film?

Student Exercise 5.3: Fairy Tale Analysis

Take a fairy tale, like *Little Red Riding Hood*, or *Rapunzel*. Analyze the story.

Student Exercise 5.4: Formulating the Play's Main Idea

Once you have completed analysis on your play, develop its main idea. Follow these steps:

1. List the themes prevalent in the play.
2. Select a single theme that resonates within you most strongly.
3. Relate that theme to yourself, your feelings about life and art, and the play; why do you resonate strongly with this theme? What is stirred inside you? Note these things.
4. Write a short, personal statement from your point of view that communicates the theme of the play and the writer's reason for writing it.
5. Keep it short, succinct, and in a cause-and-effect format.

Student Exercise 5.5: Developing a Radical Concept

Conceptualize a production of one of Shakespeare's plays, purposefully setting it in another era. Radically reinterpret the play using your identified super-objective, conflicts, and themes. Defend your choices textually and then write a clear concept statement meant to convince your artistic director that this production is the one they should produce.

Suggested Reading

Aristotle, *Poetics*. Translated by Joe Sachs. Newburyport, MA: Focus Publishing, 2006.

Ball, David. *Backwards and Forwards: A Technical Manual for Reading Plays.* Carbondale, IL: Southern Illinois University Press, 1983.

Burgoyne, Suzanne, and Patricia Downey. *Thinking Through Script Analysis.* Newburyport, MA: Focus Publishing, 2011.

Ingham, Rosemary. *From Page to Stage: How Theatre Designers Make Connections Between Scripts and Images.* Portsmouth, NH: Heinemann, 1998.

Chapter 6
Research

Why Research?

Directing a play involves more than merely blocking the actors and making sure the curtain goes up on opening night. In order to unlock the play's creative potential, the director must embark on a journey of discovery, learning as much as possible about the play. Armed with detailed knowledge, a director can more fully imagine the play onstage and begin the process of conceptualization. The greatest nutrient for a healthy imagination is knowledge.

The director must:

- Be an expert in all subject matter related to the content of the play;
- Understand the culture, history, society, and morality of the period in which the play is set;
- Have a psychological understanding of the characters;
- Explain any references made in the script to the society at large or other literary sources;
- Develop a visual and psychological concept for the play that can be communicated to the artistic team and the actors.

Assembling Research

It is important to be organized as you research. Gather all of the textual and visual research, noting information about the images as necessary, and put that material in your DPN. Use this information as a personal resource as you build the case for the concept you will present to the artistic team. Also, share the images with your actors. What inspired you will inspire them as well.

Representational vs. Inspirational Research

There are two kinds of visual information that can be useful.

First, **representational visual images** are those that give the director specific visual information. This is what a designer uses to create the designs and what a director uses to get a true sense of what things really looked and felt like. For example, if you are directing *Lysistrata*, view pictures of Ancient Greece, including pictures of the Parthenon.

The second type of information is from **inspirational research**. These are images that are abstract or unrelated to the source material, but inspire emotions or a psychological sense of the atmosphere, nature of the period, or content of the play. This can come from anywhere and take just about any form. When working on a play, be sensitive to stimuli. Be open-minded, as you might be surprised where ideas might come from. Research is exciting!

Where to Look

The Internet Whatever the internet may lack in terms of quality is made up by quantity. Your local librarian may help you find a dozen or so quality books on your subject, but Google is going to display thousands of web pages at time. Therefore, it is important to be organized as you search, by either printing images and documents or saving them to an appropriately labeled folder.

A useful internet search begins by entering terms (such as the time and place of the play) into Google and searching "images." You may copy and store these images in a file on your desktop, just be sure to verify what the images depict by also checking their web page sources. Often, the website associated with an image will give you further useful information.

By doing a regular internet search, you will also find a myriad of textual research on just about any subject, which you can print out and use in your DPN. You can do general searches and specific searches. You can find historical information, cultural references, and much more. There is no limit to the amount of knowledge that awaits you on the internet.

The Library Go to your local library, find books with images of life during the historical period you are researching, and scan or make copies if it is allowed for research purposes. Most images are protected by copyright, so only use the images for personal research. Never include these images in publications of any kind without insuring they are not copyright-protected.

The Bookstore Especially for fashion or modern architectural research, the bookstore is full of books and magazines packed with images that might be useful. Purchase the ones that have what you are looking for and cut them up for inclusion in your DPN research.

Newspaper Archives Most libraries maintain microfiche original editions of newspapers going back over a hundred years. If you are looking for a specific story you can usually target a newspaper that might have information. Consult a librarian for assistance.

Observation By observing people, you can find real human beings that possess the essence of characters from the play. Even if the play is in set in the past, you may still discover characters through observation.

Oral Research If you want to get a sense of a period or what life was like at any given time in the recent past, talk to people who lived at that time, or find someone locally or on the web who might have been there or witnessed a key event important to the play. Interviewing experts and witnesses of times past is a very powerful way for a director to get a true sense of period.

Movies and Video Depending on the period, viewing films and documentaries will provide detailed insight into the behavior, art, and culture of the period. Lest your imagination be stunted, avoid viewing a movie made from the play you are directing. Instead, view films set in the same period.

Museums Art museums and history museums offer images and exhibits that can provide historical and cultural context. These are a great first-hand way to experience culture form other periods.

Travel If the setting is a real place and you have the time and money, consider visiting the setting of the play you are directing. For example, if you are doing *Hamlet*, you can actually visit Elsinore Castle. This option is pricey and a luxury, and always a lot of fun.

Categories of Research

Character

The Character's Background Each character has unique personality traits, backstory, and habits. For example, Amanda in *The Glass Menagerie* comes from a genteel southern background, probably lived on a plantation, and was spoiled and well cared for as a child. What was that life like? To understand Amanda, the director needs to understand the world she came from. This can be accomplished by viewing movies about young girls who grew up wealthy on southern plantations, or reading books, or viewing paintings. If the past is recent enough, oral interviews with real people who have experienced similar lives can provide insight.

Educational Systems Each character was educated in some manner. Find information about how people at the time were educated.

Socio-Economic Status What is the character's socio-economic status and what does that mean in the context of the period? Being rich in India in 2011 is a very different than being rich in Edwardian England. What are the specifics of each character's socio-economic status and what did that mean in the specific period? What activities comprised their daily lives? What was important? Have they fallen from that status, or risen? And if so, how was that change of status experienced?

The Social Order What social order defines the morality of each character? How powerful was the force of the social order and how does it affect each character?

Discourse What academic theories (e.g., psychological, developmental, evolutionary, historical, biological) were prevalent in the general discourse of the character's period and how can those theories deepen a director's understanding of the character's motivations, desires, behavior, and tactics.

Place

The Physical Location Look for images that pertain to the external and interior environments.

The external location could be an island in the South Pacific, or the slums of London in the nineteenth century. For example, in *The Glass Menagerie*, look for images of tenement slums of St. Louis, circa 1937. For *Angels in America*, look for images of neighborhoods in New York and Salt Lake City, in the 1980s, as well as pictures of Antarctica.

If a play takes place before photography, look at paintings and sculptures. You may have to sort through a great deal of materials to find pictures that both accurately represent what was true about the general environment and that are closely related to the location of the play.

Interiors Determine where the play is set, and research interiors or specific outdoor settings that could serve as possible settings for the play. For *A Little Night Music*, consider country gardens and summer vacation homes in Sweden at the turn of the twentieth century. For *The Glass Menagerie*, consider the interiors of tenement apartments in the 1930s.

Architectural If the play contains specific architectural references to a setting, such as the Parthenon in *Lysistrata*, collect images of those structures.

Fashion A great deal of information exists about clothing styles worn over the past five thousand years. Find pictures of the clothing the characters would have worn. Make sure to find pictures that are accurate to social status, season, and specific location.

Furniture Consider what type of furniture is appropriate for the locations of the play. Collect images of suitable pieces. Again, be sensitive to social class, location, and styles popular in that location.

Props Study pictures of important props required in the play.

Historical

Events What are the important events that affect the characters in the play or the plot? Consider important political, cultural, and financial events. For example, are the characters affected by a war or financial crisis, by an important holiday or schism in the church?

Forms of Employment How do people make money, what kind of job force exists?

Religion Are there any religious factors that affect the characters in the play or the plot? If so, how?

Technologies What are the available technologies that influence the way people live and behave?

Speech and Dialect Is there any historically specific diction or syntax? Consider how it differs from contemporary dialogue and what role it plays in the drama.

People Get a sense of what people looked like in the period. Gather a general assortment of images, and then create a collage for each major character. In the collage, include inspirational pictures that capture the essence of the character as well as specific images for costume, hair, make-up, etc.

Cultural

Art Who were the popular artists, and what were the popular trends and movements in the visual and performing arts?

Fashion What trends were considered fashionable? What was "the norm"? What was influencing fashion?

Design What were the trends in furniture design and architecture? Who were the leading designers?

Theatrical Trends What was popular? How were shows being produced? What was the prevalent dramatic structure?

Music What were people listening to? Who were the popular musicians of the period? What were the popular musical styles?

Popular Entertainment What forms of entertainment were popular among the masses? What were the popular sports?

Textual

Context When was the work written, who wrote it, what else was being written at the same time, was it revolutionary?

References Are there any references to other works or historical or social events? If something is referenced in the play, know what it is, how it relates to the text, and if necessary, how to pronounce it. The play may reference literature, art, other cultures, and history.

Societal Impact Are there themes, characters or plot events that have societal reverberations in modern society, and if so, how and why?

Playwright Biography How does the playwright's personal story influence the play?

Era Transposition If you are moving the play to another period, what are the events of the new period that might have parallels or thematic similarity to the original setting? Identify the parallels and relate them to the original source material to make sure it translates appropriately.

Student Exercise 6.1

Identify the time and location of the play you are working on. Following the steps above, research the play in one or all areas, and create a presentation for your class that includes images and explanations.

Student Exercise 6.2: General Research

For each of the following periods, research the historical, cultural, or textual aspects following the guidelines detailed in this chapter. For each category, create a file on your computer and save images and information in those files. Then, create a power point presentation illustrating your research for each period and category.

1. Ancient Rome
2. Medieval France
3. World-War-Two Fiji
4. Small Town USA, 1950
5. New York City, September 15, 2001

Chapter 7
Concept

What is a concept? A director makes decisions, taking a universe of possibilities and narrowing them down into concise ideas. Based on work done in the analysis of the text and the daydreams of imagining, the director makes decisions about specific **concepts** in the play.

> **Concept:** a plan or intention; an idea or mental picture of a group or class of objects formed by combining all their aspects.

These concepts take two forms: the psychological and the visual.

The Psychological Concept

The psychological concept defines the director's approach to the internal action of the play, from shaping character and relationships, to directing the actors through the conflict, climax, and resolution. It also defines how the play's super-objective will be brought to life and what the director wishes to express through the performance.

The Visual Concept

The visual concept is a statement that defines approaches of the director and designer to the external action of the play, including the set, sound, costumes, lighting, special effects, and props. After the director has personally explored the text, a series of meetings with the designers follow and it is in these meetings that a visual context for the play is refined. A visual strategy leads to a stage environment that supports the psychological concept of the play.

Developing the Psychological Concept

To formulate the psychological concept, the director states the super-objective and themes of the play as identified in analysis (Chapter 5). From these, the director chooses what the play will focus on, writing it in the form of a concise **focus**

statement. When the director has formed the focus statement, he or she should consider how the focus statement applies to each character and write a statement for each. These focus statements, along with consideration of the will of the characters, combine to form the psychological **concept statement**.

> **Focus statement:** a sentence describing what the director wishes to focus on in the production.
>
> **Concept statement:** a description of how the focus statement will be realized in terms of both the physical world of the play as a whole and the psychological approach to take with each character.

Guided Example: *The Glass Menagerie*

1. State the super-objective and themes

Write the super-objective and a list of themes, followed by a short synopsis of the script.

Super-objective: To be free.

Themes: inability to accept reality, the power of memory to alter the truth, escape, love, survival, abandonment, disappointment.

Action summary: *The Glass Menagerie* is the story of a disillusioned family whose lives once held great promise. Abandoned by their father, they live in a small tenement walk-up in St. Louis in 1937. It is a memory play. Tom Wingfield has left home years ago and remembers the final days he lived with his family. The story focuses on the visit of a gentlemen caller who is an old classmate of Laura's. Amanda hopes that he will marry Laura.

2. Choose the one or two most relevant themes

This decision can be an intellectual one, based on the theme that is most socially relevant, or it can be an emotional decision, based on the director's taste.

Relevant themes: disappointment, survival

3. Think about those themes

Why did you choose them? What is the social relevance? What is the emotional relevance? Note an explanation.

I chose these themes because *The Glass Menagerie* is about surviving disappointment, and the lengths to which human beings will go in order to cope. Socially, it is relevant for today's audiences insofar as there are many single-parent households struggling to survive in our often unforgiving world. Personally, I find the will to survive empowering and what I want to focus on.

4. Write a short focus statement

I will focus on the characters' will to survive.

5. Explain reasons for this focus choice

Talk about how the production can bring these themes alive.

I am fascinated by what these characters do to cope. In my production, I will reveal the positive side of their will to survive. I don't want it to be a play about disappointment in an obvious way. I want the audience to feel the character's hopes and dreams upon curtain's rise and not be warned of the impending disappointment that ultimately will come. This is a world of hope and possibilities, of dreams never abandoned.

If the audience hopes along with the characters, then the devastation of not realizing those dreams will be much more powerful. If the audience expects disaster, when it comes it will not be powerful.

6. How will the focus statement determine how you shape the characters?

If each character lives in a world of hopes and dreams for as long as possible, the audience will sympathize with them, root for them. In each case, I want the characters to unapologetically seek what will make them happy.

Psychological Concept Worksheet page 1
Themes
1. Super-Objective: _____
Themes: _____
Action summary: _____
2. Relevant themes: _____
3. Why relevant?: _____
Focus Statement
4. Focus Statement: _____
5. Why do you want to focus on this?: _____
6. How are the characters shaped by the Focus Statement?: _____
7. Character Focus Statements:

Character	Focus Statement

Identify common theme in characters' Focus Statements: _____

Figure 7.1
Sample worksheet outlining formation of psychological concept, page 1

7. Create character focus statements

Based on #6, create a character concept statement for each character, ending each with a "character focus" statement.

Tom Tom dreams of traveling to foreign lands and seeing the world. He hopes to get Laura married and make sure his mother is taken care of so he can leave with a light heart. Tom will focus on tying up loose ends at home so he can leave.

Laura Laura dreams of being loved, but does not believe she will ever find love. So, to survive, she finds solace in her music and her glass animals. She desperately wants to find someone to love her but fear paralyzes her. Laura will focus on staying safe in a scary world.

Amanda Amanda dreams of her children's success in the world. She hopes to marry off Laura and wants Tom to succeed. She dreams that her children will one day take care of her. Amanda will focus on getting Laura married and forcing Tom to be responsible.

Jim Jim dreams of a married life with his sweetheart and great success in business. He hopes Laura and Tom find happiness because Jim is a good-natured person that hopes for the best in all things. Jim will focus on giving Laura confidence.

8. Identify a common theme to the character focus statements

Hopes and dreams.

9. State the will of the characters

Make a general statement about the will of the characters, and then a specific short statement about each character's will (will = the level of intensity employed in the pursuit of their desires).

General I want the characters to pursue their objectives shamelessly, with no apologies. They don't question their motives or desires.

Specific Tom and Amanda have strong wills that clash relentlessly. Laura has a different kind of will: she is strong-willed in her drive to escape from the world, but very weak-willed in her ability to face her fears. Jim has a strong will tempered by a deep kindness.

Psychological Concept Worksheet page 2

Statements of Will

9. General statement of will: _____

Character's Will:

Character	Short statement of character's will

Focus Statement

10. Character's actions in terms of Focus Statement:

Character	Action

11. The Psychological Concept Statement: _____

_____
_____
_____
_____
_____
_____
_____
_____

Figure 7.2
Sample psychological concept worksheet, page 2

10. Apply focus statement to character's actions

Using the focus statement from #4 and apply it to the behavior of each character and the choices they make. Start with a general statement, then give specific examples by character.

General I want to focus on the characters' will to survive. Every decision they make, every deed they do will be motivated by the will to survive.

Specific Laura quits business school because it is killing her. Tom goes to the movies because he will suffocate if he stays in the apartment; Tom invites Jim to dinner because he wants to find a husband for Laura so he can survive. Amanda drones on about the importance of chewing food because she wants her children to be strong and survive in the harsh world; Amanda sells magazines to put food on the table; Amanda wants dinner to be perfect because she believes it will help seduce the gentlemen caller who is Laura's only salvation.

11. Write your psychological concept statement

Restate your focus statement from #4. Using the ideas in your "quality of will" statements from #10, work out how you will be influenced by the focus statement in the direction of each character. Add a final statement of what you, as director, will focus on and explore in a more general way.

I want to focus on the characters' will to survive.

I will direct Tom to be very melancholy in his memory monologues, so we can see into his heart and feel his regret. The love he felt for his family will be clear in the monologues, and there will be a sepia-toned ennui as he remembers. But in the play's scenes, he will be unapologetically strong in his desire to be free. I want to see his agony at being a prisoner in a world he detests, like a caged animal fighting to be free. He will stand up to Amanda and not fear her.

Amanda will be intensely attached to her past. Whenever she remembers her golden youth, she will glow and be happy, transformed. But in the other moments, she will be tough as nails, desperate to get Laura married. I will tell the actress that "nothing can stop Amanda from achieving this; her very survival depends on it." She is a ruthless manipulator when the need arises.

Laura will have two sides to her personality; a calm and centered side that we see when she listens to music or plays with her animals, or when all is well between Tom and Amanda. Then, the other side is the one dominated by fear. Her fear will be palpable, obsessive and uncontrollable.

Jim will exude confidence. He will be the kind of person that sees inside of people, understands what they need. He is kindness personified, and an example of the kind of life that true goodness can create.

The will to survive is powerful and exists in us all. Tennessee Williams was a survivor and his characters are all marvels of the will to survive. I can relate to and want to focus on this aspect of the story.

Developing the Visual Concept

The most important step in developing a visual concept is starting with a clear psychological concept. The director, sometimes in collaboration with designers, develops the visual concept from the psychological concept, determining what the play will look like and providing the physical context in which the characters exist. Ultimately, it will be the job of the designers to design the set, costumes, and other physical elements of the play, in concert with the visual concept. Forming a clear and concise visual concept ensures that the director will be prepared to participate in the design meetings discussed in Chapter 8.

Remember, the director does not design the set, costumes, or any other physical element of the play.

Research will provide the intellectual stimuli needed to begin the process of creating a visual concept. Using the information below, note ideas for each category and be ready to discuss these ideas with your design team.

Visual Concept Worksheet

Setting

1. Indication in play:

Location in script	Setting indications

2. Stage Configurations: _____

3. Locations:

Scene	Location	How to realize location

4. Influence of Psychological Concept: _____

5. How many entrances?: _____ Doors? _____ Windows? _____

6. Furniture, architectural elements, props: _____

Figure 7.3
Sample worksheet outlining formation of visual concept, page 1.

Setting

At what point in time is the play set? The playwright will provide some information. However, the director is not necessarily bound to that. Most modern plays should be set in the precise time intended, but with earlier scripts, it is possible to make the story relevant to modern audiences by transposing the setting to a different period.

Transposition

To consider transposition to another period, the director should ask the following questions:

- Does the original period have any special significance to the themes of the play or to history? *If yes, you must not change the period of the play.*
- If the period is transposed, are the themes preserved? *If not, you must not change the period of the play.*
- If a play is moved to another period, will this illuminate themes intended by the playwright in a way more accessible to modern audiences? *If yes, then transposing the play to a new period can be powerful.*

Transposing a play to a different period can make for very potent storytelling. On the other hand, altering a play for the wrong reasons can undermine the very story the director is trying to tell. If the director changes the period or historical context, the decision should be rooted in the text, supported by analysis.

A Good Example: *A Doll's House* in the late 1950s

Major themes in Ibsen's *A Doll's House* include the subjugation of women, the sacrificial role of women, parental obligation, reliability of appearances, and societal expectations. By setting the play in the late 1950s, a director transports a woman who lived in a male-dominated society in Norway to a period in America where males also dominated in much the same way.

Originally set in late-nineteenth-century Norway, both periods share common issues, e.g. preceding women's liberation movements. Because the themes translate well to a fifties world, the transposition is defensible.

A Bad Example: Setting the musical *Hair* in the 1990s

Major themes in the musical *Hair* include youth revolution, drug use,

A production of *Hair*, set in the 1960s

the Vietnam War, and the "hippie" identity. If *Hair* is transposed to any other time, the specifics of the Vietnam War, the first American war opposed by a majority of Americans, is lost.

The revolution of young people in late 1960s was unique, bound in the historical events of that time. Shifting to another time would risk demeaning the lives of those characters. Ultimately, a director would be hard-pressed to defend this transposition.

Where is the Play Set?

Upon close inspection, the director may find the setting of the play communicated via descriptions and indications in the dialogue. Be sure to pay close attention to any descriptions provided by the playwright, and note the following before you enter into discussions with the design team:

1. **All Indications Given in the Play about Setting** These can come from descriptions by the playwright or statements by characters.
2. **Stage Configuration** While developing the concept, a director need not be bound to a particular stage configuration. Yet keep in mind that whatever the concept, it will eventually have to be realized on a specific stage configuration.
3. **Locations of All Scenes and How You Will Realize Each Location** Decide on a general overall location and then specific scene locations. These can be exactly as the playwright described, or altered to fit your concept. Don't let budgets constrain your imagination as you develop a visual concept. That comes later. A visual concept has nothing to do with money, and everything to do with imagination. Even if a play is set in five locations it can work on a unit set.

> **Unit set:** a stationary set that serves as many different settings; different scenes are created by lighting, moving furniture, or playing in different areas.

4. **How Does Your Psychological Concept Affect the Design?** Consider how the psychological concept influences the setting, lights, and costumes. For example, if *The Glass Menagerie* focuses on the characters will to survive and you want to create a sense of hope and possibility as the curtain rises, the visual concept may reflect this hope through soft colors, touches of beauty, and orderliness amidst a clearly decayed environment. The design can create the sense of hope and the characters' will to survive by embedding these ideas visually. A drab, colorless and dingy environment will not create a sense of hope.
5. **How Many Entrances, Doors, and Windows Do You Need?** Every production needs entrances and exits. The concept does not depend on this

information, but as the set is designed, these elements come into play. Style of the doors and windows can be integral to your visual concept. For example, Lorca's *The House of Bernarda Alba* is the story of a mother who incarcerates her daughters for seven years in their home after the death of their father, in keeping with Spanish tradition. In a recent production of this play, the door was thirty feet high and made of stone. It had a massive, impenetrable feel that defined the visual concept of the show and created a visual metaphor for the entrapment.

6. **What Furniture, Architectural Elements, and Props are Necessary?** Every play has specific physical needs that can help shape your visual concept. *The Glass Menagerie* needs a fire escape outside a window, a front door, an area for the dining room table, and a living room area. There must be a picture of their father, and candles that Amanda lights when the electricity goes out.

Atmosphere and Visual Concept

"Atmospheres for the artist," Michael Chekhov wrote, "are comparable to the different keys in music. They are a concrete means of expression."

Atmospheres exist everywhere on the physical plane and are layered and dynamic, not static. Just as actors need to observe human behavior, they must also sensitize themselves to the atmospheres through which people move so they can re-create them for the theatre.

> **Atmosphere:** a palpable, pervasive tone or mood that is external in nature, and thus felt and seen by the audience, albeit influential on the internal life of the characters.

Chekhov explains that by creating the atmosphere, and then allowing that atmosphere to af-

Figure 7.4
Visual concept worksheet, page 2.

Visual Concept Worksheet page 2

Atmosphere

1. Desired impact of atmosphere: _____

2. First moment: _____

3. Changes in atmosphere: _____

4. Final atmosphere: _____

Style: _____

5. Notes: _____

fect speech, movement, and feelings, the actor "reveals the content of the performance." Consider the following example:

You wake up happy to be alive, you just won a hundred bucks at lotto, and you are feeling great. You go to your friend's house and interrupt the funeral of his father. You had no idea he died. You walk into his house full of your own joy, but enter an atmosphere of mourning that is undeniable. It doesn't change the fact that you are joyful, or that you just won the lotto, but your behavior will change as a result of the atmosphere. You will not jump for joy when you see your friend. Instead, you will hug him, warmly. Aware of his sorrow, you will control your joy and speak in hushed tones. Atmosphere directly affects behavior.

How Does Atmosphere Play into Concept? When you talk to designers, communicate your feelings about atmosphere as an external influence. Explain the impact you want their work to have on the audience and why that is important.

We will discuss the use of atmosphere in the design process in a later chapter. For now, the important issue is to consider certain atmospheres as we create a visual concept.

Impact of the First Moment When the curtain rises, or in the case of an exposed set, there is an immediate emotional reaction among the audience. The lights and set combine to create an atmosphere that impacts the entire experience of the audience from that moment onward.

In the case of *The Glass Menagerie*, it is the atmosphere of hope that pervades and sends us on a journey of anxious expectation that something good will happen. When it doesn't, the pain of the characters' disappointments is intensified.

The design creates this atmosphere. In terms of concept, the initial atmosphere is critical to the designer incorporating the director's psychological concept into their design.

Changing Atmospheres Throughout the play, atmospheres change. Usually done with lighting, subtle changes can affect the actor and the audience. Depending on the concept of the production, moment to moment changes in atmosphere are important.

Final Atmosphere What we leave the audience with is the final atmosphere. As we reach the end of the journey, what is the atmosphere onstage? How does it impact character behavior and how does it impact the audience? What will be the last image?

Style

In order for designers to create their work, they must have a sense of the play's style that is in harmony with that of the director. Style is both objective, defined by the period, and subjective, existing as an instinct in the director's head. Style choices are found through research, experience, and imagination. Some simple visual style choices include:

Spectacular: big-budget realization of a visual concept

Minimalist: simple, low budget, minimal set and prop elements, enhanced use of lighting

Realistic: creating a real, lifelike feel

Naturalistic: a kitchen-sink realism that focuses on minutia

Splashy: very over-the-top, colorful, and exuberant, like a Las Vegas show

Funky: modern feel, "East Village bohemian"

Multimedia: using multimedia techniques

Or you can create your own style and give it a new name. The style of the visual concept is limited only by the material you are working with and your own imagination.

Final Thoughts

Before beginning discussions with actors or designers, the director should have a very clear idea of his or her psychological and visual concepts.

However, given that theatre is a collaborative art, a good director values the contributions of the design team and relies on their expertise in the formulation of the visual concept. A director does the necessary homework, comes to the table well-prepared with strong ideas, then, in the wonderful collaboration, "plays" with others and creates something greater than the sum of its individual parts.

Always stay open to input from designers, who are experts at creating visual concepts.

Student Exercise 7.1: Daydreaming, Part 1

1. Daydream. Pick a play with which you are familiar.
2. Close your eyes and visualize a play on stage.
3. Pick a moment in the play, maybe the first moment, or the climax, or the last.
4. Think of a line from that moment; the characters in that moment.
5. Let your mind wander; allow for images to float in and out of your mind's eye.
6. Capture the images that appear.
7. Don't censor, be free in your association.
8. As ideas come to you, jot them down, then daydream some more.

9. Think about the play as you fall asleep.
10. Note down any ideas you have when you wake up in the morning.
11. Let the play live inside you.

Student Exercise 7.2: Daydreaming, Part 2

1. Once you begin to have ideas, imagine the play on a specific stage.
2. Note the props, furniture.
3. Note entrances and exits.
4. Note lighting style.
5. Note costume ideas.
6. Note any impressions that lead to a concrete visual style.
7. Formalize a visual image for that moment.

In Your DPN

Carry your DPN everywhere you go. As you are working on a play, inspiration will come at the strangest times, and you don't want to miss an idea. Write them all down.

Inspiration has to be captured. Good ideas are like slippery fish; they can get away very easily, never to be seen again!

Suggested Reading

Chekhov, Michael. *On the Technique of Acting*. New York: Harper Collins, 1991

Schiffman, Jean. "Creating Atmospheres." *Backstage*. July 10, 2007.
    http://www.jbactors.com/actingreading/backstageatmospheres.html

PART II:
WRITTEN WORD TO THREE-DIMENSIONAL WORLD

Chapter 8
The Visual Collaboration

Working With Designers

Implementing the visual concept of a production is a direct result of the collaboration between designers and the director during the process of pre-production. While it is not always important that everyone agree initially, discussions during pre-production allow all parties involved to contribute to the process of realizing the vision for the project.

In general, the process of realizing the visual concept follows this order:

1. The producer hires the director and designers.
2. The director reads, researches, and conceptualizes the play. Similarly, the designers do their homework to get ideas about the show.
3. If both parties work in the same location, the director may want to engage in informal conversations with the designers to bounce some ideas around. If not, the director may have little interaction with designers prior to first design meeting.
4. The first design meeting is when the director and individual designers formally meet to discuss the director's ideas about the play. This could also happen by email or by phone.
5. After the first meeting, designers work on developing sketches, sometimes consulting with each other. Designer and director might talk during this period to refine ideas.
6. In the second design meeting, the designers present their sketches or thumbnails, which is followed by discussion and planning for further refinement of design plan.
7. The designers refine plans based on second design meeting. If the plans are still far from completion, the second design meeting can be repeated if needed.
8. At the final design meeting, all parties agree on the final visual concept and specific scenic, lighting, and costume designs.

The following chapter will clarify these steps and provide the insight to prepare and handle the design process from the director's point of view.

The ideal way to work with a designer is to communicate freely and frequently.

Types of Designer Collaborations

As the design discussions begin, consider how the designer approaches working with you. In my experience, I have found there are three kinds of design collaboration models. Directors are likely to encounter all three throughout the course of their careers, but the third is the preferred and most likely. The following is a description of each and how to handle them.

Model one: designer has no ideas

Situation The designer wants the director to tell them what to do. They come to the process with no concept, minimal experience of the text, and no ideas.

In this situation, it is necessary that the director take the lead by doing the conceptual work and planning for the designer. In the case of an inexperienced designer, or one who doesn't bring any ideas to the table, understanding the design process will enable the director to take the lead and move things along.

Be prepared to:

1. Present your ideas with full research support.
2. Be specific.
3. Have design ideas ready to start the discussion.
4. Excite the designers about your ideas.
5. Let your ideas become everyone's ideas.
6. Encourage the designer to begin creating their own designs based on initial discussions.

Model two: designer forcing their ideas

Situation The designer has a concept and is determined to see it realized, ignoring any input from the director.

The overzealous designer is uncommon as a good designer always seeks input from the director. If the director and designer have different ideas, they will have to find common ground that will satisfy both parties. The designer's concept might be brilliant. Hear the designer out and consider the idea. If the designer is married to the idea and will not budge, don't be bullied! Otherwise, you might end up doing a production you don't believe in. Try not to get frustrated and angry. Find a way to convince the designer to listen to your ideas and find middle ground. Ultimately, the designer's job is to use their expertise to translate the ideas of the director into physical reality. Remember, the director has the last word and the power to determine the visual concept. Exercise that power if necessary.

The following is a scenario involving a bold designer determined to force his ideas on you:

1. Designer presents sketch or model at the first design meeting that defines a very specific concept.
2. If you love it, skip 2-7. If not, ask the designer to defend the rationale for the concept.
3. Force the designer to be specific. The director has a right to a clear explanation and defense of the idea.
4. Because a designer should not present an idea that forces directorial concept or staging without the director being on board, the director has every right to override the idea. Use this as a defense if you don't like the idea.
5. Be open to the designer's idea. It might be a great one. Even if you discard the idea, you might retain parts of it.
6. If you don't like the idea, gently explain why, and ask the designer to consider other ideas.
7. If the designer will not consider other ideas, go to the producer and ask that the designer be replaced. Have strong reasons to support this bold move.

Model three: collaborative model

Situation The director and designers have done their homework, are prepared to discuss ideas about the show, and seek the collaboration of their peers to create something that best reflects the input of all.

Collaboration is the preferred way to work. The third model proceeds in the following way:

1. Designer comes to the meeting with a few sketches or ideas.
2. Director brings research and concept statements.
3. Dramaturge brings research and textual analysis knowledge.
4. There is a discussion of pre-conceived ideas, the genesis of new ones, and finally, together, the group reaches consensus about a direction in which to move.
5. Designers go home and start working on formal thumbnail presentations of their sets, costumes, lights, props, etc.
6. Throughout the remainder of the process, the director holds everybody true to the ideas agreed upon.

Meeting with Designers

Before the First Design Meeting

Informal conversations between director and designer can happen anywhere and anytime—a moment in the hallway, a quick phone call, a text, an email. Without scheduling a formal time and place, directors can use these interactions to begin the process of discussing concept ideas with the designers.

Speaking to the designers informally before the initial scheduled meetings will allow all parties to enter into the design process with an awareness of each other's ideas. It establishes the process of communication, making everyone comfortable with each other.

As you discuss your concept, share your ideas with designers and listen to theirs. Let ideas evolve. If everyone starts moving in the same direction before the design process actually begins, the process will go more smoothly.

Remember, a production is an expression of all the artists involved. Directors who respect the design team always benefit from the trust they engender.

In the collaborative process, never discount the input of others, but stay firm if you believe in an idea.

Design Meetings

Formal design meetings are called by the production manager, but designers and directors can meet anytime informally.

Keep in mind the following outline indicates the process for an "ideal" world in which everyone has the time to devote to a series of meetings. In the real world, situations vary greatly. Sometimes meetings are held via email or phone. Timelines also vary. Some very busy companies are working a month in advance of the first rehearsals, while others start a year in advance. Be flexible.

Informal meetings

- Talk about what you hope to achieve through this production.
- Discuss demands of the play: budget, timeline, talent pool, entrances and exits, levels, playing area.
- In what era will the show be set?
- Begin discussions about concepts.

Subsequent informal meetings

- Designer presents some basic thumbnail sketches, research boards, color palette, collages, and other support materials.

- Director provides constructive feedback, further refining the visual concept.

As the designs are formulated, the director has to keep an eye on the following:

- Historical accuracy
- Movement and staging issues: sightlines, entrances and exits, levels, placement of furniture, balance, scene changes
- Atmosphere: color, mood, lighting
- Costumes: Are there issues with costume changes? Will the costumes allow the actors to move freely? Are they reflective of the personality of the characters? Of their socio-economic status? Would they have these clothes in their closets?

First design meeting

Design meetings are called by the production manager. Attendees include the director, designers, stage manager, and assistants.

- The director presents concept ideas, general approach, research, and personal feelings about the show.
- Designers present their working ideas and any sketches or research they have prepared.
- Everyone discusses the show and ideas that emerge, allowing for free exchange of ideas.
- Designers have what they need to begin the formal design process
- Meeting concludes and date is set for the next meeting.

Don't be afraid to speak up. Once a design is finalized, changes are hard to make.

Second design meeting

- Designers present their sketches for discussion.
- Participants discuss presentation.
- Director and designers agree to the revisions and the designers go back to work refining their ideas.
- Meeting concludes by identifying specific revisions required and by setting a date for the next meeting.

Compliment the designers on their work. Don't be afraid to express concerns about the designs. Ask for what you need in terms of sketches or models so you can accurately assess the designs.

Final design meeting

- Designers present their final renderings or models followed by discussion.
- Last minute requests are made by the director.
- Everyone agrees to final ideas.

- Deadline for changes is set. After the set date, no more changes can be made. Request this deadline to be as late in the process as possible.
- Meeting concludes with director's approval of the final designs.
- Designers can move into the implementation phase. This means handing off the designs to the technical director to begin budgeting and drafting, or to the costume shop.

Director's Checklist for Final Design Meeting

❑ Make sure the revisions correct issues brought up in the last meeting.

❑ After this meeting, major changes are extremely difficult to make, so look closely at everything from every angle. Remember, this is it!

❑ Make sure the design enhances your production.

❑ Ask questions.

❑ If you need more revisions, don't be shy. Tell them what you need and why.

❑ Remember that the bulk of discussions with the lighting designer won't happen until you are in tech rehearsals on the set.

From Design to Tech

After the designs are finalized, production begins in the shops. In order to make sure the concept is being realized accordingly, it is important that the director understand and track the overall process of how the designs are prepared and ultimately produced. This process involves cooperation between many people, from the designers to the production staff. A description of these roles and how they relate to the director and each other is shown in figures 8.1 and 8.2. In addition, the process of realizing scenic, costume, and lighting design are each described below in the form of a ten-step outline.

Ten Steps: Realizing the Scenic Design

1. **Rough Sketches and Thumbnails** The designer creates initial, quick sketches that communicate basic visual ideas. It is important the designer take into account shape and texture, architecture, composition and balance, color, period details, and style.

2. **Renderings** At the second and third design meetings, the designer will provide extensive color realizations of the design ideas, called renderings.

3. **Models** In addition to or in replacement of renderings, some scenic designers create 3-D realizations in small boxes, done to scale using appropriate materials to depict the furnishings and scenic elements.

4. **Ground Plans** An overhead view of the set is produced by the designer.

5. **Elevations** Scale drawings of the set are produced by the designer.

6. **Budget** The **technical director** (TD) budgets the materials and labor needed to build the show.

7. **Drafted Plans** The TD drafts plans indicating how to build each individual component.

8. **Schedule** The TD schedules the build and orders materials, hires labor.

9. **Building Process** The set building process begins when materials arrive and the shop is ready. During this process, all the elements of the set, including flats, stairs, doors, levels, pieces that fly in, and other elements are built and painted. Often they are built in parts and assembled on stage.

10. **Load-in** When it is time to load-in, the elements are brought to the stage, assembled, and final touch-up painting and set dressing is finished. Ideally, the set should be ready by the first **tech rehearsal**, but this is rarely the case. Usually things get finished at the last minute, literally. For **spacing rehearsals**, the director needs the main elements of the set to be in place, including all entrances and exits, staircases and levels. Painting and dressing are not yet necessary.

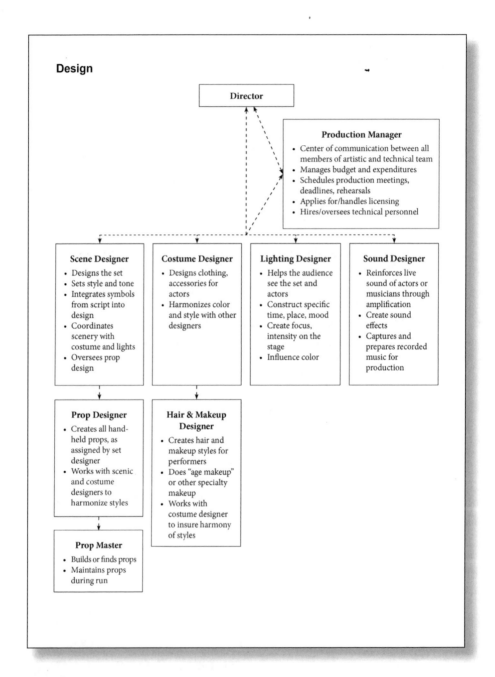

Design

Director

Production Manager
- Center of communication between all members of artistic and technical team
- Manages budget and expenditures
- Schedules production meetings, deadlines, rehearsals
- Applies for/handles licensing
- Hires/oversees technical personnel

Scene Designer
- Designs the set
- Sets style and tone
- Integrates symbols from script into design
- Coordinates scenery with costume and lights
- Oversees prop design

Costume Designer
- Designs clothing, accessories for actors
- Harmonizes color and style with other designers

Lighting Designer
- Helps the audience see the set and actors
- Construct specific time, place, mood
- Create focus, intensity on the stage
- Influence color

Sound Designer
- Reinforces live sound of actors or musicians through amplification
- Create sound effects
- Captures and prepares recorded music for production

Prop Designer
- Creates all hand-held props, as assigned by set designer
- Works with scenic and costume designers to harmonize styles

Hair & Makeup Designer
- Creates hair and makeup styles for performers
- Does "age makeup" or other specialty makeup
- Works with costume designer to insure harmony of styles

Prop Master
- Builds or finds props
- Maintains props during run

Figures 8.1 and 8.2 (p. 62)
The organization of the production from design to implementation. Includes personnel and their responsibilities. The solid arrows represent the flow of information down the chain of command, e.g. the scene designer oversees the prop designer. The dotted lines represent collaborative relationships, e.g. the director presents the concept to the designers, and the designers present their sketches based on the concept to director.

Production

Designers ⇄ **Director**

Production Manager
- Center of communication between all members of artistic and technical team
- Manages budget and expenditures
- Schedules production meetings, deadlines, rehearsals
- Applies for/handles licensing
- Hires/oversees technical personnel

Assistant Director
- Duties vary based on needs of director, production (range from getting coffee, lunch to running rehearsals in director's absence)

Stage Manager
- Runs rehearsals, calls breaks, organizes props and furniture
- Creates the prmpt book, notates blocking
- Calls lines to actors during off-book rehearsals
- Handles cast discipline issues
- Schedules costume fittings, keeps track of rehearsal materials (if rented)
- Facilitates communication between production manager, tech staff, and designers
- Handles rehearsal scheduling and actor contact
- Insures overall quality of show

Technical Director
- Oversees all technical aspects of production
- Manages building of the set
- May do drafting of scenic elements
- Oversees load-in and load-out
- Oversees Master Electrician and carpentry staff, trains crews

Assistant Stage Manager
- Assists Stage Manager
- Creates and manages sign-in sheets
- Does "scene shifts" in rehearsals

Run Crew
- Run fly system backstage
- Change sets
- Supervised by Asst. Director/ Deck Manager

Dressers
- Maintain costumes
- Dress actors during quick changes
- Move costumes
- Ensure actors are dressed correctly

Wig Masters
- Maintain wigs during run
- Styles wigs per design

Light Board Operator
- Runs light board
- Pushes "go" button on the board

Sound Cue Operator
- Pushes "go" to play pre-recorded sound cues
- Maintains wireless equipment
- Installs batteries nightly in mic packs
- Distributes mics before each show, collects after
- Runs sound check
- Runs sound
- Reports to Sound Designer

Master Electrician
- Hangs instruments per lighting design
- Installs wiring; maintains lighting instruments

Master Carpenter
- Primary labor in building sets
- Manages any over-hire labor
- Builds set, furniture

Ten steps: Realizing the Costume Design

1. **Rough Thumbnail Sketches of Characters** The costume designer visualizes ideas for character appearance.

2. **Research** Collected photographs and illustrations indicate ideas for each character.

3. **Final Renderings** Full color drawings of the costumes each character will wear are done by the costume designer. Attached to each rendering are samples of the fabrics that will be used in the costume, known as **fabric swatches**.

4. **Rent/pull, Shop or Build** Depending on the size of the organization and the budget, the costume designer will either begin building (or renting/pulling/shopping) costumes. Costumes can be rented in accordance with the desires of the costume designer, often saving time and money, but sacrificing control. Many modern costumes are purchased and then renovated to fit the particular needs of the production. If costumes can't be bought or rented, they can be built, which requires a costume shop and skilled seamstresses. If the clothing will be built, the designer will send off the renderings and swatches to the shop supervisor so they can begin construction.

5. **Measurements** The measurements of all the actors are taken.

6. **Fittings** As costume creation is in progress, the actors come in for fittings. Once costumes have been fitted, the finishing touches are completed. Wigs are ordered and styled. Make-up designs are conceived.

7. **Costume Parade** Some companies do a "parade" where actors dress in their outfits and show them to the director, one by one. Many designers don't like this process because it shortens the amount of time they have to create the costumes. Keep in mind, seeing a costume out of context and without the advantage of theatrical lighting can affect the way a costume appears.

8. **Publicity Shots** Often the publicity department needs to take publicity shots, so a few costumes might be fitted and readied early to facilitate publicity photos.

9. **Tech Rehearsals** Some directors prefer to run early techs in costume (before the first dress rehearsal). The costume shop must be advised of this in advance. Otherwise, costumes are generally worn for the first time at the first dress rehearsal. Even after that, changes and alterations can still be made, but not easily.

10. **Throughout the Show's Run** During the run of a show, the costume department will oversee the cleaning and mending of costumes, and **dressers** will work backstage and take care of the costumes during the show and on a daily basis.

The designer often will cut and replace a costume that looked great on paper and in the shop, but looks wrong onstage. Directors request this as well. It can cause some tension, but if a costume looks bad, it is ultimately the responsibility of the director to bring it to the costume designer's attention and work with the designer to resolve the problem.

Lighting

1. **Creation of the Light Plot** The lighting designer creates a plan organizing all of the lighting instruments, indicating direction, color, and focus. Instruments consist of individual lights that will illuminate the stage, e.g. spotlights, Fresnel, ellipsoidal, strip lights, footlights, scoops.
2. **Light Hang and Focus** The lights are hung and aimed, according to the lighting plot.
3. **Final Light Plot** The lighting designer prepares a final light plot for the production sometime before load-in.
4. **Instruments** The production manager orders necessary instruments, including gels and gobos (patterned inserts for lighting).
5. **Run-throughs** The lighting designer attends run-through rehearsals late in the process.
6. **Load-in** The lighting design implementation doesn't really begin until load-in, when the master electrician hangs and circuits the instruments according to the lighting plot indications.
7. **Focus** The lighting designer oversees the focus of all the instruments. The actual focusing is the job of the master electrician.
8. **Setting Light Cues** Before or during rehearsal with actors, the individual lighting looks are created. A show consists of many cues. Once approved by the director, they are set and entered into the stage manager's **prompt book** and called by the stage manager in performance.
9. **Recording Cues** Once the cues are finalized, the stage manager writes the numbers in the prompt book. The cues will be programmed into the light board—a computerized keyboard and monitor run by the light board operator.

Lighting can make or break a production. Lights influence, sometimes in subconscious ways, the overall atmosphere of the production and impact of each moment.

Through discussing with the director the feel of the overall show, individual scenes, and specific moments, the lighting designer can get a clear idea of what the director wants. Then the designer uses the plotted lighting instruments to "design" the look of each cue. If there are important moments in the play that require special lighting effects, make sure to discuss those moments with the lighting designer in design meetings.

It is a very exciting process when the director sees the actors in light. The "theatrical" world comes alive and the work always seems to "come into focus."

Changes

After the final design meeting, the set and costumes go into production; nevertheless, during the process of rehearsal, things will arise that require changes in the designs. Changes must be soundly reasoned, affordable, and able to happen given the time and labor available. It is easier to change something if it hasn't been built yet. Costume and prop changes are common, especially costume changes which can be made up until opening (unless it's an entire concept change).

Final Thoughts

Remember that designers are artists like you and their work is equally important. They can make or break a show—so always be respectful. Communication is important. Be articulate. Know their language; know about what they do. Listen, stay open-minded, and be willing to compromise, but remember you don't have to compromise.

Visit the shops frequently. Look at the work being done, support the work being done, but more importantly, make sure it is being done according to your expectations. If you see something unexpected, don't wait! Talk to the designer or PM immediately. The sooner a problem is caught, the easier it is to solve.

In Your DPN

When you meet with designers, it is important to take notes. In your DPN, be sure to record any ideas that emerge, approaches agreed upon, revisions to be made, thoughts you might have, and dates of subsequent meetings. If you need to refer back to an earlier meeting, you will have a written record.

Chapter 9
Casting

Great directors would agree that success depends on making good casting decisions. Regardless of the amount of money you spend, or the quality of your designers, or even the talent of your cast, the wrong actors can devastate the production.

What do I mean by "the wrong actor?" This statement doesn't refer to talent. A good director has an intuitive sense of each character and what makes that character tick. If the actor can't embody that essence, then they are wrong for the part.

An example of an actor who found that essence is Elizabeth Taylor as Maggie in the film of *Cat on a Hot Tin Roof*. This was the perfect marriage of actor and role. She embodied the essence of William's "cat" and made an indelible mark on the portrayal of that character.

However, in the misguided film version of Sondheim's *A Little Night Music*, the same actress was unable to capture the soul (or sing the role) of Desiree Armfeldt. It had nothing to do with age or waning powers. Although she was physically suited to the role, she was never able to capture Desiree's "essence."

Casting is an art unto itself. This is why many directors who can afford the luxury hire casting directors. A good casting director saves the director the painstaking process of initial screening auditions and brings to the project the ability to find the "right" actors—to recognize that spark or certain something.

Auditions are a difficult way to assess potential. Actors are rarely at their best and many talented actors don't audition well. But with experience, a director can recognize talent and skill despite the brutal environment of the audition. After years of auditioning actors, the ability to spot the "essence" and to identify "talent" becomes second nature. Most experienced directors need fifteen seconds with an actor to know whether they are right or not. But in some cases, what is not immediately apparent can surface through a series of auditions.

Ultimately, what a director looks for is the "essence." A director develops an innate sense of each character's essence through the process of research and exploration. Directors envision physicality, but the essence trumps physicality in all but the most specifically drawn characters. Keeping an open mind can lead to surprising and astonishing choices.

For example, I was casting a production of *Once Upon a Mattress*. The lead female is traditionally cast as a feisty firecracker of a girl, generally a skinny, small woman whose big voice will surprise the audience. I was looking for that small, skinny girl when a large-sized actress came in to audition. She was nothing like the ac-

tress I had imagined in the role: initially, I considered this actress for the Queen instead.

Wisely, she had chosen material that showed her feisty side. Her audition was charming, funny, and caught me by surprise. It never occurred to me that a larger actress in the role could be funny—especially when cast against a scrawny, small prince, which is how I cast it. I took a chance and cast her. She played the role as if she thought of her-

self as small and shy, which made the bombast even funnier. She was marvelous and made the show work. It was her essence, her inner spark that made it work. Had I stuck to my original conception of the role, the show would never have been as successful.

Don't make hasty decisions, but keep an open mind when casting. You never know in which direction the winds might blow.

Identifying Your Needs

To prepare for the audition, create a list of all the characters being cast. Referring to your character analysis, list the attributes of each character, including:

- Age range
- Physical requirements and characteristics demanded by the text
- Dialect skills required
- Physical skills required (such as dance, pratfall ability, tricks)
- Personality and "essence" statements

- Note any special requirements of the role, including nudity if it exists
- For musicals: vocal range

Organize this information in a chart to reference during auditions.

Creating Casting Sheets

Create a sheet for each role, using a page for each in your notebook, with the notes for that role in the left-hand margin. To the right of the margin, list the actors that suit those requirements, i.e. who you plan to call back. You might also note what material you ask each actor to prepare for callbacks, or anything else you want to remember regarding the actor. Write what you want to remember; with so many auditions, recalling details is difficult.

An example of a casting sheet appears as figure 9.1. This is condensed. Let each role have its own full sheet of paper so you have plenty of room to make notes.

Casting Notices

Writing a Casting Notice

A quality turnout for an audition depends on a descriptive casting notice. It is important that it include all the information needed by an actor, including time, date, and role information. The better the casting notice describes what you are looking for, the more apt you are to find it.

Casting Sheet

Production: Tony Kushner's *Angels in America*

Role	Actors	Callback materials
Prior Walter		
Age: 20s–very early 30s	*Notate actors here*	*What scenes would*
Emaciated or thin	*that you want to call*	*you like them to read*
Lighter Aryan features	*back for this role and*	*at their callback?*
Essence notes: have to sympathize with him, feel his pain; should be able to play transparent emotions; has to cry onstage; emotional vulnerability and availability; convincing as someone dying of AIDS; flamboyant; able to handle playing drag;	*notes about them*	
Louis		
Age: 20s–very early 30s	*Actor names and*	*Scenes*
Fairly good looking	*notes*	
Has to look very long speeches		
Should look Jewish; darker features		
Has to be pathetic at the same time as he is cold and unfeeling; lost in his own paralyzing intellectualism; rationalizes his selfishness;		
Must be willing to engage in graphic scenes of sexual violence		
Has to kiss another guy.		
Joe Pitt		
Age: Late 20s	*Actor names and*	*Scenes*
Good looking, looks like a Mormon	*notes*	
Blonde, blue-eyed boy next door with authority		
Formal type; looks at home in a suit and tie; hiding a virulent inner life; able to present one face to the world while fighting a demon inside him; should not be flamboyant in any way.		
Has to kiss another guy.		
Harper		
Age: 20's	*Actor names and*	*Scenes*
Attractive, yet can look unhealthy and unnerved	*notes*	
Unraveling; has to play impending sense of lunacy; dreamlike; easily accessed emotions; able to handle very fast shifts in emotion; funny without knowing it; innocent; simple; deeply sad.		

Figure 9.1
Sample casting worksheet
to be used by director during auditions

Director's Checklist for Writing a Casting Notice

❑ Name of the play

❑ Writer and Director

❑ Company name

❑ Location of the production and rehearsals

❑ Location, date and time of auditions

❑ Materials required for the audition

❑ Roles and descriptions; what roles are open

❑ How to submit for the audition

❑ Whether union or non-union, paid or unpaid

❑ Identify type of audition: open call, by submission, agents' submissions only, etc.

❑ Special requirements such as nudity, smoking, etc.

Depending on where you are, the casting notice can be in paragraph form for submission in publications like *Backstage* and *Show Business Magazine*, as a flier, or online blurb. Here are two examples of submissions you would list in a trade paper format:

Example #1: Non-Equity principal casting for Red Apple Theatre's production of Tony Kushner's *Angels in America*

> Red Apple Theatre Company announces auditions for all roles in M. Wainstein's production, opening on October 13, 2010 at the Red Apple Theatre, 104 East 42nd Street, New York City. Roles available: Prior Walter—20s to early 30s, emaciated, emotionally vulnerable, obviously of Anglo descent; Louis, his partner—late 20s, Jewish New Yorker, verbose, ignorant of how actions can harm others; Joe Pitt—20s, Mormon from Salt Lake City, corporate, leading a false life; Harper, his wife—20s, a pill-popping mess. Please prepare two contrasting one-minute monologues and be prepared for cold readings. Auditions at the Ansonia Hotel, 72nd and Broadway, suite 1509; Thursday, August 10th. Submissions accepted by email only. Send pic and resume to angels@mac.com. No open calls; by appt. only. All roles paid, rehearsals and performances. Show runs October 13, open-ended; performances Wednesdays through Sundays.

Example #2: Equity principal auditions casting for Red Apple Theatre's production of Tony Kushner's *Angels in America*

> Red Apple Theatre Company announces auditions for all roles in (your name)'s production of Tony Kushner's *Angels in America*, opening on October 13, 2010 at the Red Apple Theatre, 104 East 42nd Street, New York City. Roles available: Prior Walter—20s to early 30s, emaciated, emotionally vulnerable, obviously of Anglo descent; Louis, his partner—late 20s, Jewish New Yorker, verbose, ignorant of how actions can harm others; Joe Pitt—20s, Mormon from Salt Lake City, corporate, leading a false life; Harper, his wife—20s, a pill-popping mess. Open call at Ansonia Hotel, 72nd and Broadway, suite 1509; Thursday, August 10th at 10am. Sign-in begins 8a.m. Sides will be available at audition. Bring pic and resume. Run open-ended.

Advertising your Casting Notice

Internet

The internet is full of casting sites. Do a Google search to find them. If you are looking to attract actors nationwide, or to attend auditions in New York City, primary casting sites are:

- *Backstage*: Click the casting/jobs button and then go to "find talent: Casting Center." You will need to create an account. http://www.backstage.com/bso/index.jsp.
- *Show Business Weekly*: You should subscribe to access all functions. http://www.showbusinessweekly.com/casting/casting.shtml
- *Playbill.com*: There is a $24.95 charge for running each individual notice. http://www.playbill.com/jobs/post/
- *Craigslist.com*: Most Craigslist sites have local casting categories. This is better for local searches. No charge!

Print

Backstage print edition: widely read by actors seeking employment, but it is limited to the New York area. Some film.

Show Business Weekly: Also widely read among New York actors, but limited to New York and regional auditions. Some film.

Casting locally

- Local casting hotlines
- Facebook
- Local newspaper

- Craigslist.com
- Posters and fliers
- Word of mouth
- Notice of auditions on your company's website

Types of Casting Calls

Equity Principal and Chorus Auditions Equity has strict guidelines for professional auditions. Generally they are advertised in Backstage and on the Equity casting boards. They are limited to equity actors, although non-Equity actors can attend and request to be seen. If there is time non-Equity actors might get into the audition, but they have to wait for an opening. All auditions for Equity productions must be registered with Actor's Equity.

Agent Submissions Larger productions and regional theatres will invite agents to submit clients. The casting director will coordinate with the agents and schedule the auditions for the director, which are generally held in a big city, usually New York.

Non-Equity Open Calls (also known as Cattle Calls) Open calls have no set appointment times. Actors come to the audition and sign up for a number. Ideally, a sign-up sheet will be available to actors many hours before the audition. Actors wait for their turn, and that wait can be hours or even days.

Large Unified Auditions Each region has its own theatre organization. For example, in the Southern USA it's the Southeastern Theatre Conference (www.setc. org). They all hold auditions in a centralized location, where dozens of companies seeking actors audition hundreds of actors seeking work. Most states also have annual state-wide auditions as do large cities.

Non-Equity Auditions by Appointment Either through submissions of headshots or email contact with the company, actors are scheduled in 3-5 minute intervals. This way the actor can schedule their day, and the producer has a good idea who is coming and how many will be auditioning; it is more convenient for all involved.

The Audition

Preparing for the Audition

There are a number of things the director must do to host an audition, from securing a space to printing signs and sign-in sheets. This section explains each of those things and how to do them.

Director's Checklist for Preparing an Audition

❑ Rent or arrange for the audition room (also for call-back auditions).

❑ Request or arrange for the tables, chairs and music stands you will need.

❑ Determine the time for the auditions, and the length of each audition.

❑ Create an appointment grid if auditioning "by appointment" and a way to receive and schedule appointment requests. Email is the best means; it is easy to monitor and every communication can be saved for future reference.

❑ Hire or arrange for a hall monitor.

❑ Hire or arrange for a reader if needed.

❑ Create the sign-in sheet (for all types of auditions).

❑ Hire a good accompanist for musical auditions.

❑ Prepare sides or any musical materials you might want to distribute or use during the audition. Have plenty of copies on hand to distribute.

❑ Put together your casting worksheet.

❑ Create signage you might need to direct actors from the main entrance of the building to the audition room.

❑ Create a one-page description of the play and production that actors can read while waiting.

❑ For cattle calls, make sure to have a holding room where actors can wait.

Additional items for College and Community Theatre Casting

❑ Create an audition form that captures information about rehearsal conflicts.

❑ Make commitment clear, especially rehearsal times and run dates.

Rent or Arrange for the Audition Room Depending on the location of your audition, you will either have a room available to you or you will have to rent a room. If you are auditioning in a big city such as New York there are many such facilities that rent by the hour or day. Prices can range from $25/hour to more than $100/hour.

If you are auditioning in a college or community theatre setting you most likely will have free access to audition spaces. Make sure they are big enough and have a separate area where the actors can wait. Reserve the spaces through the building managers.

To find a space in New York (or locally) do a Google search for "New York Audition Spaces" or "New York Audition Studios." Selected internet resources for studios in New York City are displayed in figure 9.2.

Figure 9.2
Resources for
securing audition
spaces in
New York City

Name	Website
New York Music Spaces.com	http://nycmusicspaces.org/music_search.html
New York Performing Arts Spaces	http://nycpaspaces.org/show/about/welcome.html
From the Actor's Yellow Pages	http://yellowpages.backstage.com/products/list-products.php?category_id=81
Simple Studios in New York	http://www.simplestudiosnyc.com/
Ripley Grier Studios	http://www.ripleygrier.com/
New York Dance spaces	http://nycdancespaces.org/dance_search.html

Obtain Tables, Chairs, Music Stands Request or arrange for the tables, chairs and music stands you will need. You will need at least one long table and a few chairs. The director, choreographer and other production staff sit behind the table and the actors perform several feet in front of the table. Make sure actors have access to a chair.

Determine Time and Length of Each Audition Before you create your appointment grid, determine how long you want each audition to last. The audition notice stipulated the requirements for the audition. Consider the time needed for each actor to fulfill those requirements and plan accordingly. If two one-minute monologues are requested, you will need at least 3 minutes per actor, leaving time for entering and exiting and chatting if needed.

Create Appointment Grid Using a Word™ table or Excel™ spreadsheet create an appointment grid if auditioning "by appointment," and a way to receive and schedule appointment requests. Create a column for the time, the actor's name and their contact information. Make sure to capture contact information as you might need to send informational emails to the actors prior to or after the audition.

Hire or Arrange for Hall Monitor You will need someone to receive actors outside the audition space. They will handle the sign-in process, walk-ins, making sure the actors have their pictures and resumes ready, and giving them information they will need for the audition once inside the room. You can often find a volunteer for this.

Hire or Arrange for a Reader If you are doing cold readings, one actor at a time, you will need a reader to read with each actor. The reader will sit near your table and read all the other lines in the scene. The stage manager can also serve this purpose. The reader should not "act" with the actor, but remain neutral.

Create the Sign-in Sheet When the actors arrive, they note their arrival on the sign-in sheet. The sign-in sheet should list all the appointments and leave space for initials beside each actor's name. Have a copy of the list in the room and with the hall monitor. In the case of an open call with no appointments, prepare a grid of numbered spaces next to which the actors can sign their names and secure their places in the queue.

Hire a Good Accompanist for Musical Auditions It is critical to hire a pianist who is a skilled sight-reader and has experience playing auditions. This person can cost from $25–$150 per hour or it can be the musical director or rehearsal pianist for the production. Book them well in advance! The great ones are always busy.

Prepare Sides or Any Musical Materials You Might Need If you are doing cold readings you will need to prepare **sides** for the actors and the reader. Sides are cuttings from the play of two- to three-person scenes. Have plenty of copies available with the monitor so actors can look at the materials while they are waiting. Label each scene by character and organize them for quick access. If you will ask actors to sing from the score of the show, you will need to prepare copies of the sheet music for the songs you want them to sing.

Put Together Your Casting Worksheet Bring your sheets, extra paper, copies of the play, and pencils to the audition.

Create Signage to Direct Actors to the Room If the room is difficult to locate, post signs at the entrance door to the building and wherever else it is needed to help the actors find you.

Create a One-page Description of Play Create a one-page description of the play and the production that actors can read while waiting. Especially in college and community theatre, this description serves to familiarize the auditioners with the show as well as the rehearsal and performance schedule. Sometimes the time commitment is too much. It is best that potential cast members know the schedule in advance so they can evaluate whether they should audition or not. You can also state rates of pay or if the show doesn't pay, the roles being cast, information about the theatre company, the rehearsal schedule, show dates, etc.

Create an Audition Form with Conflict Information In college and community theatre situations, actors will have conflicts with rehearsals. At the audition, capture this information. If an actor has too many conflicts, ask them if they can rearrange their schedule should they be cast. They might be able to eliminate many conflicts if they want the part. When you are creating your rehearsal schedule, the conflict information is important. Create a simple form that captures name, contact information, and conflict list. Use the table (figure 9.3) as a guide.

Name	Email Address	Conflicts
John Abernathy	(633) 212-2020 jabernathy77@gmail.com	Thursdays 5 PM-8PM
Ken Johnson	(633) 266-4763 Ken.johnson658@yahoo.com	Mondays (November)
Rebecca Novak	(418) 344-9489 Becca9856@hotmail.com	Saturday, Oct. 3

Figure 9.3
How to organize an audtion form

Audition Format for a Non-musical Play

Monologues or Cold Readings? Both a monologue and cold reading can tell you a lot about an actor's suitability for a role.

Monologues can reveal what actors can do with material they have fully prepared. The performance of a monologue reveals information about an actor's self-image, and how he or she performs under pressure. However, even the most seasoned pro can go afoul in an audition situation (how they handle problems can be very telling). Even if the monologue is great, always have the actor also read from the script. Some audition extremely well with their carefully selected material, but are not great actors. Readings can be done at the initial audition with the reader, or at callbacks.

In a **cold reading**, the director furnishes the actor with dialogue from the script to read with either another actor or a reader. Using material from the script helps the director assess the suitability of an actor for a specific role. The more time the actor has with the script before the audition, the more accurate the assessment of their potential. If there is no way to have dialogue scenes available beforehand for actors to prepare, give them a few minutes in the hall to look it over before they begin.

Welcome the Actor Every actor is nervous at an audition, so try to make them feel at ease. Do what you can to make them comfortable. Welcome them, smile, and engage in light conversation. It is to the director's advantage that the actor feels relaxed.

Observe Watch the audition; don't let your mind wander. Don't spend time during the audition looking at the resume! If you like the actor, make notes in the appropriate places on your audition worksheet. Decide the role(s) for which the actor would be well-suited, and which they should prepare for callbacks. Ask them to do a second monologue if you want to see more. Talk to the actors you like. Try to get a sense of what working with them might be like. Be selective about who you invite to the callback.

Give Direction If you are interested in an actor, give them an **adjustment**.

> **Adjustment:** a change in choice or tactic. For example, if the actor does a monologue with one strong choice, give them a different choice and see if they can make the change.

Giving an adjustment allows you to test the actor's ability to take direction. How they deal with the adjustment also provides insight into their sense of their collegiality and collaborative nature. If you like an actor, let the actor know and ask them to prepare specific materials for callbacks. Don't forget to thank each actor for their time.

Make Notes Directly on Resumes This is very useful if you are seeing a lot of actors. I assign point values on the top right hand corner of the resume, along with the role or roles they might be suitable for. For the ones I am very interested in, I make additional notes on my casting sheets. Later, it is easy to sort out the strong candidates by arranging the resumes by ranking numbers.

Look at the Resume A resume might or might not be a factual list of what an actor has done. Some young actors may pad their resumes, i.e. add fictitious roles and companies. However, given the ease of checking the veracity of a resume, most are honest. Look at the directors the actor has worked with. If you are familiar with one, call for a reference.

The resume also gives you a sense of the actor's experience by the number and quality of the credits listed. If you are casting a major leading role and the actor has only done chorus in musicals, you might question whether this person is ready for the job.

In the case of college and community theatre, consider the conflict form. Make sure the actor's availability is suitable.

Dress Professionally A director's professional appearance is important. Represent yourself well.

Don't Eat, Drink or Talk During Auditions This is very rude. Don't do it!

Look for Warning Signs These are red flags that might indicate an actor who will cause problems if cast:

- Bad or indifferent attitude
- Can't take or resists direction
- Ill-prepared
- Sloppily dressed
- Talks about the other offers he/she is considering
- Sloppy resume
- Rude to the hall monitor (make sure hall monitor tells you about rude people)
- Overly obsequious or forced pleasantness
- Late for appointment

After the Audition: Callbacks

Go Over Your Notes Look at your notes immediately after the audition. Note who you liked, consider potential casting choices, and make notes accordingly. Doing this when the names and faces are fresh is best.

Decide Who Will be Called Back From the notes, decide whom you want to see again and what you want to see them do (if you haven't already assigned them callback material). Give the information to the stage manager to contact the actors and tell them what to prepare. Don't require memorization. If someone does memorize, that tells you about what kind of commitment they will make.

Organize the Callbacks by Roles You will want certain actors to read roles with other actors. Determine who will read with whom and which groupings of actors you wish to see work together. With the help of your stage manager, figure out how you will organize the callbacks in the most expeditious way.

Because each character has relationships with other characters, make sure to read "potentials" together to see how they work together and what kind of chemistry exists.

By Groups of Two You can schedule actors by scene. In this scenario, you call two actors back at the same time and have them read together. Decide the scenes they will read and let the stage manager copy those scenes and notify the actors. Ask them to arrive early to run the scene with their partners. The downside of this approach is seeing each actor with only one partner.

In Larger Groups You can call five or ten actors back at a time and have them read with different partners in different scenes for as long as you wish. When they arrive, assign the first scene and set of scene partners and let everyone go into the hall to rehearse. After they perform, change partners and scenes and have them perform again. You can eliminate actors you are not interested in or keep everyone until the end. Some directors like to pare down to the actual actors they want to cast and have them read with each other to get a sense of the actual ensemble they are casting.

Don't rush this process. Do what is necessary to cast your production in the best way possible. If you have to schedule a second callback, do so.

After the actors are excused, go over your choices and double and triple check to ensure you haven't overlooked anyone.

When you are absolutely certain of your choices, announce the cast and have the stage manager or casting director contact the actors or their agents to offer them the roles. Have a backup plan for each role in case actors are unable to accept the job. Cast understudies if you are able to.

If you still need more time with certain actors, schedule another callback. Wait to announce your decisions until all roles are cast.

Depending on the venue type, post a cast list.

If you can, contact the actors you have not cast, via email or phone, to let them know they have not been cast and to thank them for their time. It is a nice courtesy.

Casting Musicals

For most musicals, actors must sing and move well. Therefore, you need to add two components to the audition process: singing and movement auditions.

The Vocal Audition

Instead of doing monologues or cold readings at the first audition, a vocal audition is a good way to quickly screen for non-singers. Ask performers to prepare one or two short, sixteen-bar selections that show their range. Schedule them in two- to four-minute blocks of time. Request they bring music prepared for an accompanist.

Don't request that actors perform music from the show for their first selection. Encourage actors to sing in the style of the show, using music they are comfortable with. You can ask them to prepare a song from the show as their second selection or have music from the show on hand. If you like someone you can ask them to sing music from the show.

If you want to call an actor back, tell them what song you want them to prepare for the callback and provide the sheet music if possible. In addition, give them sides for specific characters so they can prepare readings as well.

At the vocal audition, assess the following:

- Vocal range and voice type: the lowest note in their range to the highest
- Musicianship: do they make music or just noise?
- Vocal quality: is their voice beautiful, well produced?
- Phrasing skills: Do they breathe in the middle of words? Are they able to create fluid phrases that make sense and tell the story?
- Ability to incorporate character into performance: Do they have range as actors? Are they performing as themselves or creating characters?
- Stage presence: Do you want to watch them? Are you compelled to watch them?

If you like the actor, you can offer an invitation to callbacks before he or she has even left the room. Tell the actor what you want prepared for the callback, and make a note of the request on your casting worksheet. If you are considering the actor for the chorus, ask him or her to attend the dance audition or movers' call.

If you ask actors to prepare certain songs for callbacks, have copies of those songs (organized by character) available to hand out at auditions. Give them some time to learn the song. Tell them the song doesn't have to be memorized, but they should be familiar with it. If they do memorize the song, take note! Hard workers usually memorize.

Most directors don't invite actors to callbacks at the audition. Instead, the stage manager contacts the actors and communicates to them what the director wants at callbacks. In that case, the actors find their own way to learn the music. Most show-tune sheet music can be found at www.1800sheetmusic.com. iTunes is a treasure trove of recordings. Regardless, make sure to have copies of the requested songs on hand at the callback.

Movement Auditions

The Dance Call The choreographer or an assistant runs the dance call, at which the auditioners are taught a short combination that reflects the skill level required and style of the show. Before the dance call, give the choreographer the resumes and ask them to notate on the resume, on a scale of 1–10, the dance ability of the performer. Although each choreographer has a unique way of evaluating dancers, what ultimately matters is that the director can understand the notations. Through this process, the director and choreographer will work together to cast the show.

Dancers Only Call If you need a trained dancing chorus in the show (a group that dances but doesn't need to sing), or strong dancers that sing, schedule an open dance call and don't require the dancers to attend singing auditions.

The Movement Call The movement call is a type of dance call, also run by the choreographer, at which actors are evaluated for their ability to handle simple dance movement or musical staging. The combination is simpler and more about style than triple pirouettes.

The director can attend the dance or movement call to observe the abilities of those under consideration.

The Callback

The callback audition includes a combination of requested vocal auditions such as assigned songs from the show, and readings from the script (in the same way described for non-musical auditions). At this point, the director assesses a selected actor's suitability for the various roles and chorus positions being cast.

Generally the choreographer will schedule their own callback if it's a dance-heavy show involving a dancing chorus.

Testing the actors' acting abilities is crucial. They've already proven they can sing and move. The callback is the time to evaluate their acting abilities, how they harmonize (literally and figuratively) with other performers, and whether they will be able to handle the role.

If the show calls for duet or harmony singing, test harmonizing and blending skills. Have materials ready for the singers to learn that is not only simple but will showcase their abilities (or lack thereof). This is critical in a show like *Forever Plaid*, where the entire show consists of tight, four-part-harmony singing.

Final Thoughts

Don't rush the casting process. This is the most critical decision you will make. Do as much as is required to accurately assess the actors' ability.

Imagine possible casting groupings: how will they work together? If you are casting a family, consider similarity of physical appearance.

Finally, chemistry is extremely important to a successful ensemble of actors. Whether they are playing lovers, friends, family, or enemies, how the actors relate to each other has a great effect on the final result. Use your intuition and trust your inner voice.

PART III: REHEARSALS

Chapter 10
Preparing for Rehearsals

A show's success relies on an organized, exciting, productive, and creative rehearsal process. If rehearsal isn't stimulating and fun, the show will suffer. "Fun" in rehearsal can be fun in the usual sense of the word, but it can also be the joy of accomplishments born of hard work. Rehearsals are often painful, emotional, and draining, but as artists, we revel in the journey of the creative process.

Having a clear plan for the rehearsals will free the actors and the director to concentrate on bringing a script to three-dimensional life by providing a structured environment. Many directors, especially back in the 1960s, believed that structure was detrimental to the creative process. While free and unstructured rehearsals can lead to interesting results, structure enables the creative process by freeing the brain and heart to focus solely on the playmaking.

Director's Checklist: Preparing for Rehearsals

❑ Organize the rehearsal schedule (integrating actor conflicts).

❑ Make rehearsal plans.

❑ Prepare a DPN or prompt book for recording detailed blocking notes.

❑ Organize the rehearsal props.

❑ Define the roles and responsibilities of the stage managers.

❑ Use daily sign-in sheets for larger shows (see figure 10.1).

❑ Clearly communicate expectations to the actors.

❑ Set rehearsal rules, including specified break times (see figure 10.2).

❑ Compile a contact list.

❑ Display ground plans and elevations on the wall, easily visible.

❑ Create a safe environment that grants the freedom to explore, take risks, fail and act like a fool.

❑ Request that the actors prepare for each rehearsal and set goals.

Rehearsal Schedules

The rehearsal schedule will depend on the particular situation in which you work. This section will first provide an overview of particular considerations for different types of productions (i.e. Equity, non-Equity regional/summer, community/college), and then detail how to build rehearsal schedules in a step-by-step fashion.

Production Name: _____

Company: _____

Logo:

Please initial the appropriate square when you arrive.

Actor names	Date	Date	Date	Date	Date

Figure 10.1
Sample sign-in sheet for taking attendance at rehearsals

Scheduling for Different Types of Theatre

Equity or other professional theatre

Most often, actors are on call for all rehearsals in Equity or professional theatre. They are required to attend whenever called. Conflicts are not an issue; actors are employed by the production, and unless they have negotiated release time for other projects, they are expected to be at all scheduled rehearsals during the work week, which is Tuesday through Sunday, usually 10 A.M.–6 P.M. But in repertory and summer theatre situations, days and times may vary.

During tech and final rehearsals, Equity stipulates that longer rehearsal days may be allowed, to provide the time needed.

Eight Out of Ten Eight out of ten is a schedule wherein actors can be scheduled for up to eight hours in a ten-hour work day (e.g. 9 A.M.–1 P.M., one-hour lunch, 2 P.M.–6 P.M.). The actor doesn't have to be called for the entire eight hours, but the maximum amount they can work is eight in any given ten-hour period.

Ten Out of Twelve Ten out of twelve is a standard call for technical and dress rehearsal periods. Actors can work a maximum of ten hours in any given twelve-hour period, allowing an hour each for lunch and dinner.

Breaks Give five-minute breaks every hour, or ten minutes if you work for an hour and a half. The stage manager calls the breaks by gently reminding the director it is time. Make sure your stage manager understands, if you are in the middle of working on something, to wait until a suitable break in focus, even if you go over five minutes.

Rehearsal Rules

1. Ten minutes early is on time.

2. If you are going to be late, call the stage manager as early as possible to inform them of the situation and your expected arrival time.

3. Warm up on your own prior to starting.

4. Be prepared.

5. No complaining.

6. No cell phones.

7. Breaks on the hour or hour and a half.

8. No "directing" other actors!

9. If you are having problems, speak up!

10. Please finish eating before rehearsal begins or eat on breaks.

11. Do not come to rehearsal high on anything except art!

12. Come to rehearsal with goals and plans.

13. Bring something to read or otherwise occupy yourself in case we are running late or you have to sit around.

14. Being an artist is a great gift, don't take it for granted

15. If you need help, ask for it.

16. Have fun, don't take anything too seriously.

Figure 10.2
Rehearsal rules

In a repertory or stock situation, if the Equity actors are appearing in one show while rehearsing an upcoming show, they are restricted to rehearsing two hours on a two-show day, and six hours if they are on a one-show day.

Generally, the schedule distributed to the company is posted daily on the call-board. Because the actors expect to be there every day, the company doesn't need to be given a long-term schedule. At the end of each day, the director informs the stage manager about the following day's schedule, and it gets posted on the board and sent via email. Sometimes a guest, such as a fight choreographer, will come in for a few days. In these cases, the sessions need to be scheduled in advance; otherwise, the schedule evolves daily depending on the needs of the production.

Nevertheless, a director can and should still map out their plan for the rehearsal process to ensure the show is ready on time.

Non-Equity regional or summer theatre

The most grueling of all work experiences for directors and actors is non-Equity summer stock. There are no rules protecting actors, and in some unforgiving situations, actors work up to fourteen hours a day with minimal break time. In most cases, actors are rehearsing one show while performing another in a season of five to ten shows that rehearse for one to two weeks per show. In some cases, actors don't get a day off for weeks. If hired to direct for a company like this, try to direct a show early in the season when everyone is still fresh!

Scheduling rehearsals is tricky because the schedule must take into account the actors' other daily commitments and duties such as working in the box office or performing a children's show. There are no limitations on the length of calls or the times scheduled. Keep in mind the intensity of the actor's work schedule. Don't call actors if they are not needed and organize the schedule to maximize their participation when called.

On two-show days, actors are usually free for a maximum of two hours in the morning before lunch. Actors save energy for the full day of performances ahead of them. On two-show days, if you must rehearse, schedule work that doesn't require a lot of energy: review blocking and dance numbers and run lines. If possible, avoid blocking new scenes or intense acting on these days if the schedule allows, and avoid calling actors with large parts in that day's performances. In fact, avoid rehearsing at all.

If you must rehearse, you can call afternoon rehearsals between the matinee and dinner, but don't expect focus or energy.

In one- or two-week stock, the current show usually closes on Sunday afternoon and the next show opens early in the following week. The tech crew strikes one show and stays up all night loading-in the next. The cast comes onstage sometime Monday to space the show and give the crew a few hours to sleep. By Monday night, the show is in tech and can open as early as Tuesday or as late as Friday. Some opening nights are the first time the show runs without interruption. Stay calm and organized, and be prepared.

College and community theatre

College students have a thousand things going on. The same is true for working folks who volunteer for community theatre productions. Even if the director insists on no conflicts, most participants' lifestyles make that impossible. Generally, it is better to cast a good actor with a few conflicts than a mediocre one with no conflicts.

Once cast, use the information about conflicts from the audition conflict form, and confirm with each actor that those conflicts remain irresolvable. Often, actors will clear their schedule once they get the role, but if there are always irresolvable conflicts, work around them.

As you create the schedule, have the list of conflicts at hand so you can schedule scenes that don't include the absent actors, if possible.

Creating the Schedule for a Non-musical Play

Preparation work

The following example applies to college and community theatre productions, but can easily be adapted to fit all circumstances. Given the hectic lives of students and community theatre actors, giving them a full schedule in advance will allow them to schedule their lives around rehearsals.

Steps for preparing to write a rehearsal schedule:

1. Break the play down into French scenes, wherein each "scene" includes a specific group of actors.
2. For musicals, add songs and dance numbers to the breakdown. Make sure to consult with the musical director and choreographer to determine time needed for music and dance rehearsals.
3. Make a list of all scenes (songs and dances), and which of the cast are involved in each.
4. Note for each scene the amount of table time and staging time you will need, expressed in "hours."
5. Given the length of the rehearsal period, decide when the first run of each act should occur.
6. Note dates for crew views, techs, dresses and opening.

Schedule the "landmarks"

The rehearsal timeline is made up of a series of landmark dates; these dates form the skeleton of the schedule. The landmark dates for both a musicals and non-musicals appear in figure 10.3. In order to create the rehearsal schedule, the director ought to begin with a grid containing each rehearsal day, like the one shown in figure 10.4. Be sure to note the conflicts and location of each rehearsal. Then, the director determines the placement of the landmark dates according to the rules that follow. For more on scheduling rehearsals, consult the examples listed at the end of the book in Appendix 3: Example Rehearsal Schedules.

Figure 10.3
Rehearsal
schedule
timeline

Rehearsal Schedule Timeline Landmarks	
Non-Musical	Musical
First day	First day
Table readings	Musical rehearsals
Blocking rehearsals	Dance and staging rehearsals
Off-book	Off-book
Run-through and work-through period	Run-through and dance brush-up period
Crew view day	Crew view day
Final run-through in rehearsal space	Final run-through in rehearsal space
Spacing rehearsals onstage	Initial spacing rehearsals onstage
Technical rehearsals	Technical rehearsals
Final dress	Final dress
Opening night	Opening night

For a non-musical:

1. **First Meeting** Schedule the first meeting on the first day of rehearsal with the whole company for designer presentations and the first read-through.
2. **Already Scheduled Rehearsals** Rehearsals that are already scheduled or determined by the production may include crew-views, techs, dresses, previews, and the opening. Enter these into the grid.
3. **First Run-through** The date of the first run-through should occur between half and three-quarters of the way through the pre-tech period.

4. **Table Reading** Consider how much time you have between the first rehearsal and the first run-through. Decide how much table reading time you can afford during that period. Schedule table rehearsals for the first days of rehearsal (for non-musicals). Break down the table rehearsals into full readings and scene work. For the scene work days, schedule each scene and the actors required for that scene. Check to make sure you are not running into conflicts. Try to schedule actors back to back so they aren't sitting around for an hour between scene calls. End the table reading period with a full, uninterrupted read-through.

5. **Blocking Rehearsals** After the final table read, schedule blocking rehearsals, scene by scene, indicating on the grid which actors are called. Try to schedule actors back to back, avoiding long breaks between their calls. Next, begin breaking down each block of rehearsal into the French scenes you outlined in the preparation work. Each scene should be scheduled for the amount of time you estimated in your preparation work. Keep in mind that although it is best to proceed chronologically, you must also respect the actors' time. Double check conflicts for each day so you can work around actors that are unavailable. Scheduling with the actors' convenience in mind can get a little tricky, but nothing is worse for an actor than rehearsing a scene, then having a two hour break, then rehearsing another scene, then having another break, etc. Be respectful of everyone's time even if it means rehearsing scenes out of order.

6. **Stumble-throughs** Every time you block a chunk of the show, schedule both

Schedule

Day 1			Day 8		
Conflicts:			*Conflicts:*		
Time		Agenda	Time		Agenda

Day 2			Day 9		
Conflicts:			*Conflicts:*		
Time		Agenda	Time		Agenda

Day 3			Day 10		
Conflicts:			*Conflicts:*		
Time		Agenda	Time		Agenda

Day 4			Day 11		
Conflicts:			*Conflicts:*		
Time		Agenda	Time		Agenda

Day 5			Day 12		
Conflicts:			*Conflicts:*		
Time		Agenda	Time		Agenda

Day 6			Day 13		
Conflicts:			*Conflicts:*		
Time		Agenda	Time		Agenda

Day 7			Day 14		
Conflicts:			*Conflicts:*		
Time		Agenda	Time		Agenda

Figure 10.4
Production worksheet

a stumble-through rehearsal and a time for reviewing those scenes before moving on to new material. After blocking each act, be sure to schedule a stumble-through and work-through rehearsal before proceeding to the next act. Remember to keep an eye on the time you have left before you have to begin the run-throughs. The blocking and stumble-through period ends the day before the first full run-through. Plan accordingly.

For a musical:

1. **First Meeting** Schedule a first meeting on the first day of rehearsal with the whole company for designer presentations, immediately followed by the first music rehearsal.

2. **Already Scheduled Rehearsals** Rehearsals that are already scheduled or determined by the production may include crew-views, techs, dresses, previews, and the opening. Enter these into the grid.

3. **First Run-through** The date of the first run-through should occur between half and three-quarters of the way through the pre-tech period.

4. **Key Runs** Schedule dates for the run of first act, second act, and full show, based on how much time you determine each will take.

5. **Musical Rehearsals** Look at how much time you have between the first rehearsal and the first run to get a sense of the time available for the staging rehearsals. Schedule the musical rehearsals first. If some of the cast is not in a musical rehearsal, you may plan dance or staging rehearsals concurrently, but remember that music takes precedence at the beginning.

6. **Read- and Sing-through** Once all music is learned, the director should schedule a read- and sing-through of the entire show with all cast present. Invite designers to attend.

7. **Staging and Dance Rehearsals** Schedule staging rehearsals, allowing time to read and discuss the scene before blocking. In order to use time wisely, the director should concurrently schedule dance and staging rehearsals—granted they don't use the same actors—in different spaces when possible.

8. **Stumble-throughs** Schedule stumble-throughs as soon as each act is blocked and choreographed. This should be followed by a work-through period before moving on to the next act. Rotate between full-cast work-throughs and principal-only work-throughs, in order that the director may focus on scene work without the distraction of the ensemble.

9. **Music Reviews** Periodic music reviews should occur during staging and run process.

10. **Full Runs** Schedule full runs to begin eighty percent of the way through the period between first rehearsal and tech. Schedule time during the runs for TBA scene work as well as music and dance brush-ups. You'll need the extra time!

Review the schedule

Don't forget: Always double and triple check to make sure that you have allowed enough time for each task, and that you have worked around conflicts. Have the stage manager double-check the schedule before publishing it.

Preparing the Rehearsal Room

Director's Checklist: Setting Up the Space—What's Needed

❑ Rehearsal props and furniture

❑ Water and accessibility to bathrooms

❑ Director's table and chairs

❑ Table or other storage for props

❑ Rack for rehearsal costumes

❑ Chairs for actors and artistic staff

❑ Ground plan

❑ Set renderings

❑ Costume renderings

Rehearsal Props and Furniture

Representative furniture and props are required when blocking begins. A list of all rehearsal props needed, by scene, should be given to the stage manager a week or so before blocking begins so they have time to gather the items. Such a list is shown in figure 10.5. Don't expect to use the real props in rehearsals. If you do, chances are they will be destroyed. Instead, use substitute items that are similar in size, weight and structure.

Ideally, if there will be a sofa on the set, there should be a sofa of corresponding size and feel for rehearsals. The same goes for chairs and tables. Furniture is set as indicated on the ground plan. Create as accurate a representation of the real scenic elements as possible, paying close attention to the distance between items.

Props can be anything that approximates the size, shape, and weight of the item. Ideally, a prop should be the same kind of item or a replica of the item itself. In some cases, you can use the real thing as long as the rehearsal process will not cause damage or wear.

The prop table

In order to manage the props themselves, the stage manager should have a table set up in the rehearsal hall. Use tape to divide the top of the table into sections and in each section, place one prop. Label each square to indicate the prop that belongs there. The same setup is used for a backstage prop table during performances.

Place the prop table in the same relative location to the playing area as it will be in performances. Props are removed from the table when used and replaced by the actor or stage manager when finished. Impress upon the actors that props should never leave the table except when being used and should always be returned.

Prop List

Scene	Prop name/description	Character	Hand	Set	Dress

Figure 10.5
Rehearsal prop list to be filled out by director and given to stage manager

Rehearsal Costumes

When rehearsing a period piece, or when the style of the clothing has a significant impact on the way characters move or behave, insist on using rehearsal costumes. Actors can bring in appropriate clothing to serve as their own rehearsal costumes, or better yet, the shop can supply costume pieces to be worn in rehearsals. Shoes are especially important in developing physicality. Require actors to wear shoes that are similar in feel to their costume shoes. If someone is playing a formally-dressed businessman or woman, they shouldn't wear sneakers.

Example: A Restoration comedy

Supply the ladies with corsets and long dresses, or hoop skirts if called for, and appropriate footwear. When using hoops, only the actual hoop is needed for rehearsal. Actors need to get used to working around the awkwardness of wearing a hoop. For men, vests, waistcoats and hard-soled shoes will allow them to experience the influence of their costume on physicality. Depending on the period and the costume design, require as little as a pair of specific shoes or an entire costume. The idea is to have the actors wear clothes that give them the same experience as their costumes. Store them on a rack in the rehearsal hall, available to the actors as they arrive.

The Director's Table

Once the ground plan is taped and furniture is set, place the production table where the audience will be in relation to the stage. If the stage configuration is three-quarter thrust or in the round, the production table can move from place to place, allowing the director to see the show from all the vantage points. Chairs are needed behind the table for the director, stage manager, assistants, choreographer, and anyone else who needs to be there.

Make sure there are an adequate number of chairs in the room for the actors and other personnel. Place the chairs out of the way—off to the side, as far away from the action as possible, is best. Insist that all bags and water bottles be kept out of the way of the work area.

On the wall behind the director's table, hang a ground plan, set and costume renderings, and any other visual materials the actors should view during rehearsals. The ground plan should be easy to reference.

Taping Out the Rehearsal Hall

Before staging rehearsals begin, the stage manager, following the ground plan supplied by the designer, uses different colored tape to create a landscape map of the set on the floor of the rehearsal hall. Solid lines represent walls; broken lines represent doorways. There are a number of ways to tape. As long as the stage manager clearly explains the chosen method to the actors and keeps it simple enough to follow, it will work.

The taping should delineate entrances and exits, walls, furniture, windows, archways to other rooms, closets, and stairways. In multi-scene musicals, different colors of tape can indicate different scenes.

In rehearsal halls that can't accommodate the entire set, it is better to have a partial set outline with accurate distances than to "shrink down" the set to fit the room. The actors need to develop a sense of the actual space.

Final Thoughts

Preparation and organization are the keys to starting rehearsals off on the right foot. A rehearsal schedule and an organized rehearsal space provide the structure in which creativity will thrive.

In Your DPN

Along with your prop list, be sure to create a list of the cast with every member's contact information gathered from auditions, like the one in figure 10.6. Whenever you need to contact cast members individually or collectively, you will have this list in your notebook to refer to.

Also, build your rehearsal schedule in your notebook, where you can amend and refer to it as needed. At the end of one day of rehearsal, a quick glance in your notebook will allow you to remind the actors of the upcoming agenda.

Cast Contact Information

Name	Role(s)	Contact Information	Conflicts

Figure 10.6
Form for capturing contact information for the cast

Chapter 11
The First Rehearsal and Table Work

Part III of this book addresses rehearsals, while Part IV gives particular treatment to rehearsing musicals. In early rehearsals, the processes are different, but once the show is staged, the rehearsal process for both is the same. This chapter, along with the next two, deals specifically with plays.

The First Rehearsal

The director sets the tone for the entire rehearsal process at the first rehearsal. By appearing organized, informed and in control, everyone involved in the show will feel confident and at ease.

With your stage manager, prepare an informal agenda.

Director's Checklist: First Rehearsal Agenda

❑ Welcome the cast and staff.

❑ Meet and greet: introduce the cast, artistic staff, and designers.

❑ Present the concept.

❑ Call on designers to present their work.

❑ Call a break.

❑ Hold a first read-through.

❑ Lead a discussion.

❑ Discuss what to prepare for second rehearsal.

The Welcome Speech

If there is a producer, he or she may open the meeting, welcoming everyone on board and wishing the cast and staff well in their pursuits. If not, then the director assumes this responsibility. In opening remarks, welcome everyone, tell them how thrilled you are to be working together, talk about what the play means to you, and share any other pertinent information, but save concept statements for after the meet and greet.

Introductions, Concept, and Design Presentations

Have everyone identify themselves and their role in the production. Make sure not to leave anyone out.

Briefly discuss the play, your initial reaction to the script, the concept, and other information of importance. Research can be presented by the dramaturge. Keep this short and to the point, allowing the designers to elaborate on the physical concept in their presentations.

Get people excited and in sync. Set the tone.

Designers, one at a time, present their sketches and other visual material to demonstrate their plans. Many designers don't like to do this, but it is important for everyone to share in the collaborative effort and to understand the world of the play as conceptualized by the designers. It will guide choices in rehearsals. If designers don't want to participate, ask them to send their assistants.

Once you break the ice and get through the formalities, take a break and let everyone chat for a while. Designers usually leave after the break, but invite everyone to stay in the room for the first read-through.

First Read-through

If you are working with professional actors, just launch into the first read without discussion. The actors, if experienced, will know how to handle the first read-through. However, in college or community theatre situations, you will want to set these ground rules first:

- No performing. Avoid showing off.
- Keep it simple and honest.
- Have an enjoyable experience, laugh.
- The Stage Manager reads the stage directions.
- Avoid discussion during the break between acts.
- After the read-through, talk about the show, share reactions, and have a lively, thought-provoking discussion.
- The cast notes their initial reactions and what they want to accomplish.

Things the director should avoid at the first read-through:

- Expectations of any kind
- Directing the actors
- Exerting any influence whatsoever over the process

After the read-through, talk about the show, get reactions from cast and have a lively, thought-provoking discussion, but avoid setting anything or asking anyone to make commitments to any choices. Leave things free and open. The first read-through, like the director's first reading, is primarily "for pleasure." The point is to let the play wash over the cast and see who goes where.

A director must **observe***! Observe the actors, listen to the script through the actors mouths. Don't watch your script, watch the actors. See what begins to happen naturally.*

Even at the first rehearsal directors will gain insights. Write them down in your DPN. If something occurs to you, note it in the script. Every time you hear the play, expect to have new ideas. *Record them*!

Ending the Rehearsal

As you wrap-up the first rehearsal, remember to do the following:

- Set a date for being off-book.
- Talk about the rehearsal process and expectations.
- Let the stage manager speak as needed.
- Indicate what to prepare for the second rehearsal.
- State the time and place of the next rehearsal.

Table Work

Table work is useful for all rehearsal processes, but is primarily used in rehearsing non-musical plays. While methods described below can be used in rehearsing musicals, due to the nature of musicals, there rarely is enough time. In Part IV, table work is treated as part of the musical rehearsal process.

Why Table Work?

Before actors get on their feet, exploring the play without distraction is essential to the future shape and quality of the final production. Table work offers the chance for actors to explore and become familiar with the text as well as for the director to "direct" the script and the actors. At the table, the actors have complete freedom to explore the play and their characters in a way that unleashes their imaginations. It is a time of discovery, inspiration, and exploration.

Professional actors use table work to become familiar with the text, develop their characters, and begin creating relationships with the other actors. Especially in classical theatre, getting comfortable with the words is the first step in the technical process. Actors can play with dialogue and scenes with the other actors, try different approaches, and work on difficult passages, all without the encumbrance of staging. In non-realistic theatre, table work is vital to hashing out meaning and subtext.

At the table, the director observes and guides the actors, explaining important references made in the script and clarifying passages that have meaning beyond what appears on the page. A director observes the nature of the emerging relationships between actors and their characters, quietly cajoling them in the right direction and giving them just enough insight to ignite their imaginations and go deeper. Together, the director and actor consider the objectives and tactics at the table.

With less skilled actors, the director teaches, asks questions, and assists actors with finding their performances. Working with very inexperienced actors requires the director to direct beats, discuss objectives, and clarify conflicts. Sometimes it requires working beat to beat, i.e. breaking each beat down and discussing what specifically is happening in each beat. It is critical that actors understand what they are saying, what is happening, where the conflict is, and where they stand in regards to the conflict.

While most good professional actors will uncover the emotional life of each moment, the journeyman actor, unless naturally gifted, needs a director's push to get to the truth. That push can come through various methods, including exercises outlined in this book. Using common sense and trusting the inner voice to guide the rehearsals is the director's best bet. When there is a moment that is not working, observe, consider, and reach inside your own imagination for what you can offer to help the actor.

The director engages with the actors, encouraging them to listen to each other, and develop an understanding of the text. For younger actors, listening may be difficult, but it is the key to establishing relationships, fostering spontaneity, and ensuring that table work stay simple and honest.

Regardless of the experience of the actors or director, working at the table allows the group to mutually define the world of the play and to become part of that world.

Table Work Continues

The journey the director has taken from first reading for pleasure, to second reading and analysis, to research and conceptualization, is now the journey the actors must make. In other words, the director is like a teacher whose own personal readings serve as a lesson plan at the table. Yet, like any good teacher, the director must allow the class to arrive at the answers on their own accord. Impart your knowledge of the play through gentle guidance; don't force it.

At the second table rehearsal, start breaking down the play into smaller working units as you would in analysis (acts, scenes, beats), allowing the actors to wrap their mouths around the words, clarifying the meanings in the text, identifying and working conflicts, and developing relationships.

For the second reading, start at the top and begin reading through the play, in a way similar to the first read, this time stopping when one of the following issues needs to be addressed. The reading can take all day or it might go quickly. The important thing is to take the time you need to work on the details. If there is dialect required or period-specific style work, discuss that and begin integrating it immediately into the table readings. Whether you have a dialect coach or the director coaches, accent work begins immediately.

Seven questions to guide actors through table work:

1. What relationships is your character involved in? What is the nature of these relationships?

2. What are the characters' objectives? Work through individual beats.

3. What are the conflicts (conflicting objectives) and how do they affect the dramatic action?

4. What is the play's super-objective? How do they relate to the individual characters?

5. What is the mood and atmosphere of each scene?

6. What is the rhythm of the action, i.e. what makes the highs high, the lows low, and the climaxes climax?

7. What is the subtext?

As table work continues, keep in mind these seven questions and be sure to do the following:

Clarify Text References Every play has references to world events, local references, period-specific references, and words in other languages or that might not be in the daily lexicon of the actors. Using either the director's or the dramaturge's research, stop and explain the references, demonstrate correct pronunciation, and clarify the meaning of difficult passages.

Clarify Understanding of the Text Make sure the actors understand what they are saying.

It will be apparent when they don't. If it is a non-realistic play with absurd language or the language of Shakespeare, talk about passages that are difficult to understand. The director can explain the meaning or ask the actors to explain. This is critical when rehearsing Shakespeare or period pieces with inexperienced actors. *The performers must understand what they are saying and why they are saying it.* Without that understanding, there can't possibly be truth in their performances. Table readings of Shakespeare or a play like *The Way of the World* by Congreve requires a complete breakdown of every beat to clarify meaning. It can take two weeks just to get through these kinds of plays.

Finding the Truth in Every Moment While it is a tall order, the success of your play rests on believability and that begins with the actors being truthful. The word "truth" is bandied about and often misconstrued. It is a buzzword in modern theatrical practice, but its theatrical definition is really quite simple. Actors have to believe in what they are doing and own the words, behavior, and feelings of their characters. Many of the exercises offered later in this chapter and in later chapters offer the director tools to help the actor find the truth in each moment. *You can't fake it in the theatre.*

Directing Emotional Moments Many directors, especially in musicals, tend to race past the individual emotional moments. It is the director's job first to identify those critical moments where the underlying fabric of the play's emotional center is revealed, and then to ensure that those moments are fully realized, not rushed, and directed for maximum emotional impact and adroit storytelling.

For example, when Jim tells Laura she is beautiful in her own way, allow the compliment to be fully absorbed by Laura. The audience needs to see and feel that compliment course through her veins and change her forever. That moment can't be rushed.

Encourage Discussion If actors are confused about what is going on, stop and talk about the scene. Ask questions instead of providing easy answers. Facilitate the discussion, allowing actors to discover for themselves the meaning or point of a scene. If they veer of course, ask a question or make a comment that nudges them in the right direction.

After each read-through, talk about the play. Let the actors do most of the talking. As they engage among themselves, they are building relationships and ensemble. The director can guide the discussion as needed, but let the actors connect.

Observe During table reads, watch the actors closely. Don't keep your nose in the book. Know the play well enough to be able to watch what the actors naturally bring to their characters. Great insight can be gained from the discoveries actors make as they read the play. Make notes about moments that are naturally working well, and the moments that will need work. Begin to consider how to approach problem areas in future rehearsals.

Solve Acting Problems Working at the table allows the director to focus in on problems without the encumbrance of blocking. Every actor is going to have strong and weak moments. The table is the time to solve acting problems. If actors aren't listening, deal with that at the table. If they are being dishonest or they are forcing the role, work with them at the table using exercises to help them overcome these problems. You may not solve every problem, but persistence and support combined with practiced, specific guidance can really make a difference.

Set Goals Right before breaking, set the agenda for the next rehearsal and reiterate the schedule. For the third read and beyond, break the rehearsal into scenes so that actors who are not working don't have to sit around waiting. You can spend as much time as you have with each scene. Use the table period to delve deeply into the minutia of the play, until every detail has been considered.

Final Table Reading

The table work period culminates in a final reading that is uninterrupted, incorporating all of the work done at the table. The play should come alive and the basic emotional life, relationships, conflicts, and objectives should be expressed clearly and convincingly.

Once blocking begins, directors start the slow and painful process of losing control as external elements are introduced, *so get it right at the table.*

Directing Different Types of Scenes

Getting it right at the table depends on the director's ability to direct different types of scenes. The section lists different kinds of scenes and table-work approaches to each.

Expository scenes

Usually at the beginning of the play, scenes of exposition introduce the main characters, conflicts, and plot lines. The pace is usually even, setting the base line tempo from which things will vary as the play progresses.

How to Direct Keep things interesting while telling the story. Clearly communicate the important information in these scenes, creating mood and atmosphere, establishing relationships between characters, and ensuring the conflicts are strong and compellingly introduced. Identify what is important about these scenes and emphasize the details. Keep the pace moving forward but make sure the important points are clearly expressed.

Rising action scenes

The rising action scene is where the major conflict of the play is launched. In *Hamlet*, this would be Act One, Scene Five, when Hamlet encounters his father's ghost. The Ghost tells Hamlet of Claudius' betrayal which sets the plot in motion.

How to Direct Heighten the scene's importance through pacing, mood, and directing Hamlet's intense emotional reaction. This scene hooks the audience. Directing this scene requires intensified tempo, higher stakes, and a heightened connection between Hamlet and the Ghost. Create tension/release moments that build to an internal climax that is unmistakable. The higher stakes force a faster pace. Isolating the individual moments helps focus the scene and clarify the conflicts.

Transitional scenes

Transitional scenes are those that connect more important scenes. In musicals, the classic transitional scene is called an "in *one*," usually consisting of exposition or transition between climaxes. Up until the 1960s and 1970s, the stage was divided by side hanging borders into *one*, *two*, *three*, and sometimes *four* areas, with one being the closest to the downstage apron. While the large sets were being changed in areas *two* though *four*, a drop would fall and the actors would act "in *one*." There they would perform a short scene that allowed for the scene change behind them to occur. Not much is established in these scenes; they might include a reprise, a scene between two characters, or a travelling scene.

In a play, the transitional scene is a scene of lesser importance that connects scenes of greater importance.

How to Direct Each transitional scene defines its own approach. The tempo is generally normal, and there are no climaxes or important occurrences. Transitional scenes provide an opportunity to relax the intensity. Identify the main action of the transitional scene and focus on important points that are made. Keep them simple and sharply focused.

Climactic scenes

Conflict comes to a boil in climactic scenes. Although there are scenes with minor and major climaxes, usually the play has only one "major climactic scene." Identify that scene and the high points through analysis, understanding how they fit into the structure of the play.

How to Direct Direct the actors with high energy and intensity. Know exactly which moments are the most important and ensure those moments are clear, not rushed, and the full impact is experienced by the characters. If the actors don't bring the depth of emotion required for these moments, talk to them and use the exercises at the end of this chapter to help them find the truth and fully express it. Don't be afraid to mine the depths of these moments.

Falling action scenes

Falling action scenes are similar to transitional scenes but occur after a climactic scene. The dramatic intensity decreases and the result of the climactic scene is more fully revealed.

How to Direct Slow the pace down, bring the energy down. Think "reflective" as opposed to "active." Let us see the impact of the climaxes on the characters and how they behave as a result.

Dropping action scenes

Dropping action scenes are defined by a fast and sudden change in intensity from high to low. Playwrights use the contrast to make dramatic points.

How to Direct Let the pace slow. The quality of the energy changes, but don't let it drop. Focus on the main point of action in the scene. If there is important exposition or one important incident that changes the course of the plot, make that shift clear.

Suspense scenes

Suspense scenes are defined by prolonged periods of unrelieved tension. Don't confuse this with mysteries or thrillers which have suspenseful scenes. This type of scene is more about emotional anxiety than fear of death.

How to Direct Find the highs and lows as well as the quick and unexpected changes in intensity. Make staging choices that heighten the relationship between characters and that change the balance of power. If there is a climax at the end, build to that climax but never let the audience feel a sense of resolution. These scenes keep the audience on the edge of their seats. The conflict is palpable: we don't know what will happen and that sense of not knowing creates the suspense that is compelling. If the actors appear as if they know what is coming, the suspense is lost. Focus on playing the anxiety of the unknown, even if it is a comic scene.

Table Work Exercises

The following exercises are ideal for the table-reading phase of rehearsals, but can also be used once the actors get on their feet.

1. Working Beats Exercise

Stanislavski developed a system of breaking down dialogue into "beats," or units of action that are short sections of dialogue that change when the objective changes. Beats can follow action objectives or a change of need or emotion.

Physical beats of a scene can be broken down like this: a character enters the room, takes off his jacket, pours a cup of tea and opens his computer. There are four beats of action, with the objectives of "enter the room," "take off the coat," "quench thirst," and "check email."

However, more commonly, the important work on beats is discerning in dialogue when the emotional or need-based objective changes. In analysis work, a director breaks down a script into beats and notes the objectives for each character in that beat. At the table, the director "directs" those beats, ensuring actors are "acting" their objectives and that the action is focused.

Knowing what the character wants in each beat allows the director to "direct" the actors towards those outcomes. In a long scene with a lot of dialogue, as in a Chekhov play, identifying beats, objectives, and obstacles is what keeps the plot moving forward and the situations compelling.

While you don't have to direct every beat in the entire play, it is useful to work beats when the work of the actors is not clear.

Problem: Actors are having trouble finding the conflict in a scene.

Goal: The actors know what they want in each beat, how that conflicts, and therefore are able to keep the plot moving forward and the situations compelling.

Steps:

1. Identify the conflict in the scene; talk about it.
2. Identify each actor's major objectives in the scene.
3. Demonstrate how the objectives clash and cause conflict.
4. Discuss character tactics and how each character is behaving; how does that behavior cause conflict?
5. Run each beat individually, with the goal of establishing clarity of objective and tactic and how and why those change.
6. Work the scene beat by beat, identifying objectives and tactics as they change.
7. Ratchet up the conflict.
8. Run and re-run beats that are not working, giving the actors direction and adjustments.
9. Continue only when the beat has been "clarified," and the conflict is clear.
10. Make sure the actors are listening. (See next exercise.)
11. Once the beats are clear, run the whole scene to see if the work has "stuck."

2. Repetition Exercise (A Take on Meisner)

As in the famous Meisner exercise—where actors repeat their observations about one another, back and forth—the primary activity in this version is to listen and respond, repeating the same phrase over and over. Use the repetition exercise when there is a moment that is not working. Isolate the two lines at the heart of the beat in the problematic section: the first is a line said by the first character and the second is the response of the second character. The chosen lines should be a maximum of 5-8 words.

Problem: A section is not working because the two actors are not listening and reacting spontaneously.

Goal: Listening is facilitated and an emotional connection occurs. The raw truth of the moment is revealed and experienced by the actors. The scene will gain a new and honest emotional life.

Steps:

1. Explain the method of the exercise and the goal.
2. Identify the two lines that the actors will repeat.
3. Tell them simply to repeat the two lines without any expectation or desire for results.
4. Explain that it might seem odd, and boredom might set in, but the goal is just to listen and react with no obligation to "act." Encourage them to emotionally go wherever the exercise takes them.
5. Run the lines back and forth for as long as necessary until something starts happening. Line readings will change as the actors listen and react to each other. It might start with laughter, self-awareness, or boredom, but once past all that, something will start to happen.
6. Watch for "forced acting"—this exercise is about listening and responding truthfully with no obligations. Start the exercise over if the actors are forcing their responses.
7. Allow the repetition to go wherever it naturally goes.
8. If actors start to laugh or get angry, encourage them to follow that through.
9. Once something real starts happening, keep repeating to intensify the truth of the moment until it is undeniable. The line readings will gain deeper intensity and feel "real".
10. Once they find the emotional truth, say "Go." At that moment, they jump right into the scene without skipping a beat, taking the emotional place they discovered and letting it influence the dialogue.
11. If they lose the emotional truth and start "acting" again, stop them, point out the problem, and start over until they can carry the truth they discovered into the scene.

3. Making It Personal

In this exercise, the director asks the actor to make the subject "personal." Stanislavsky's use of the phrase "as if" proceeds from the same premise—act as if it were your story, or happening to you, not another person.

Problem: An actor's performance is not believable.

Goal: The actor connects emotionally to a given moment, experiences that moment in a truthful way, and then expresses that experience in their performance. The actor experiences emotional truth.

Steps:

1. Ask the characters to "make it personal,"—make the moment about themselves or "as if" it were happening to them.
2. If necessary, ask them to bring personal experience to bear on the moment and to recall how they felt. This is known as **substitution**.
3. Ask them to imagine what it would feel like if they were in this situation and how would it make them feel.

Example: *The Glass Menagerie*—the actor playing Tom is not believable in the opening monologue

> The director wants the actor to exude a sense of ennui as well as longing for the chance to rectify the mistakes Tom feels he has made. Ask the actor if he can relate in any way to Tom. If he can relate, ask him to express how Tom feels by bringing the actor's own personal experience to bear, by recalling a time when he felt similar to Tom. If the actor can't relate, ask him to imagine how it would feel if it had happened to him. Help him to connect emotionally but in a real way by making it personal.

Directors, be careful not to push an actor too close to something in their life they are not ready to handle such as the death of a parent or close friend. When using substitution, it is safest to use experiences further in the past that are not difficult for the actor to deal with anymore.

4. Playing the Subtext

Problem: Actors are playing the superficial action of the scene but not bringing the emotional sub-currents alive.

Goal: The actor discovers the real emotional motivation underlying a moment or scene which leads to a tactic that allows them to become truthful and multi-dimensional.

Steps:

1. Identify the subtext of a section of a scene for each character.
2. Have the actors create a short statement that expresses that subtext or "what the character really wants or is really thinking"—keep it short and to the point.
3. Run the scene, vocalizing the subtext statement (saying it out loud with full emotional commitment) before saying each written line of dialogue.
4. Go through the entire section of the scene this way—subtext statement then line, subtext statement then next line. Make sure the subtext statement is said with full emotional commitment each time, informing the delivery of the text line.

5. Go back and replay the scene without vocalizing subtext. Tell the actors to "think the subtext loudly."

6. Finally, run the scene without saying or thinking subtext. Hopefully the work of the exercise will subconsciously inform the acting and bring the subtext alive.

7. Note how it changes the relationship and influences the moment-to-moment reality.

Example: *A Doll's House*—the blackmail scene between Nora and Krogstad

The problem is the actress playing Nora is too calm and composed. She isn't helped by the dialogue, which hides her inner torment. Beneath the composure is a panicked woman. Choose as a subtext statement, "please don't do this to me." Krogstad's subtext is "I will suffer no longer."

Before each line in the scene, both actors say their subtext out loud with fully vocalized emotional life allowing that to influence each line that follows. Nora will say "Please don't do this to me," and then her first line. Krogstad will do the same. Run the entire section of the scene this way. Watch how it influences choices and their relationship. Then, run the scene with time to think but not speak the subtext line. Finally, run with no conscious thought of the subtext.

5. Objective Work

This is slightly different than working beats because its sole purpose is to put the objective to work.

Problem: The action is not moving forward.

Goal: The actors play their objectives and develop tactics, activating the action.

Steps:

1. Restate the objectives of the scene and the super-objective of the characters.

2. Define each actor's objectives for the first beat—make sure it is an active verb, not passive.

3. Relate scene and super-objective to the beat objective so the actors understand the big picture.

4. Discuss the conflict of objectives between the characters.

5. Play the first beat—the only obligation is to fully play the objective.

6. Discuss how the actors can best play the objective and define a tactic.

7. Repeat the beat, employing the tactic.

8. When that beat is working, go to the next beat and repeat. Continue through the scene.

Example: Two actors struggle to create the action of the scene

> The objectives are "to hurt" and "to please." The first actor tries "to hurt" the other actor (with words) and the other tries "to please" the first actor. How do these clear and strong choices create tension and energy between the characters? The first actor uses a demeaning tone and stands above the other actor; that is the tactic. The second actor cries and holds the other actor's leg; that is their tactic.

6. Ratcheting Up the Conflict

Problem: The tension/conflict of a moment between actors is lacking.

Goal: The conflict between characters is intensified.

Steps:

1. Identify objectives and tactics.
2. Define the conflict specifically for each character in relation to the other character.
3. Do an improvisation around the conflict, off script.
4. When the improvisational interaction becomes real, jump into the scene.

Example: A mother and daughter are arguing because the daughter has been walking in the park every day instead of attending business school.

> The mother's objective is "to scold" and the daughter's objective is "to assuage." The mother's tactic is to scream and circle her daughter. The daughter's tactic is to nod her head and hide her face, and never look at her mother.

> Have the actors pick a parallel situation to which they can both relate. The young actress spent the night with a boy when she actually had claimed to be with her girlfriend. The mother got a call from the girlfriend during the night asking where her daughter was. The mother is furious. She attempts to assuage her anger by hurting her daughter, scolding her. The daughter wants to placate her mother to shut her up. The actors start the improvisation. The director coaches them as needed to focus the conflict and raise the stakes. They finally get into a very tense argument and become emotionally connected. The director tells them to jump into the script, which they do, and the conflict is there, simmering as they read the scene that a moment ago was void of conflict.

A Note on Improvisation Exercises

It is counterproductive to move too far away from the text. Every improvisation in rehearsal should center on a specific section of text or a problem between actors. Improvisations must have a clearly stated purpose and goal and not steer too far away from given circumstances of the play.

Other Table Reading Work

Dialect and Speech Work

It is vital that actors speak with accurate accents if they play characters from other regions or countries. If the director is not an expert, then a speech coach is brought in. If there is no budget for a speech coach, two excellent resources are listed at the end of this chapter in the Suggested Readings. Whatever you do, make sure the accents are authentic or don't use them. A badly executed accent can destroy believability.

Problem: An actor's performance is not believable because of an inaccurate accent.

Goal: The accent is real and doesn't distract.

Steps: TBD by speech coach or resources in Suggested Readings.

Wander Reads

In order to transition from the table to the stage, the director may want to hold a wander read. After the final table read and before the first blocking rehearsal, the actors read through the script on their feet, carrying their books and improvising blocking.

Problem: the actors' performances feel constrained because they need to get out of their chairs and move.

Goal: the actors get a feel for natural staging dynamics; the director discovers some organic staging moments, and records them for further use in staging rehearsals.

Steps:
1. Set up the ground plan in the rehearsal hall
2. Identify all entrances, exits, furniture and any props
3. Explain that the only difference between this and the final table read is that they are on their feet.
4. There are no expectations about movement.
5. Sit, stand, do whatever is motivated, while maintaining connection to the other actors.
6. Director notes anything that happens organically which they might want to use in the show.

In Your DPN

Keep the "Director's Checklist: First Rehearsal Agenda" in your DPN. Work from this page as you lead the first rehearsal meeting. When it comes time to present your concept, you can refer back to your concept notes.

During the first read-through and the discussion that follows, be sure to take notes. The same goes for all subsequent table work, as the director will gain insights throughout the process. As you wrap up a rehearsal meeting, record what is to be prepared for the next rehearsal, as well as any dates and times decided on. Refer to your rehearsal schedule if needed.

Suggested Reading

Blumenfeld, Robert. *Accents: A Manual for Actors*. New York: Proscenium Publishers, 2002. This is an excellent resource that breaks accents down into simple sounds. No need to learn the International Phonetic Alphabet.

Stern, David Alan. *Acting with an Accent*. New York: Dialect Accent Publishers, 2003. This is the most comprehensive and best source for accurate information and recordings of accents. Tapes can be ordered on Amazon.com or at Stern's website, http://www.dialectaccentspecialists.com/store/index.php/cat_1.

Chapter 12
Staging Rehearsals

Rehearsals are artistic playgrounds where creativity and imagination are unleashed. If the rehearsal environment is stifling, then creativity will be stifled!

Once the table work is completed, the staging process can begin. This chapter, which explores staging rehearsals, is applicable to both plays and musical scenes. The basic foundation is such that it applies to all genres.

What does it mean to be creative?

Creativity implies the discovery of unique and original ideas.

The goal of the rehearsal process is to discover unique qualities in the group of people assembled. These discoveries guide the choices that result in the final production: an expression, through the words of the playwright, of the voice of every member of the group.

Staging, or **blocking**, defines the actor's relationship with the set, props, furniture, entrances and exits, and of course other actors.

> **Blocking:** the choreography of movement of the actors established by the director or actors.

Dynamics of relationships are realized in three dimensions by the placement of actors on the stage. The "art" of directing is in creating pictures on stage from moment to moment that bring the story alive and make the meaning of the playwright's words clear.

Staging methodology varies greatly. Every director has a unique approach to staging and the nature of a play also dictates staging style. If it is an experimental or anti-realistic piece like *Waiting for Godot*, a more improvisational approach works better than pre-planned staging. On the other hand, a realistic, structured play with many scenes and characters generally requires preparation and decision-making in advance of rehearsals.

The key to good staging is discovering or identifying what is true and important about each moment and allowing that to directly influence movement choices.

Good staging enhances the character relationships and conflicts, creates tension and release of tension, and reflects the inner life of the characters and their desires.

Elements of Staging

Dynamics

Every interaction has a **dynamic**—the nature of the relationship between two or more characters expressed physically by their placement. As the director and actors explore the staging, pay close attention to the dynamic between the actors.

Physical relationships play a critical role in establishing strong emotional and psychological reactions in the audience. Different parts of the stage have different properties. Generally, downstage and center stage are the most powerful places. For example, placing one character downstage right and another mid-stage center gives the actor at center stage more focus in the scene, because the actor downstage right has to look upstage to see the other actor. The actor downstage right has been **upstaged** by the other actor. By experimenting with different spatial relationships, the director and actors discover where the powerful positions are in each moment.

> **Upstaging:** When the positioning of one actor forces another actor to turn upstage in order to engage in conversation. Avoid this.

To create the dynamic that articulates the conflicts and relationships which exist between characters, a director uses his or her imagination to set the placement of actors at the start of the scene. Imagining the visual elements of the play is a process that began during the reading process and became more defined during conceptualization. Continue that process when staging the scene, visualizing in the mind's eye how it will begin. Directors can also refer to their analysis notes on characters, conflicts, and relationships to help the imagination process.

One way to approach blocking is by using an improvisational approach. The director places the actors at the start of the scene, and then through improvisation discovers the rest of the scene's staging. The scene unfolds, and the director observes the actors as they discover a continuous dynamic relationship while moving through the scene. The director keeps what works and makes the adjustments as necessary to achieve the desired result, based on the improvised organic choices of the actors. It often takes a lot of trial and error to find the right solution.

The actors' physical relationship to each other includes issues of distance, levels (height relationship), stage placement, and how much of each actor we see.

Example: Act 1, Scene 2, *The Glass Menagerie*

> Amanda is coming home to confront Laura about the lies she has been telling for the past several weeks, when she was supposed to have been at the business college. Amanda is furious, hurt, and determined to trap Laura.
>
> The dynamic is dominant predator vs. innocent, cowering victim.
>
> The director places Laura in the middle of the floor playing with her animals, and Amanda in her coat towering above Laura, creating a dynamic of dominance and submission. The director tells Amanda to circle Laura, who has nowhere to go or hide, like a predator stalking its prey. Laura is unprotected, like the animals; they could be shattered at any moment. Because Laura is center stage, the focus on her is strengthened as we watch her react to Amanda. The heavy coat on Amanda gives her added layers of protection. Laura, dressed in a nightgown, is vulnerable. The actors use this stated dynamic to discover organic blocking choices.

Student Exercise 12.1

Using a scene from a play you are working on, define the dynamic of the scene's first moment. Imagine a spatial relationship between actors that seems to capture the essence of the defined dynamic. Then start the scene but omit words. No speaking, just movement. Think through the scene, fleshing out the spatial relationships between the actors from moment to moment. Coach from the side, stating the next moment and the dynamic they should look for. Do this for the whole scene. Then go back to the beginning and add dialogue to see how the discoveries of the exercise influence both the spoken dialogue and the relationship between the characters.

Actions (Objectives)

When developing staging, actors require a clear understanding of action. The director gives the actor specific physical activities, such as "cross to the table and drink water," or "immediately confront your partner, nose to nose."

But actions are more than just activities. Actions happen both internally and externally between the actors. The activities above are "to cross" and "to confront," but the actions are "to quench thirst" and "to demand answers." The actor does the physical movement in order to satisfy the character's immediate desires or objectives.

The scene's major action is defined by scene objectives. Sometimes called **motivation**, the objective "motivates" the action. A director should have in mind one major action for each character in each scene. Minor actions exist and can be discovered in rehearsal. But for the sake of clarity, focus on the major action in the scene.

Before staging a scene, discuss the "action" of the scene, define what each character wants/needs, and how they attempt to achieve their goals (tactics). Encourage the actors to offer their thoughts on the scene's major actions/objectives.

Actors should only move when motivated to do so. There must be a strong reason for every movement, directly influenced by character relationship, pursuit of objectives and dynamics.

Example: Define the action of Act 1, Scene 2, *The Glass Menagerie*

> The action for Amanda is to enter and confront Laura with the truth, forcing her to come clean; for Laura it is to deflect Amanda's anger. Laura sits on the floor, engrossed in her animals; Amanda circles Laura, getting closer and closer to her until she gets the reaction she wants. The action of confronting Laura gives rise to the physical movement of circling. The action of deflecting Amanda's accusations leads to stooped posture, hovering over the menagerie, and continuously turning her back to her mother.

Student Exercise 12.2

Choose a two-person scene and define each character's action. Discuss the action, and define objectives and tactics. Without specifically determining every movement for each actor, allow actors to improvise movement choices. First, run only the entrance and first two lines of the scene. Repeat the entrance and two lines, trying different choices with each attempt. Keep changing the movement until the actors find blocking that brings the conflict alive immediately. Then go onto the next beat, improvising the scene to the end. For each beat, play with movement choices and dialogue to find the potent movement that raises the stakes and allows maximum character intensity.

Focus

The key to good blocking is clear, easy-to-follow storytelling. Central to good storytelling is focus; helping the audience to know where to look.

Especially in large crowd scenes such as those found in musicals, the directorial choices determine focus: where the audience directs their attention.

As was mentioned earlier in reference to dynamic, there are certain areas of the stage that are more powerful and visually apparent than others. Down center, especially on the apron, is the most powerful and prominent position on the proscenium stage. In the round, there is no down center, so center stage becomes the position of most power. On a thrust, there are several positions of primary focus because there are three audience vantage points.

There are moments when the director wants the focus to be on a specific actor. A simple example is blocking one actor to sit facing upstage watching the other actor. The focus will be on the actor speaking, not the seated actor. Such obvious choices should be chosen carefully and be motivated. Most often, focus is achieved through much more complex and subtle means.

The general rule is to place the actor who you want to pull focus closest to the audience, with eyes and face in full view. However, this is not a hard and fast rule. Sometimes the upstage actor will pull focus if everyone downstage is facing upstage, watching him.

If everyone onstage is facing to the side and one actor is facing downstage, that actor will pull focus. If there is a group in one place and an actor alone apart from it, that single actor will pull focus. As you set each moment, look at the stage and determine where the focus is, then adjust as needed.

In larger group scenes focus is created through actor placement, lighting, costume color, and where the attention of the onstage actors is focused. If everyone onstage is looking at the actor at center, then the audience will look there too.

In a musical chorus scene, the leading actors' costume colors differ from the color palette of the chorus, which draws attention. A spotlight follows the leading actor in the chorus number, i.e. focus by illumination.

The leading actor, especially in dance numbers, stands downstage of the group in the center. The group can be placed in clusters of several actors, say in family units, while the lead is either alone, or paired with the other lead in the center, or downstage on the apron area. This forces the audience to focus their attention on the characters advancing the story.

The tricky thing about focus is that it shouldn't look like staging choices are made solely for the purpose of forcing focus. It should not be obvious at all, but seem natural and organic to each moment.

Example: Act One Finale, *Anything Goes*, in the round

Reno Sweeney, the principal, is dancing with the entire chorus in the show's title number at the end of Act One. She starts the number as a solo, in the center of the circular stage. The chorus is crouching down around her in a circle; she is visible above them; and audience attention remains focused on her. The tap section begins. Reno moves to the edge of the stage and the group assembles behind her. With each pattern their position shifts to a different quadrant of the circle, so by the end of the first tap section they have performed to every side of the audience. When Reno resumes her solo, everyone onstage moves into the aisles, leaving her alone onstage. When the chorus dances with Reno again, a circular lift stage center raises out of the floor lifting Reno above the chorus, ensuring central focus and creating a great moment. When Reno leaves the stage to allow the chorus to dance, they share focus, playing to all sides of the audience; there is no central focus. When Reno reenters with a big flourish, she reestablishes her focus. She is dressed in bright yellow which contrasts the blue and pink hues of the chorus costumes. Two spotlights shine on her from different angles.

Example: Act 2, Scene 7, *The Glass Menagerie*, proscenium

The Gentleman Caller and Laura are seated on the floor. He is doing his long speech to Laura about confidence. She sits on the edge of the sofa facing slightly upstage at Jim. He is behind the sofa, looking at her, but his face is full front to the audience. We can see the side of her face and her reactions. The candle is on a perch behind the sofa, just below his face, adding a visual dimension to the focus. We can see both, but we are focused on Jim.

Student Exercise 12.3

Choose a scene already staged. Go through the script with a pencil and notate where focus should be. Run the scene; note what pulls focus. Compare your notes with what was actually drawing your attention. Isolating each beat of focus, shift around the staging to accomplish your focus goals. Depending on the configuration, make sure to check the focus from every angle. Play with focus; try different spatial relationships to find the strongest staging choice.

Relationships

Relationships are defined by dialogue as much as they are by how characters physically relate to each other. A director's job is to analyze character relationships and enhance them onstage in a way that tells the story clearly and effectively.

First, how do characters move in relation to each other? Relationship is defined by the way they touch, or don't touch, the way the distance between them changes, where they are on the stage, who is in the power position, and how they move in reaction to movement of the other actors.

For example, in a dance duet, like the type seen in so many Fred Astaire movies, the couple dances in love-soaked harmony, twirling, spinning, dipping, and waltzing. The elegance of their choreography captures the essence of their relationship as they vary from very close to far apart and rushing back to each other.

Example: Act 1, Scene 2, *Hamlet*

Hamlet is in the big hall with his stepfather, his mother, and members of the court. One approach to this scene is to limit the movement of all characters but Hamlet. Once the court has taken their places and Hamlet enters, his movement is loose and jerky, which stands in contrast to the stillness of his rigid parents and members of the court. The movement pulls focus to Hamlet and also brings out his anger and frustration, at odds with his parents' fear and unease. The choice creates a relationship dynamic that is clear and compelling and it is articulated without a word spoken. He makes everyone nervous, and the audience feels their distress.

The second aspect of blocking that expresses relationship is spatial relationship. The physical placement of the actors on stage and in relation to each other speaks volumes about how they feel about each other and how they relate.

Example: Scene between Sky and Sarah, *Guys and Dolls*

In the musical *Guys and Dolls*, when Sarah and Sky are in the mission together, alone for the first time, he is wooing her. Even though she is very different from his usual girl, she intrigues him. She is a "mission doll": shy and conservative. As the scene begins, they are apart. She keeps her distance from him as he tries to get closer to her. It's a cat and mouse game. He circles her, corners her and she escapes. He moves in, she runs away. If you turn the volume off, the audience will still understand what's going on.

Then, they sing, begin to fall in love, and the distance between them diminishes slowly, until they reach the climax of the scene and kiss. The tension the audience feels is palpable and the release when they kiss is satisfying. Even though it's a romantic scene, it's also a suspense scene; will they or won't they? Who will ultimately prevail? The back and forth swings in momentum keep the audience on the edges of their seats until that final kiss that relieves the tension.

Student Exercise 12.4

Go through a scene you are working on and analyze the change in relationship between the characters from start to finish. Note in your script where the changes occur, and the nature of the changes, such as "she walks away from him because she's angry and needs space." Put the actors on their feet and play with the "relationship" plot, moment to moment, focusing solely on blocking choices that reflect the "relationship plot."

Run the scene silently once, no dialogue, only movement. Does your movement capture the journey of the characters from start to finish and clarify the essence of their interaction? Add text and do it again.

Conflict

Enhancing the conflict through staging choices is one of the director's most important tasks. As in the example of Amanda circling Laura, the staging reflects the conflict in physical terms.

Because conflict is at the root of drama, reflecting conflict in the staging serves to heighten the drama and draw the audience in. There are major conflicts between the protagonist and antagonist that are pervasive throughout the play, and there are beat conflicts that are minor and change frequently. It is the minor conflicts—the conflict inherent in every moment—that you want to focus on.

In each scene there is a conflict that is introduced and resolved (or not resolved). As the scene proceeds beat by beat, that conflict is unraveled and exposed, creating the drama of the scene.

The director first analyzes to understand the nature of the conflict, the characters involved, the introduction, climax, and resolutions, and then directs the scene to amplify the conflicts for the audience to aid in both their understanding of the story and their interest in the characters.

Conflict is intensified through movement, pace of movement, and spatial relationships. If two people are angry and fighting, they won't be seated closely on a couch. The continuous changing of their spatial relationships, their posture, and their stage placement develop the visual drama.

If two actors are angry and fighting, they move quickly and don't get close unless it is in a threatening way. If one is more powerful than the other, the powerful character is placed in the dominant position in their duet of movement.

If the conflict is understated but intense, then the blocking subtly captures that intensity through slower, more cautious, more dangerous, or tenser movement.

Example: "The Waltz for Che and Eva," *Evita*

> A dance duet that demonstrates hatred (unlike that of Fred and Ginger) is "The Waltz for Che and Eva" in *Evita*. The duet is a twist on the traditionally romantic waltz, but the movements are harsh, hard, and soaked with venom instead of love. They move in unison, but there are unexpected movements that surprise and make us nervous, exaggerating their conflict. By performing a waltz usually reserved for lovers, but using movement antithetical to a love duet, the irony heightens the conflict and makes their dislike for each other palpable.

Student Exercise 12.5

Set up an improvisation on a scene that has a clear conflict. Assign a start position to each actor on the stage. Identify one as stronger than the other. Have them start moving in a circle. Only the stronger actor can change direction or blocking pattern and has to force the weaker actor, without physical contact, to move as they are moving. Begin running lines as the improvisation continues, and see what happens.

Entrances and Exits

Plays are full of entrances and exits. In farces, there are lots of doors; in musicals, the chorus all comes in at the same time, often seemingly out of nowhere. Every scene is marked by entrances and exits.

In the prompt book, the location and timing of the entrances and exits should be noted beforehand. Usually the playwright notes where someone comes from or exits to but that information can be revised given the set or concept.

When determining entrances and exits, the director must consider the set and stage configuration. On a proscenium set, entrances and exits happen from offstage, either through a door or portal or from the wings. It is important as you work with the scenic designer to ensure you have sufficient entrances that make sense.

In three-quarter thrust, actors can enter upstage through the set, or from the house through the aisles onto the stage. In the round, entrances are always from the aisles, unless there is a trap door on the stage.

Musicals have their own challenges. Because the entire chorus in classic musicals often enters en masse for the town scene or big dance number, the director must find ways to make the introduction of so many characters make sense. For more information on this topic, see Chapter 17: Staging Musical Scenes.

The general rule is to vary entrances so that everyone doesn't file on together and to make choices that feel real and motivated.

Example: The "Wells Fargo Wagon" number, *The Music Man*

> In *The Music Man*, when the "Wells Fargo Wagon" number starts, the motivation to enter is clear; everyone wants to see what treasures the wagon is bringing. The script makes it possible for the director to stagger entrances. By breaking the chorus up into family units, with a mother, father and a few kids in each group, you can stagger entrances by family, one by one, so that you can establish each family as a unique and real group with its own interests and personalities. Once they all get onstage, the audience has had a moment with each and it feels real and not forced.

Sightlines

The director, while staging the scenes, must consider **sightlines**. Working in each stage configuration, the director has to think about how the staging will be viewed by different parts of the audience. The director must consider: how much and which part of the stage can the audience see?

> **Sightline:** the view each audience member has of the stage.

Having a model close by is helpful. A director can hold the model up at eye level and look into it from different angles to see where the problem areas might be.

It is also helpful to change where the director sits during rehearsals. If working in three-quarter thrust, having a chair on each of the three sides of the stage area and moving between those seats during staging helps avoid sightline problems.

Example: Act 1, Scene 1, *The Glass Menagerie*

> The actors are at the dinner table eating. The configuration is proscenium, but the house is very wide and has more than thirty seats in each row. At first, the director places Tom at one end of the table, with Laura and Amanda on the upstage side of the table. By moving around from side to side, the director realizes that in certain positions, Tom blocks the other actors and he has a weaker dynamic. By experimenting and moving, the director finds that when placing Amanda at the upstage-center seat of the table, Tom at the stage-right end, and Laura at the stage-left end, all three can be seen from every seat in the house, and Amanda is the focal point.

Student Exercise 12.6

Select a scene that has been blocked already and that involves furniture and other impediments. Set the stage with the representative furniture. Place five chairs in different positions in the area where the audience will be sitting. Depending on the stage configuration, you could place all the chairs in front of the playing area (proscenium), on three sides (three-quarter thrust) or on all four sides (in the round). Run the blocking for the scene, watching each time from a different chair. Note where the sightline problems exist for each chair, correct them, and recheck them to be sure that no new problems have been created.

Stage Pictures

What is a stage picture? Michael Bennett was the master of the **stage picture**. His stage placement for *A Chorus Line* was meticulous. Because the stage pictures he created for the show are so iconic, his original blocking book is the prized possession of only a chosen few directors. When remounting Bennett's staging, the stage pictures are just as important to the overall show as the choreography.

> **Stage picture:** the totality of what the audience sees from their seats. Ideal stage pictures are unified, aesthetically pleasing and reflective of the inner life of the play in every moment.

The placement of people on the stage creates the scene's visual aesthetic, defines the dynamics, and captures the essence of each moment. Directors create the details of each stage picture. Especially in moments where there are a lot of people onstage not moving, there is still "movement" in the stage picture, i.e. a sense of action without actual movement.

Stage pictures should be aesthetically pleasing without being pretentious and forced.

What Makes a Good Stage Picture?

One of the true delights of directing is to create pictures onstage that are aesthetically satisfying, powerful, and resonant of the inner truth of the moment. Directors set up stage pictures in the rehearsal hall, but invariably directors will change them onstage to take advantage of the new scenic environment.

Composition What are the elements of the picture? How do the actors and set interact in the overall composition? Where are they placed?

The composition of the picture is defined by who and what is onstage and how everything interacts to create the overall impression. Michael Bennett's stage picture just before "What I Did For Love" in *A Chorus Line* placed all the dancers in peer groups, some standing, some seated, all appearing bruised and seeking comfort. Just after Paul injures himself and is taken to the hospital, they are sad and contemplating their futures. His use of groupings and levels created a composition that was soaked with the atmosphere of dread and sadness. The relationships of the dancers and the closeness they shared was made clear by where he placed everyone and the levels at which they stood or sat.

Balance and Proportion Is there balance onstage, or a purposefully unbalanced look?

In a balanced look, there are equal numbers of people and activity on both sides of the stage. In large group numbers, the symmetrical placement of people balances the stage picture. Instead of clumping lots of people together in one large group on each side, carefully selected smaller groupings create a more interesting, more realistic stage picture. Create groupings that have a shared commonality: couples and family units, friends, co-workers. Don't just throw people together to make a pretty picture. Have a reason for each placement and give the groups something to believe in by creating characters and relationships for them.

Asymmetry can also be used powerfully. An unbalanced stage picture can create strong focus and atmosphere, as well as tension.

Variety Is the same thing repeated over and over, or is the picture constantly changing?

Because each stage picture reflects a new moment in the play, no two stage pictures are going to be the same. Create variety in the way the pictures are constructed through the use of different levels, groupings, scenic elements and furniture, and patterns of movement.

Especially in large chorus scenes, create a variety of non-repeating pictures that define in each moment what is true about that moment, and use that knowledge to determine both the relationships of each group and their positioning. Each "mini-picture" should have a sense of purpose and tell a story.

Beauty Are the pictures aesthetically pleasing?

Don't be afraid to make beautiful stage pictures. Just remember, stage pictures must always reflect the inner truth of the moment—a fact more important than beauty. Beauty doesn't always mean "pretty." A beautiful stage picture can be a heart-wrenching scene of barbarity or cruelty. The beauty comes from the picture's ability to translate the emotional moment into a visual image that touches the audience.

Use the Set Use the entire stage. Don't confine people to one small area, unless that is what the designer intended. Especially in musicals, use the space! Constantly check for empty, unused areas of the stage and change the composition to fill the stage.

Sightlines Sightlines are an important consideration, to not only the overall configuration but also to individual stage pictures. Be very careful about sightlines. Move around in the auditorium when you are setting a show onstage. See your work from every angle to discover when people are being blocked.

Blocking: Discovery or Planned?

The Discovery Approach

Many directors feel planning the staging in advance compromises spontaneity. They prefer to discover blocking in rehearsal through improvisation that allows the actors to move freely and "discover" what feels natural and **organic** in each moment.

> **Organic:** Truthful, believable, and coming naturally from the given circumstances of the moment and relationship between the actors. If something is organic, it feels human and honest.

Even using this approach, every play has sections that must be planned out. The director can prepare those sections in advance. For example, the dinner scene in *The Glass Menagerie* involves eating, passing food, drinking, pouring tea, etc. While other scenes can be approached through improvisation, planning the mechanics of the dinner scene will free the actors to explore the emotional content without thinking about when to pass the plates or chew their food.

Improvisation is great way to organically discover truthful blocking, but it is not for every play or every actor. Some actors don't work well on their feet, and prefer being directed. Others love working improvisationally and have a good head for this approach. The director makes the call, and can always change midcourse.

Improvisation The basis of the discovery approach is improvisation. The director does not give the actors any specific blocking, but indicates only the scenic elements. Therefore, the actors move wherever their inspiration leads them. Through trial and error, the director determines what works best and then sets blocking choices.

This approach can be very effective in discovering often surprising and organic staging, but it also can be problematic for actors unable to work both sides of their brain at the same time. That is to say, it can be either a dream or a train wreck. With most experienced actors, working improvisationally comes naturally. They are able to live in the moment and explore the set and blocking choices while remaining truthful and adept at interacting with the other actors. With student or inexperienced actors, providing structure is sometimes necessary to allow actors to focus on interaction and emotional life.

If the actors can't "feel out" the blocking and connect to the material at the same time, the director will be better served by the planned approach described later in this chapter.

During improvisational blocking rehearsals, directors should watch very closely as the actors explore the staging possibilities. Note what works as you actively participate in the process with the actors, discussing the staging choices after each run. Do they feel natural to the actors? Do they look natural? The goal is to discover blocking through improvisation.

Blocking Outline Improvisation is helped by having a loose blocking outline that provides a structure for the improvisation. The director gives the actors the basic architecture of the blocking, with a few specific targets to hit, and the actors fill in the blanks. This gives the actors a sense of the scene before they begin to improvise from point to point, as well as making it easier to be free, to discover, and not to have to think too much.

Setting the Choices After improvisations to discover the blocking, the director sets choices, and the stage manager records the blocking in the master prompt book. There comes a point in the work on each scene where the improvisation ends and the blocking is considered set, or finished. That doesn't mean blocking will never change, but the expectation is to repeat the set blocking in runs from that point forward. If actors have "aha" moments and want to try something new, let them. The discovery process never ends, but the blocking process does.

Due to its unpredictability, improvising the blocking in an actual performance is only done in improvisational theatre. In final rehearsals, there is no more improvisational blocking. If an actor has a new idea, they may bring it to the director, who may incorporate it through a quick rehearsal. In such a scenario, the stage manager then informs the lighting designer of the change.

Actors need structure so their acting can be free and spontaneous. After the show is set, the "improvisation" that continues is more about living moment to moment truthfully, hearing each response from the other actor as if for the first time without having to worry about where the next cross will happen.

Rehearsal Process for the Discovery Approach

1. Set the room with rehearsal furniture and props, placed according to the ground plan. Make sure distances between furniture pieces are accurate. If you don't have enough space to tape the entire set on the floor, tape down the area where the primary staging will occur and work outwards from there until you run out of space.

2. Read through the scene once in chairs with actors, much like a table reading. The purpose is to get the actors relating and listening to one another, and to give them a chance to re-familiarize themselves with the scene. It's a warm-up.

3. Explain the ground plan to the actors and show them the renderings so they can visualize the set. If they can envision it, they will understand it, and it will help them make good choices.

4. Tell them to freely explore blocking choices as they go through the scene. Explain that you will not give them specific blocking. Rather, you will let them "make it up" as they go along and see where their instinct takes them. Impress upon them the importance of moving only when motivated.

5. Discuss the main action of the scene for each actor and how that action might spur behavior and movement.

6. Discuss potential business for the actors that will be part of a scene so they can incorporate that business in the improvisation.

7. Discuss scene dynamics, relationships, and power positions. Make sure they understand the dynamic of their relationships.

8. Give them the basic architecture for the scene; tell them where to start, explain any specific required blocking, and ask them to use those moments as guideposts.

9. Place the actors in their starting positions.

10. Impress upon the actors the importance of moving only when motivated to do so!

11. Begin the scene. Stop and start as needed, especially when the blocking gets awkward. You can side-coach and make suggestions, but ideally you will leave the actors alone and observe what choices they make.

12. Make note of anything that works well.

13. Run the scene a few times, repeating blocking that worked well and continuing to explore the rougher sections.

14. Continue this process until the actors have found organic choices for the entire scene. This will require input from the director, but let it go for a while before getting involved and making decisions for the actors. Always let those decisions come from what you see them doing naturally.
15. Once you have found what works, set the choices and repeat them a few times.
16. The stage manager notates the final blocking in the prompt book

The Planned Approach

This method is suited for plays with complex staging requirements or short rehearsal periods, or for directors who prefer to plan staging in advance. This requires knowledge of the ground plan, the play, and a sense of the movement that will be natural to the characters.

Even using the planned approach the director will not be able to nor should plan every moment of the show. Regardless of how much time and energy the director puts into pre-planning, some of the staging will inevitably need to be worked out. Leaving minor details to be discovered and staying open to changing major sections that don't work is critical. Don't over-plan! Remain open to discovery and to revising plans based on those discoveries.

Imagining and Organizing Blocking When working on a scene with just a few actors, the director can imagine a picture of the scene, and go through it in their imagination, envisioning the blocking and notating the movements using blocking short-hand in their DPN. Read each beat; analyze that beat for dynamics, conflicts, and relationships; and finally, visualize movement that tells that story. Note it in your book using charts and blocking notation (see the section "blocking notation" later in this chapter).

Visualizing the Blocking By closing your eyes and daydreaming or visualizing the scene in your mind's eye, you can allow your imagination to reveal the blocking. This won't solve every problem, but it's an exercise that utilizes the power of the director's imagination.

Student Exercise 12.7

1. Read and be thoroughly familiar with the scene.
2. Make an outline of the scene's major actions.
3. Close your eyes.
4. Visualize both the set and the actors in your mind's eye.
5. Proceeding beat by beat, daydream your way through the scene.
6. Let the actors move from place to place.
7. Record what you saw.

Using the Ground Plan For those who have difficulty daydreaming, use the ground plan as a guide. Have the production book, the ground plan, and a 2-D rendering or 3-D model at hand. Constantly referring to the ground plan, begin to determine the movement beat by beat.

Student Exercise 12.8

1. Make multiple copies of the ground plan (or plans if the scenes change).
2. Place a single copy of the ground plan on the page opposite each page of the play text.
3. Consider dynamics of the scene, and how they influence the blocking. What movements or spatial relationships are mandated in order to realize dynamics?
4. Consider the main action of the scene. What are the objectives of each character and what movements will they make to achieve those objectives?
5. Consider stage business and incorporate that into blocking choices.
6. Consider the relationships of the characters and find ways to define those relationships spatially and through movement.
7. Does the playwright require any specific blocking? If so, incorporate that into blocking choices.
8. Take all the information and begin a blocking plan. Decide where the actors start on the stage and notate their placement on the first ground plan page.
9. Going from beat to beat, incorporate all the information above into the blocking of the scene.
10. By letting capital letters represent each character and arrows designate direction of movement, diagram the scene on the ground plans. (See figure 12.3)
11. Write numbers in the text to correspond to a movement noted on the ground plan. Label both with the same number so you can easily jump to the ground plan to see what is indicated for each moment.
12. For each new page, notate where the actors begin on that page and then diagram the movements through to the end of the page.
13. Work though the entire scene, mapping out each movement until you reach the end.

Figure 12.1
Diagramming
movement on the
stage. Actor starts
at position 1, enters
through doorway,
crosses to
position 2, then X's
to sit on couch.

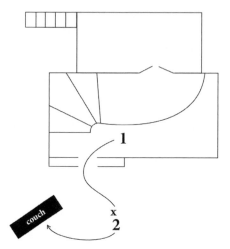

Keep in mind that things can change! This is just a place to start. When you have real actors working in space, what you planned on paper might not work. Use your plans as a starting point. If they work, use them. If not, find what works and make the changes in your book.

Many Characters Onstage at Once For plays that have more than eight actors in a scene, try creating small square cut-outs and writing the name of a character on each cut-out. Place the cutouts on the ground plan and move the cutouts around to help you organize the staging and keep track of each actor. This way, you will always know where everyone is, what their traffic patterns are, and where they end up. It is a great way to organize a crowd scene. As you move the cut-outs, diagram the specific track in your DPN for each character.

Using a 3-D Model If the designer has provided you with a model of the set, using small paper cut-outs of the actors, physically manipulate the cutouts to get a visual idea of the movement. This is especially useful when you have a lot of people onstage. Follow the steps for using a ground plan and apply to using a model.

The advantage of this method is the opportunity to consider sightlines. Position yourself on eye level with the model and get the same view as the audience.

Adding Actors—"Putting the Scene on its Feet" In rehearsal, you will translate blocking from notes in a book to human actors working on a taped set in a rehearsal hall. Follow these steps.

1. Set the room with rehearsal furniture and props, placed according to the ground plan
2. Explain the ground plan to the actors; show them the renderings and model.

3. Read through the scene once with the actors in chairs, to re-familiarize them with the text.

4. Discuss the main action of the scene and determine objectives, motivated major movements and placements.

5. Discuss potential business for the actors and how that business would work and why it's necessary.

6. Discuss scene dynamics to establish their changing relationship throughout the course of the scene.

7. Place the actors in their starting positions.

8. Begin blocking the scene; have the actors begin their lines. When you get to a place where a movement is planned, or you suddenly have an inspiration for the actors to move, tell them what you want them to do and let them do those lines again with the requested movement.

9. Allow the actors to play with your choices. They will find ways to make your choices natural for themselves.

10. Give the actors the freedom to move if motivated.

11. Work through the entire scene this way, giving them the blocking, letting them run the blocking with their lines, and then moving on to the next section.

12. Once fully blocked, run the scene and watch carefully.

13. Notice and change anything that doesn't feel right.

14. Stage manager notates the final blocking in the prompt book.

Blocking Notation

The director can notate blocking plans in many ways: by inputting the script in the computer and typing out the plans in the columns; by placing a ground plan page opposite each script page in the production book; by notating in the margins; or by just winging it with no prior notes. The only hard and fast rule is that the notations be clear, accurate, and easy to read and understand when you are in rehearsal.

	Backstage			
In three	UR	UC	UL	Off left
In two	R	C	L	
In one	DR	DC	DL	
	Thrust/apron			

Figure 12.2
Diagram showing areas of the stage

Figure 12.3
Standard blocking
notation

Symbol	Description	Symbol	Description
L	Stage left	@	At
U	Upstage	O	Around
R	Stage right	CoX	Counter
D	Downstage	fr	From
C	Center	↘	Look downstage left
X	Cross	↗	Look upstage left
XDR	Cross downstage right	⌐ ¬	Look at each other
XDL	Cross downstage left	Ɍ	Rise
CUC	Cross upstage center	Ş	Sit
off	Off stage	⊢	Stop
Ent	Enter	Ҟ	Kneel
Ex	Exit	G→	Give
ExUC	Exit up center door	⨼	Lie down
bf	Before	⊢	Chair
af	After	⊓	Table
. . . . .	Pause	⊞	Window

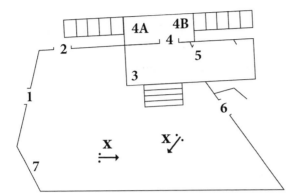

Figure 12.4
Diagramming
position and
direction

HAMLET, ACT ONE, SCENE TWO

H starts sitting on ledge
C & G are on thrones USC on platform
L kneeling on floor below

C x DC to L **1**

G x SR to H **2**

C - Claudius
G - Gertrude
L - Laertes
H - Hamlet
X - Court members

CLAUDIUS
Take thy fair hour, Laertes; time be thine,
And thy best graces spend it at thy will!
But now, my cousin Hamlet, and my son, --
HAMLET
[Aside] A little more than kin, and less than kind.
KING CLAUDIUS
How is it that the clouds still hang on you?
HAMLET
Not so, my lord; I am too much i' the sun.
QUEEN GERTRUDE
Good Hamlet, cast thy nighted colour off,
And let thine eye look like a friend on Denmark.
Do not for ever with thy veiled lids
Seek for thy noble father in the dust:
Thou know'st 'tis common; all that lives must die,
Passing through nature to eternity.
HAMLET
Ay, madam, it is common.
QUEEN GERTRUDE
If it be,
Why seems it so particular with thee?
HAMLET
Seems, madam! nay it is; I know not 'seems.'
'Tis not alone my inky cloak, good mother,
Nor customary suits of solemn black,
Nor windy suspiration of forced breath,
No, nor the fruitful river in the eye,
Nor the dejected 'havior of the visage,
Together with all forms, moods, shapes of grief,
That can denote me truly: these indeed seem,
For they are actions that a man might play:
But I have that within which passeth show;
These but the trappings and the suits of woe.

Figure 12.5
An example of a
page from
blocking book

Classroom Exercises

Classroom Exercise 12.9: Dynamics Exercises

These exercises are useful to discover how dynamics affect staging, and how staging affects dynamics. They are classroom exercises and not useful in rehearsal.

1. Using six actors, place them in a line, shoulder to shoulder standing about one foot apart. Note who takes focus—no one! Place five upstage and one downstage, note how the actor downstage takes focus. Play with various configurations of the six actors and see where the focus is strongest, where it is the weakest, and how the dynamics can be varied through various configurations.

2. Using two actors and a chair, place one actor on the chair and the other in different places in relationship to the person on the chair, both standing and on the floor. Note how the dynamics change as the placement changes.

3. Using five actors and a few boxes to stand on, play with levels. Place one box upstage center with an actor standing on it. Place the other four actors in each corner of the stage area. Note where the focus is. Move the box around and add other boxes. Note how the stage dynamic changes and how you can find stronger and weaker placements.

4. Using five actors, two boxes and a chair, place actors in different areas of the stage either standing, on a box, sitting, or lying on the floor. Playing with levels and stage positions, find powerful stage pictures and note what makes them powerful.

Extended Classroom Exercise 12.10

Take a scene from a play you are working on, or want to work on. Copy the pages, put them in a mini-production book and work on the scene to develop a blocking plan. Create a quick and simple ground plan. Use the visualization method to explore possibilities, and then notate your choices in the book.

Chapter 13
Blocking in Different Stage Configurations

A whole book could be devoted to the subject of working in different stage configurations. The following are brief considerations of each.

Proscenium

In a proscenium setting the audience views the entire show from the front. The director is working in a flat, two-dimensional aesthetic.

Considerations

Placing the Director's Table Place the table so the director sits directly in front of the rehearsal area.

Upstaging When an actor is behind another actor, the actor downstage must face "upstage" to talk, and we lose their faces. This can be useful if used sparingly. Generally, find ways to open up your actors so they can be seen by the audience.

Cheeks Because actors naturally want to face each other, this causes their cheeks to face the audience. Audiences don't want to

Proscenium with no thrust

| Wall |
| Stage left wing | **Stage** | Stage right wing |

Audience

Proscenium with small thrust

| Wall |
| Stage left wing | **Stage** | Stage right wing |
| Apron |

Audience

Figure 13.1 Blocking in proscenium

spend all night watching actors' cheeks. Audiences want to see actor's eyes. While a certain amount of facing each other is unavoidable, directors must find creative ways to open actors to the audience.

Audience Sightlines The audience seated in front but on each side of the orchestra will have a skewed view of the stage. Because they will see everything from the extreme sides, be aware of placing actors on the downstage left and right edges of the stage for long periods, where they will obstruct the view of the side-seated audience members. Watch out for obstructing the view of actors or action.

Straight Lines Avoid actors standing in straight lines. Using the entire playing space, create stage pictures that are varied and not repetitive.

In the Round

In the round, the audience views the show from all four sides or seating wraps entirely around the stage. The director works in three dimensions and there is no "front."

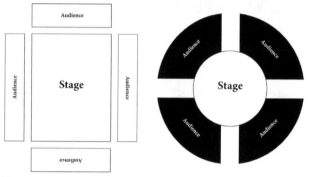

Figure 13.2
Blocking in the round

Considerations

Placing the Director's Table The table can be placed on any side but the director should move during rehearsal to allow for multiple vantage points.

Duologues In a duet scene, keep the actors moving. If they get stuck in one position, entire blocks of the audience will see only the back of one actor's head. You can vary the sightlines by using the following techniques:

- *Use levels* Seat one actor so that the audience can see the other actor over the seated actor's head.
- *Coordinate with the aisles* Nobody sits in the aisles, so if an actor has his back to an aisle, there are no sightline problems. Those seated near that aisle will have a limited view.
- *Frequently change position* By moving the actors into new positions, you change the sightlines. In the round, the audience understands they are going to see backs of heads, but by moving the actors frequently, no audience member will suffer for long.
- *Use crosses* When an actor crosses from one side to the other, and then turns back to look at the actor they have crossed away from, their face is then in view of the audience that were previously looking at the back of the actor's head.

- Keep the set low, minimal, and transparent. If you have to use furniture, use pieces that don't go above the actor's waists. Use as little onstage furniture as possible, and any hanging pieces, like windows, must be transparent.

One advantage of the round is that in it the actors don't need to worry about a director instructing them to **cheat out**!

Try to keep the actors connecting with as much of the audience as possible, and rotate the direction of the actors as unobtrusively as possible.

Choreography in the Round The round can be a nightmare for a choreographer. Every formation is based on a circle or square. Unlike proscenium, where there is a front and back, in the round, every angle is both front and back.

Using circles with actors facing out is the most effective way to stage chorus dances. If you have a center unit that rises, then the star can be placed above the dancing chorus and seen by all.

The trick is to keep the formations changing constantly, with focus always being shared by all angles. It is both challenging and fun to stage dances in the round. There is great freedom to explore patterns never used on a proscenium stage.

Entrances and Exits All entrances and exits happen through the aisles. Timing the entrances is important, as is traffic flow.

Set Changes Unless there is a system of bringing sets in from above or through traps in the floor, all set pieces are brought on and removed by carrying them through the aisles. Keep the scenic elements to a minimum and remember that anything above audience eye level will block their view. You can't place a door on a set in the round or everyone facing that door will have their view blocked. But you can place the door on the apron of the stage, directly on the aisle, where there are no audience sight line issues.

Working in the round frees the staging to be more organic and less concerned with upstaging, but at the same time the director must constantly consider angles and directions to ensure the best sightlines for the audience.

Three-Quarter Thrust, Arena

In three-quarter thrust the audience views the show from three sides. However, in many arenas, there is an upstage area that is viewed by everyone from the front, much like a proscenium.

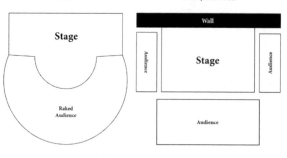

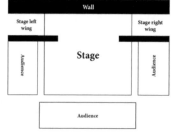

Figure 13.3
Blocking in three-quarter thrust

Considerations

Placing the Director's Table It is best to put the table in front of the rehearsal area and to have chairs on stage left and stage right to which the director can move throughout staging in order to consider the show from the three audience areas.

Upstage When staging on the upstage area of the set, the rules for proscenium apply.

On the Thrust When on the thrust, the rules of "in the round" apply with the caveat that there are only three sides to be concerned with instead of four.

Using the Downstage Area Avoid playing everything upstage; use the thrust area fully, bringing the show close to the audience and fully utilizing the entire stage area.

Scene Changes Scenery can come from the back and be brought downstage, or it can come through the aisles. Like the round, keep the scenery on the thrust to a minimum, and nothing can be above eye level.

Play All Sides Especially in dance numbers, don't stage all scenes to favor front/center audience. All three sides are the "front." Balance the use of each side.

Entrances and Exits Entrances can be made from upstage, through the aisles to the sides, and front corners of the rectangular thrust.

Use the dynamic of the thrust to intensify the relationship between actor and audience. The thrust "thrusts" the show closer to the audience and there is power in that.

Final Thoughts

Regardless of stage configuration—and you might encounter some very strange ones not covered in this section—always remember to double-check your blocking.

> **Director's Checklist: Things to Remember When Blocking**
>
> ❏ Where the audience is seated
>
> ❏ The audience sightlines
>
> ❏ Creating organic action while ensuring audience visibility
>
> ❏ Entrance and exits
>
> ❏ Scene changes

Each configuration offers positive and negatives, so make the most of what each offers. Move frequently during rehearsals to see the show from every angle.

I remember seeing a Broadway production from the front row, extreme side. At one point, four actors moved down left and sat on the apron, completely blocking my view of the stage action for more than fifteen minutes. Don't let this happen.

Student Exercise 13.1

Take a scene you are working on in directing class. Stage it first for proscenium, then for the round, and then for a thrust. Find solutions that work for each.

PART IV:
REHEARSING A MUSICAL

Chapter 14
Initial Rehearsals of a Musical

The process of putting together a musical adds several components to the director's work. Collaboration with the musical director and the choreographer, and leading the initial rehearsals are the subject of this chapter.

Working With a Musical Director

Role of the Musical Director

In opera, the musical director (MD) is king and the stage director (SD) takes a back seat. However, in musical theatre the collaboration is more equitable. The director has the final word, but both make important contributions to the overall process. In fruitful collaborations, the stage director and musical director work closely together to realize a shared vision. They discuss theme, concept, and style, and apply their conclusions to the work.

The musical director interprets the **score**, making musical decisions that support the concept. Then, the MD teaches the music to the performers. Once the performers learn the music, private and group **coaching** sessions run by the musical director focus on character and musical issues. In companies with large budgets, a rehearsal pianist plays rehearsals and the musical director conducts. On limited budgets, the musical director does both.

Duties of the musical director

- Hires, rehearses, and conducts the orchestra
- Conducts vocal rehearsals with the cast
- Interprets the score and teaches the cast music, guided by that interpretation
- Plays first keyboard in smaller companies with limited budgets
- Conducts the orchestra at performances
- Coaches singers throughout rehearsal process
- Runs musical brush-up rehearsals

Working Through the Score

In pre-rehearsal meetings, the director goes through the score with the musical director and choreographer. They discuss potential cuts in vocal or dance music and the role and presence of **underscoring**. In most cases, the only way a director becomes familiar with the underscoring is to hear it played. It rarely is recorded on cast albums. Underscoring can provide important insight to a scene's emotional life.

Working song by song, they discuss interpretation, mood, song dynamics, and how concept influences musical choices.

Interpretation

Influenced by the director's concept, the musical director **interprets** each song and instrumental section.

Score: All of the music written by the composer and words by the lyricist for the production

Underscoring: Music played under the dialogue in a scene to provide emotional texture to the scene

Coaching: When the director or musical director works on interpretation of music, not vocal technique

Interpreting: Making musical decisions about tempo and style dynamics based on discussions with the director, and then communicating those decisions to the performers in coaching sessions

Example: Rodgers and Hammerstein's *Carousel*

The concept is to create an updated version of the musical *Carousel*, setting it from 1942–1957. The creative team goes through the score in order to find ways of bringing musical influences of the 1940s and '50s to bear on songs and instrumental dance music. They decide to swing a section of the "Carousel Waltz" in the opening, and the choreographer will stage a lindy-style break. The MD suggests a vocal style that is influenced by musical trends of the early '40s, using a crooning pop style where it makes sense. They go from song to song, seeing how these choices work and where changes and cuts make sense. In Billy's "Soliloquy," the MD suggests a Bing Crosby style approach to the first two sections of the song, moving to a more legitimate style at the end to enhance the power of the song's climactic conclusion.

Cuts

Dance Cuts Made judiciously, cuts can tighten a production. In early American musicals, the audience expected long dance sequences. Modern audiences are not as apt to sit through very long dance numbers if the company doesn't have skilled dancers. The length of the dance sections impacts the forward movement of the story.

Reprise Cuts Reprises were very popular in early musicals, but often had little dramatic effect. They gave stars the chance to sing the popular tunes one more time. Cutting reprises keeps the action moving forward and focused. But in some cases, the reprise is a powerful restatement. In *South Pacific*, for example, when Emile reappears at the end and sings "Some Enchanted Evening," it harkens back to the first moment that Emile and Nelly fell in love and therefore plays an important dramatic role. Depending on how the reprise works in the overall show, the MD and SD will either cut it or use it.

Song Cuts Sometimes, entire songs can be cut. For example, in *Carousel*, "The Highest Judge of All" is often cut because it slows down the action after Billy goes to heaven and is not an integral song. In *Hair*, most productions cut "Dead End." Many publishers require that written requests for alterations are submitted for approval. Get the necessary approvals needed to alter the show before you begin rehearsals.

Updated Versions

Many shows have updated versions made popular by revivals that reinvent the show. *Carousel*, when produced by the Royal National Theatre in the 1980s, was a marvel of reinvention. If you are looking to direct the reinvented production, you'll find that the changes instituted by the Royal National Theatre are not published. If you are producing *Carousel*, Rodgers and Hammerstein Music Library sends the original 1945 orchestrations.

You can always ask the publisher if the new material is available, as in the case of the Public Theatre's production of *The Pirates of Penzance*. You can find the newer version of that production through Music Theatre International.

If the music director wishes to update the score, as long as notes don't change, approval is not needed. However, if re-orchestrations or major alterations to songs are planned, you must submit a request to the publisher to make these changes. *A publisher can shut down a show without notice if changes have been made without permission.*

Song Dynamics

Songs are moments of heightened expression. When words are not enough, music flows out of the dialogue. Songs in most musicals since *Oklahoma* serve to advance the plot. Before that, they served as diversions from the plot.

The MD and SD consider how each song advances the plot and expresses character. Unlocking the truth of each song is the first step in interpretation. Especially in musical revues, where songs are often isolated mini-plays with their own beginning, middle, and end, understanding the content of the song is the key to staging it.

Example: "Timid Frida" from *Jacques Brel is Alive and Well ...*

> First, analysis of the song reveals it is about freedom and the costs and dangers of freedom. It's about growing up and making a life, living independently, and learning life lessons the hard way, away from the repression of family and old-fashioned moral codes. It proceeds from the idea that if we are suffocating our children in our moral repression, then their natural inclination will be to engage in a lifestyle of dangerous rebellion.

> The staging of the song focuses on the loneliness and dangers of being in the big city, and what Frida sacrifices. The musical director favors a stripped down and simple vocal style using straight tone vocals and stark phrasing to capture her sense of fear and loneliness. The stage director finds a visual metaphor in a dimly lit stage, slow movements, isolation of the character, and the staging of short scenarios that heighten her initial excitement only to contrast that with a string of bitter disappointments. The other cast members play different characters in the scene. In the end, she is alone onstage, not sure how to move forward.

Discussion of Songs and Character

The musical director and stage director discuss the characters and their relationships to each other. The musical director not only uses these ideas to interpret songs and to make musical decisions, but also shares the ideas with performers in rehearsals and coaching sessions.

A good musical director not only focuses on the notes, rhythm, tempi, and singing, but also injects discussions of characterization and emotional life into the process of preparing the music.

Working with a Choreographer

In the early days of the American musical theatre, dance—like song—was not integrated into the story. *Oklahoma* by Rodgers and Hammerstein was a landmark musical, in that both dance and song first took on important roles in advancing the plot and deepening character and relationships. Since that time, characterization and storytelling have become important elements of choreography. It is not enough simply to move; that movement needs to develop the plot, characters, and relationships.

There are directors who stage their own dances but generally a choreographer works with the director, bringing a specific skill set to the staging of musical numbers.

The director determines what sections of the show the choreographer will stage. Sometimes the director and choreographer collaborate together on the staging of a dance; other times, the choreographer works independently, later showing the work to the director.

The Role of the Choreographer

The choreographer stages dances consistent with the director's concept, teaches the choreography to the cast, rehearses the dance numbers throughout the rehearsal period, and ensures the dances are well-rehearsed.

Depending on the nature of the show, the collaboration, and the individuals involved, the choreographer can simply stage dances and rehearse them, or be more involved by working with the director on staging musical scenes that don't require dance. In shows like *Hair* where the dance is mostly heightened movement integral to the storytelling, a director and choreographer work together in a less organized, more spontaneous way to discover what works. This approach relies on the natural movement styles of the cast. Although both the director and choreographer utilize their expertise to make discoveries, it is the choreographer that shapes what is discovered, finely detailing the movement.

Duties of the Choreographer

- Assists with hiring dancing chorus and general casting
- Works with director and musical director to develop the show's concept
- Interprets dances based on the concept
- Creates the dance movements
- Prepares dances for rehearsal
- Teaches dances to the cast
- Runs brush-up rehearsals
- Assists the director with musical staging as needed
- Stays with the show through opening night, overseeing quality of dances

Choreography vs. Musical Staging

Choreography is different than musical staging. Whereas choreography consists of set dance movements, musical staging is heightened movement inspired by the underscoring of a scene or the music in a song. Directors usually stage the musical scenes themselves, but sometimes using a choreographer to assist with the musical staging is very helpful. Some directors (e.g. Harold Prince) hire choreographers to do the musical staging as in the case of *Company* in 1970, where Michael Bennett is credited with the musical staging and Prince is credited as director.

Each collaboration defines its own way of working. There are no set rules. The bottom line is the good of the show, not your own ego. If you can't stage musical numbers, use a choreographer.

The Collaboration

Concept Discussions The director and choreographer discuss the dances as they relate to the director's concept for the show. These discussions influence the choreographer's development of the dances. Everything works in harmony, with all elements supporting one another. The director must be specific about concept as well as open to the input of the choreographer as they discuss the role of dance in the production.

Style Discussions Defined by the concept, each show has an inherent style of dance, which influences the creation of each musical number. The director and choreographer, having discussed and defined the overall concept of the show, then discuss both how that concept will influence the overall dance style and how it will be applied to each song.

Director's Checklist: Things to Consider for Each Dance Number

❑ Style as indicated by the music and concept

❑ Period movement and iconic dance styles

❑ Fundamental dance styles to be employed (ballet, jazz, tap, etc.)

❑ How does each dance fit into the story?

❑ Who is involved and what is their story?

❑ How does the personality of each character influence the way they move?

❑ What are the special needs of each song?

❑ How will available props be used?

Example: "With a Little Bit o' Luck" from *My Fair Lady*

> The concept of the show is to exaggerate the stark contrast between Eliza's old and new life. The director wants a raucous number that expresses the world of Alfred Doolittle as free, easy, and extremely untamed. The number is set in an alley with an ample supply of trashcan lids, broom handles, and other percussive props.
>
> The style will be inspired by English music hall, making use of the props lying around to create a percussive climax. Doolittle and friends are drunk and let loose and make noise. He is not a trained dancer but loves to dance on tables in the local pubs. He is comfortable with his body and moves easily. The style of the chorus is more acrobatic and formally executed although they should not look like trained dancers.
>
> The choreographer's concept is to use found objects in their environment to become percussive elements. At the song's climax, they slip their feet through the handles of the trashcan lids specially built to hold on to the shoes of the dancers as they dance and crash the lids like a tap dance on steroids. Others use broom handles and wood blocks to create a cacophony of noise and hysteria.
>
> This style choice fulfills the needs of the number. It also tells us about Eliza's father, his friends, and Eliza's former world. And it's very entertaining!

Give and Take The choreographer often works on his or her own, away from the watching eye of the director. When the director sees the dance for the first time, it is the time to express compliments and concerns to the choreographer. If something doesn't work, don't be shy about saying so, but support your concerns with specifics and solutions. The dance has to support the concept.

Watch for dances that expose weaknesses in the chorus. If the choreographer is trying to create something that is beyond the abilities of the performers, don't immediately stop them. Let them take the dance as far as possible; but in the end, don't allow choreography to be in the show if the abilities of the performers can't fulfill the goals of the choreographer.

Working with a choreographer is an important collaboration, one that can be joyful and exciting. Respect your choreographer, allow them the freedom to explore every possibility in their imagination, but don't shy away from being honest in your feedback. If you have to, demand changes that are for the good of the show; however, be sure to do it in a respectful and professional way.

Initial Rehearsals of a Musical

The initial musical theatre rehearsal process is broken into three parts:

1. Music Rehearsal
2. Dance Staging
3. Scene Staging

Teaching the music comes first. Then the dance and scene staging happens concurrently.

Music Rehearsals

During music rehearsals, the musical director teaches the music to the cast and coaches song interpretation. These happen first because actors must know their music for dance and staging rehearsals. With professionals this process takes about two days. In a community theatre or college production it can take a few days to a few weeks. It is important that sufficient time is devoted to learning the music. Musical brush-ups are scheduled throughout rehearsals.

The First Read-and-sing-through Once the music is learned, the cast comes together for a read-and-sing-through of the show. The musical director (or rehearsal accompanist) plays and the entire script and score are performed. Ideally, the cast members, sitting in a circle, rise when it is one's turn to speak or sing. Table reading rules that require the actors not to push or perform apply.

The first read-through is a good time for introductions and designer presentations.

Dance- and Scene-staging Rehearsals

In most musicals, it is possible to rehearse scenes and dances concurrently as long as you have two rehearsal spaces. A good rehearsal schedule maximizes everyone's time, beginning with act one numbers and scenes, followed by act one runs and then act two staging and runs.

If dance numbers are complicated and require extra rehearsal, start them early in the process. Dance can take a long time to get into the actor's bodies, so allow plenty of time for initial dance-staging and review rehearsals.

In summer stock and regional situations, rehearsal time is limited. It is essential that the director and choreographer be prepared to stage the show in a short amount of time.

Table Work There is rarely time for table work when staging musicals. Given the dance, music, and scene staging requirements, there is often barely enough time to get the show into runs before tech.

However, if you have the luxury of a few table readings, it can be of great benefit to the performers. Follow the same approach as with plays.

Even if you don't have much time, before staging each scene for the first time, read through the scene in an "expedited" table read to flesh out the action, objectives, and **through line**.

Coaching Songs: Finding the Truth in the Music

Once rehearsals begin it is common for a director to coach songs. Avoid talking about musical issues or vocal technique, which is the musical director's job.

Directors coach songs to help the actors find what is true and to solidify or clarify relationships in group numbers. In order to coach a song, the director must analyze and understand the song.

Coaching a song is like coaching a monologue in that the key to the performance is in the text and the music. The answers are all there. The rules of objectives, wants and needs, and acting beats all hold for songs.

The following is a general scenario of how the director coaches an actor:

1. The actor sings the song.
2. The director discusses with the actor the song, its meaning, and how it furthers the scene.
3. Together, they identify the through-line or story of the song.
4. The director asks the actor to identify the type of song, e.g. is it an "I want" song, an "I am" song, a love song?
5. Together, the actor and director define character objectives, desires, wants, and needs.
6. They break the song into sections and define the essence of each.
7. They discuss the needs and desires of the character, and what he or she wants to express.
8. They identify important lyrics and images and talk about what the images mean to the character.
9. If needed, the director can lead the actor in an exercise to help find what is personal to the actor. (See exercises that follow.)
10. The actor sings the song again, each time incorporating a goal to achieve.
11. In a duet, follow the same steps, defining how the relationship is expressed through the song.

Coaching Exercises

Song as Monologue Have the actor speak the words of the song as they would a monologue. Analyze the song for objectives, beats, images, operative words. Use exercises like "making it personal" (see below) to find the truth in the words. The actor will try to do the words in rhythm, but they should resist that. Make the words as natural and connected as possible. Once the actor has achieved a good level of connection, let them sing it again and discuss what changes.

Name the Sections Break the song down into 2-5 sections, giving each section a name. The name captures the essence of each section. Track the journey of the character through each section, charting where they start and finish, and where things change. Find the "aha" moments of realization in the song. Give each section an active verb to describe the objective of the character in the section. Sing each section to incorporate that verb. This is very similar to beat work in a monologue.

Listen to the Accompaniment Ask the pianist to play the song. Listen to the piano part without thinking about the lyric. What does the underscore tell you about the character and the situation? The sung line might be very legato and slow, with a patter fast underscoring. That could be the fluttering heartbeat of the lover singing a love song in a romantic way, but the music reveals they are nervous as hell. What clues does the accompaniment provide?

Defining the Arc If there are problems capturing the full arc of the song, discuss the journey of the character in the song, where they begin and end, and what they realize; how they change. Note the places in the song where those realizations occur. Sing each "realization section" then the entire song, incorporating the new arc into the performance.

Imaging Every song or monologue has an inherent string of images connected to the words. For example, in "Mary Had a Little Lamb" we have Mary, the lamb and the white fleece. Work through the song, asking the actor to associate images with words to make the song personal. Isolate the strongest images and visualize them, then incorporate the visualization into the performance. Literally "see the image."

Working the Words Just like in monologues, there are operative words in a song that inspire phrasing choices and musical interpretation. Have the actor identify the operative words and phrases and energize them as they sing the song. Discover the power in those moments.

Preparation: Emotional State of Being What happens before the song? Why does the character sing this song at this moment? What is it they hope to achieve? Define the initial emotion of the character and help the actor find that emotion and make the first moment personal. Sing from that emotional place and let the emotion change as inspired by the song and its music and lyrics.

Ask the actor to find something that inspires the defined emotion. Then, sing the song, exploring how that emotion inspires and colors the performance. If the actor is not fully personalizing the emotion, work with them to find a true emotional connection that leads into the song. Be patient and sensitive, this process can be difficult for some.

Making it Personal Like the earlier exercise, find something personal that the actor can relate to. Often actors just sing without relating the material to their own experience. Ask the actor if they understand what the song is about, and to identify the song's emotional core. Ask if they had a similar experience, or if they can imagine what it would feel like to have the character's experience. Making it personal will make it truthful. Urge them to explore, keeping it simple and honest.

Chapter 15
Staging Musical Scenes

Once musical rehearsals are completed, staging both scenes and musical numbers begins. Musical staging uses the same vocabulary as staging plays and is in many ways identical. However, there is usually less time, so the director has to be prepared to execute staging quickly with less improvisational discovery.

That is not to say that there can't be improvisation. If the director has the blocking ready and communicates the major movements quickly and effectively, new details can be discovered in rehearsal.

Know the limitations of actors. Don't stage a number that is beyond the capability of the actors performing it. Make choices that accentuate the actors' strengths and hide their weaknesses. Simple can be beautiful. Nothing is more destructive to a show than a director who shoots for the stars with a toy rocket.

The Technique Elements

Keep in mind that dances and musical staging tell a story. Choreography is an outgrowth of that story while musical staging is part of that story.

Physical Dynamics

The director asks:

1. What is the dynamic of this song or musical scene?
2. How does that influence the movement?
3. Does the quality of the movement vary or build within the song?

These answers define the approach to physical dynamic of the scene. Even a small movement can impact the dynamic of a moment. Consider the song "I Am What I Am" from *La Cage Aux Folles*. There are two major sections to the song, the second being the climactic one—it even adds a key change to heighten the sense of drama. It is a powerful number that requires emotional intensity. When the singer reaches the final verse of the song, a simple cross downstage is enough to raise the stakes and meet the demands of the song's intensifying dynamic at that point.

By trying out different things, the director can get a feel for what enhances the music and the emotional life of the scene. Some scenes require dance-like movement while others require just a few crosses or a swaying embrace.

If a song needs to get "bigger," a movement downstage as in the case of "I Am What I Am," or to a higher level can suffice. If that is not enough or doesn't make sense, the musical staging can get more energized by staging bigger and stronger movements, such as twirls, turns, sweeps across the stage, or in the case of a tap number, a concentrated explosion of tap. If there is a simple moment in the middle of the song, bring the actors close to each other. Simplify the movement; alter the lights to get more intimate—thus achieving a quieter, private mood.

Ultimately, by trial and error the director finds the most effective solution. It is a skill perfected by years of experimenting. After a while, a director begins to get an internal sense of what will work. Planning in advance will help get things started, but being flexible and patient will lead to the "right" choices.

If you are not sure where to go, get the number up on its feet. Make choices, even if wrong, so that you have something to work with. Once you see something on its feet, it is easier to find solutions. Then, you can experiment with choices until you find one that resonates.

How do you identify the right choice? When it feels right, enhances the moment, and establishes a stronger sense of character, style, and relationship, you know you've hit it.

Stage Areas and Levels

Fully utilizing the space is important. Big, open staging is a choice. For musicals, it is generally a good choice. Long segments of small, confined scenes don't suit the classics of musical theatre.

When first looking at a scene or song, try to "feel" the dynamic. It is an internal, indefinable awareness that is more intuitive than cognitive. Get a sense of the scene's dynamic. Is it big? Sweeping? Small and confined? Intimate?

Once you sense the dynamic, start translating that intuitive knowledge into staging choices. This relates both to the physical relationships between characters and the way they are placed on the set.

Determine where each character is in relation to the others and who is in a position of power or weakness. Sometimes the actors have to move out of the powerful positions to realize they were in powerful positions. Play with choices, positions, and tempo of movement to find the right dynamic.

Use levels. For example, in Hal Prince's staging of *Evita* he placed Eva high on a bridge when singing "Don't Cry For Me, Argentina," which gave her the distinct power position above the masses. The crowd was facing upstage with their backs to the audience. The military men on the bridge were in dark costumes and out of the spotlight. Eva was dressed in white, bathed in white light, and appeared almost angelic. It was a brilliant use of stage and lighting to realize the dynamic of the song, pulling focus to Eva. She made only a few simple arm movements, creating one of musical theatre's most iconic images: the raising of her hands at the end of the song. It was a very small movement but had incredible power. Prince understood the inner life of that song, the relationship that had to be created between Eva Peron and her people, and the dramatic nature of the character.

Choosing the Right Movement Style

The director and choreographer define the overall style, which they then apply to all staging decisions. Every musical has an inherent general style. Every song has a more specific style related to the show's overall style.

In order to direct the style, refer to your research. (See Chapter 6) Stories about the period (like Sholom Aleichem's source material if you're doing *Fiddler on the Roof*) provide insight into the way people moved, thought, and behaved. As the director becomes immersed in the period research, the period comes alive, and the movement style becomes clear.

Directing *42nd Street* requires a very different approach than *Fiddler on the Roof*. Both have easily recognizable styles. *42nd Street* is a thirties musical that incorporates tap, soft shoe, and other classically theatrical dance styles, while *Fiddler*, a musical that is rooted in the Russian world of the pogroms in the late nineteenth century, requires a more organic, character-driven style. Jerome Robbins understood this, using his knowledge of classical dance to create a movement style that never seemed like "dance."

First, listen to the recordings of each. The score reveals everything.

42nd Street features review-style numbers influenced by the Busby Berkeley movies popular in that period. Traditionally, the show opens with a slowly rising curtain revealing a huge chorus of tappers. Only their feet can be seen at first, beneath the bottom edge of the curtain. The curtain rises a foot or two and stops. The tap starts and we see only a hundred feet. It's a brilliant beginning that sets the tone for the whole show. A director can use that tradition or create a new one, but should understand the tradition. What was Gower Champion thinking when he made that bold choice? It was thrilling to see fifty pairs of legs tapping away, as the full stage and chorus dancers who owned those feet was gradually revealed. While a director doesn't have to "copy" Champion's choice, it is important to create a thrilling sense of Hollywood to set the mood for what is to come.

To research the style of the show, a director can view hundreds of movie musicals done in the style of *42nd Street*. The stage show is a love letter to those musicals, and those iconic period films provide the director with the best source of inspiration.

In *Fiddler*, the music is influenced by Yiddish music of late-nineteenth-century Russia. The opening number, "Tradition," is an iconic example of how the staging of musical theatre captures the essence of a show, characters, and story. The music and its rich sense of the period is a clear indicator of the movement style. Like the music, the movement has to be a mixture of boldness and intimacy that demonstrates the characters' strength as a people and their sensitivity and kindness in the face of terrible adversity. To research this style, the director and choreographer can look at films of traditional Yiddish dance style, photos, and art from the period, as well as reading the original Sholom Aleichem stories.

In the wedding scene, there is a section of music notated as the "bottle dance." The director and choreographer research this traditional dance done at Jewish weddings of the period. Like the music, the dance is very specific in tone and style. Using their own lens, director and choreographer interpret the "bottle dance," incorporating their own movement concept with the specifics of the actual dance to make a statement. What emerges is a moment in the joyous wedding scene where everything slows down, and the wedding guests focus intently on the bottles being precariously balanced. The precise movements of the men balancing bottles on their head as they crouch and move forward one large step at a time becomes a metaphor for the balancing act of their faith and their oppression.

While the style of *42nd Street* calls for a more technical approach to dances meant primarily for entertainment, the dance and movement in *Fiddler* has to feel more natural to the characters and must deepen story and character.

Finding the right style of movement is a result of thorough research, listening to the music, and understanding the text.

The Transition from Scene to Musical Staging

Musical scenes usually follow a section of spoken dialogue. The transition must be either seamless or purposefully obvious. In the case of most numbers for *42nd Street*, the more obvious the better. With a style definition that might be "zingy,

Broadway pizzazz, and lots of flash," we want it to be clear that we are moving from a scene to musical staging. The fun is in how the dialogue scene goes into the song. In a "wink wink" way, the scene moves into the song and the audience gets a kick out of the obvious and entertaining silliness.

But in *Fiddler*, that transition should be barely perceptible because songs are an emotional intensification of the dialogue scenes. The way the transition is staged enhances the style.

Staging the Opening Number

The staging of an opening number sets the tone for the entire show. In *Fiddler's* opening number, "Tradition," the characters of the play are introduced. The villagers reveal who they are and what they care about, as well as their sense of community, values, heritage, and relationships. The way they are placed and move in and out of focus is important.

From Experience: *Fiddler on the Roof*

In my production of *Fiddler*, I used a rotating turntable. Each group was assembled in a picture, and the turntable rotated to them as their verse began. It was a quarter turn each time. Then, when they sang in a round, all at that same time, the speed of the turntable increased so each group passed by center several times giving the impression that the individual groups were all part of one village.

In *42nd Street*, the opening is a tap dance done by the entire chorus. At the curtain's rise we instantly know we are watching an entertainment about tap dancers on Broadway that is light and meant for pleasure. The thrill of the hundred tapping feet is then surpassed by the set, the costumes, and the pleasure on all the dancers' faces.

Introducing the Style of the Show

In the case of *Fiddler on the Roof*, the opening number makes clear that this show, while realistic, has elements of storytelling that are non-realistic, almost Brechtian. Tevye introduces the show after a man playing a fiddle on a roof scratches out the opening tune. It is not a realistic number in structure, but it is realistic in tone.

The director has to find a way to make the presentational style ring true. The movement has to both feel natural to the characters and reveal the importance of their tradition, family structure, and values. With the help of the choreographer, the director moves the entire cast around the stage, through sections of music, dialogue, explanatory passages, a fight, and a climactic resolution.

Jerome Robbins' reverence led to a presentational structure imbued with humanity. The patterns and groupings masterfully reflected the emotional content of the story. By placing the men and women separately, he clarified the distant relationship between the sexes and articulated a community of people struggling to stay together while being ripped apart. He worked from the lyrics, but found visual poetry.

Frank Galati did the same for the opening of *Ragtime*. In a musical that focuses on the clash between races in the early-twentieth century, at the climax of the opening he placed the three ethnic groups—Jewish immigrants, upper-class white Americans, and African Americans—in a circle, facing each other as a turntable rotated. As they rotated and sang, the groups became defined by both their composition and the juxtaposition of the other groups. The contrast in their costumes, attitudes, and relationships created a visual experience of the tension of their world, preparing the audience for the journey they were about to take.

Revealing Character

In addition to style and tone, an opening number reveals information about the characters and the world they inhabit. Whether through spatial relationship, movement, tempo and rhythm, or movement style, the director finds ways to begin the story by introducing the main conflict, the main characters, and their relationships.

The director should look at every opportunity to introduce the audience to the show's main characters—their needs, desires, and what kind of people they are.

In the show *I Love You, You're Perfect, Now Change*, the opening number introduces four characters, two men and two women, in their bedrooms preparing to go out. The bedrooms are created by small clothes racks from which the characters, who begin in underwear, take clothes and get dressed.

After a Gregorian Chant–inspired choral opening, the actors strip off their robes. Underneath they are half-naked, a visual metaphor for how we all feel on a first date. During the number, they alternate between running downstage to address the audience and running upstage to grab the next garment they put on.

The staging creates the urgency and chaos associated with getting ready for a date—the nerves, the fear, the stupidity. It also allows each actor to distinguish their "base" character from which the many other characters they create will vary. By the end of the number we relate with the characters and then easily accept them in a variety of roles throughout the show.

Introducing the Protagonist, Antagonist and Main Conflict

Some shows introduce the main characters, protagonist, antagonist, and main conflict in the opening and some do not. In the opening of *Fiddler*, the protagonist, Tevye, begins and ends the number. Throughout the number, we are introduced to the people of the town, their conflicts, what they are up against, and how they survive. It is a chance for the director to create the fabric of that world. It also allows the audience to begin viewing the world of the play through Tevye's eyes, defining a point of view for the audience. Shows like *A Funny Thing Happened on the Way to the Forum*, or *How to Succeed in Business Without Really Trying* do the same with the protagonist as the storyteller.

The director looks at the opening, its structure, and the presence of the protagonist to make decisions about how to open the show. If the protagonist is present, what point of view do you want to instill in your audience? How will the protagonist be revealed? Simply? With pomp? Every decision the director makes influences the audience's point of view.

Purpose—Expository or Something Else?

In *Ragtime* and *Fiddler*, the opening is an expository introduction to the characters and main conflict. The director's job is to capture the essence of the conflict, setting the stage for the unwinding of the plot. The characters literally introduce themselves, their world, and their story.

An expository opening can seem to lack action and forward movement, but capturing the essence of the drama and communicating information is important. The director finds the "action" in the exposition while making the points necessary to the story.

Led by the protagonist as in *Fiddler*, the audience is drawn both to the character and how he interacts with the world, which illuminates both the protagonist's relationship to his world and the world itself.

Tell the story. The opening number captures the audience's attention and introduces the story. Openings can be grand events, but don't muddle plot with a lot of extravagance and cleverness. Whether it's a contemporary rock musical or *Oklahoma*, tell the story and clarify the characters and conflicts while introducing the world of the play.

If not expository, then what is its purpose? In *42nd Street*, the chorus opens the show with a big dance number. The main conflict is not introduced until later. The opening's primary purpose is to set the tone—to transport the audience to the carefree, rapturous, intense world of the 1930s and the strain and thrill of putting on a big Broadway show. We know that the show is not realistic, but rather a celebration of an iconic world where stars are born overnight and where you can tap your troubles away.

Chorus, Group, or Solo Number?

The cast requirements of the opening number define the style of the number and the impact it will have. If the show opens with a solo, as in *Cabaret* (the MC sings "Wilkommen," followed by the entrance of the Cabaret girls), it requires a different approach than a full cast number such as *42nd Street*. Often, as in *Ragtime* and *Fiddler*, the opening begins with one person and builds into a full rousing ensemble number. Finding the through line (the story of the number) helps clarify its components and tell the story.

Look at the overall structure of the opening. Does it start small and build? Does it start with a big bang? Determine the arc and then direct accordingly.

Revealing Theme

Revealing of theme is the final aspect to consider when staging the opening number. If the theme is "the power of love," build the number with that in mind. In *Fiddler*, if the theme is "love and tradition conquer all," then focus on the elements of love and tradition.

Incorporating the theme helps clarify the staging. In *Fiddler*, seeking ways to express the sentiment that "love and tradition conquer all," will lead to strong staging choices that personify that ideal. It may be subtle, but let the theme work on you and find ways to express the theme.

Fiddler's opening number begins and ends with a solo violin. Between those two moments the villagers are introduced, the relationships and love of tradition are clarified, their challenges are introduced, and they fight, make up, dance, and leave. At the end, there is that lonely violinist, perched precariously on the rooftop as a metaphor for the precarious nature of their very existence. But they survive, the fiddler never falls. The lonely fiddler on the roof is a metaphor for the Jewish people, their struggle to survive, their loneliness and isolation. Intensify the metaphor to get emotional payoff. Make sure the beginning and end are quiet moments and the climactic chorus sections are rousing and exciting. Find the arc.

By the end of the opening number, the show is well on its way. The audience should understand the world of the play, and be ready to accept the plot as it unfolds.

Staging a Scene Without Music

The process here is identical to that of staging a scene in a play, albeit a quicker one.

Director's Checklist: Steps for Staging a Scene Without Music

❑ Come prepared with a thorough knowledge of the scene and staging notated in your director's production notebook.

❑ Do a quick read-through of the scene.

❑ Discuss objectives, character and relationships, action, and through line.

❑ Explain the set; identify entrances, exits, furniture, and props.

❑ Explain your staging to the actors a beat or two at a time, then run those beats. See how they work and if satisfied, move on to the next chunk of text until you reach the end.

❑ Let the actors notate the blocking before moving on.

❑ If a section has no specific staging to be explained, let the actors move through the section and discover small movements organically.

❑ Once through the scene, work the entire scene beat by beat to cement the staging and make sure the actors are comfortable.

❑ Once all the staging is set, run the scene a few times.

❑ Focus on the movement, not the acting. If something looks awkward, change it, but allow them the freedom to find their own choices.

❑ Make sure the stage manager records the final choices in the prompt book.

Staging a Scene With Music

Things get interesting when music is added. Musical staging includes all movement done over underscored dialogue as well as solos, group songs, and chorus numbers that aren't specifically "danced." Musical numbers emanate from character and situation and they generally require bigger, broader, more emotionally-driven staging choices.

Look for the answers in the music. Whether it is spoken dialogue with underscoring, **recitative**, or a song, listen to it, feel the changes in mood, and then allow the music to inspire the style of movement.

Recitative: musical declamation of the kind usual in the narrative and dialogue parts of opera and oratorio, sung in the rhythm of ordinary speech with many words on the same note or in a pattern of notes not dependent on interesting melody.

To stage the musical section, first explain the blocking you've devised and then go through the scene with the music. Section by section, instruct the actors on the blocking and let them walk through it without singing. Once they are comfortable, add the music, and see how it feels and looks.

Get a sense of what your actors are capable of and what is natural to their bodies. Use that knowledge to create something that looks effortless and harmonizes with the style of the song. It could be normal, natural or heightened movement or even dance. It depends on the nature of the section and what the director intuitively imagines happening at that moment. The important thing is to know what your actors are capable of and comfortable with, and then use their vocabulary of movement as a starting point for the staging.

Demonstrate or explain your ideas, then let the actors repeat, changing as needed for their comfort and ease. Musical staging is more fluid and adaptable than choreography. Plan the musical staging and then use the plan as a guide, feeling your way through the scene with actors. Oftentimes, what seemed perfect in the quiet of your thought process looks awkward on the stage. Be ready to adapt.

While pre-planning is a good idea for a novice director, musical staging can be discovered in rehearsal without much planning by more experienced directors and actors.

Don't rush staging. If something you planned doesn't work, experiment to find a better solution. Rely on the actors to help find the answers. Good actors take simple ideas and turn them into visual poetry. Let the actors be your muses.

With less experienced performers, more planning is necessary and directors have to teach style. Without a lot of rehearsal, inexperienced performers can't develop that innate sense of style on their own. It is an internal awareness that can't be taught, but is "absorbed" over time. If the actors don't understand the style, then the director must take the time to demonstrate and work with them until the style appears natural and organic (or at least present). Guide actors to useful research materials to help them find the style.

Example: Staging *The Pirates of Penzance*

In a production of Gilbert and Sullivan's *Pirates of Penzance*, the concept for the style is "zany, loose and in the style of the Keystone Kops."

This concept definition influences each number.

What was true of the Keystone Kops? Their signature style is characterized by sight gags, turns, falls, bumping into one another, frenetic pace, and staccato movement. How can the director incorporate that into musical staging as well as choreography?

Consider the first entrance of the pirates. It is easy to incorporate this zany, loose approach. As they enter from the boat, the pirates tumble, bump into each other, and do a lot of big, strong movements with a strong dose of silliness and looseness of limbs. The opening number introduces this style and sets the tone for the show. The subsequent numbers in the show share this approach, adjusting as needed to suit the content of each scene as the plot unfolds.

Each character has different degrees of zaniness or lack thereof. Ruth can be played rugged but carefree, while the Pirate King is very zany and loose, and Frederick can be rigid and less free. By contradicting the style of the others, we see Frederick as more uptight, young, and insecure. Within the overall style, the trio of the King, Frederick, and Ruth contains differences of degree to which that style is expressed.

When the daughters make their entrance, the loose style is adapted to fit young girls' movements. They are light on their feet, hopping instead of walking. They are full of energy and do a lot of turns. The director "translates" the concept into the bodies and characters of the ladies which influences their movement style.

Director's Checklist: Steps for Staging Scenes With Music

❑ Consider the show's "style concept."

❑ Analyze each number for required movements, story, character, and action.

❑ Listen to the music, lyrics, and specifically the underscoring for insight into style of each number.

❑ If it is a "lead plus chorus" number, determine who is most important.

❑ Determine the style of the transition from text to musical staging.

❑ Break down the overall action of the scene into individual actions and determine what kind of movement works to realize each action.

❑ Apply your style concept to the staging and to each character in the scene to find movement that tells the story.

❑ Work section by section, explaining the staging to the actors, and letting them try it.

❑ Decide what works, what doesn't. Experiment if you are stuck, change if it is awkward.

❑ After staging each number, check that the style concept has been followed and works. If not, either change the number or re-evaluate your style concept.

❑ Run each scene a few times to set the final choices.

If you are staging a love duet, look at the lyrics; consider the two characters and the quality of their love. Is their love new? If so, they might not start close but once they get close, they'll stay that way. If they've been married for years, their staging will be less sexual and more romantic, if that is the quality of their love.

Find what is true about the situation and then translate that into staging that reflects the truth and enhances the audiences' experience viscerally through movement.

Each song has its own special key to unlock. And by unlocking that key, the director and actors unlock that element of the plot.

The staging must not only seem natural, but it must serve to help unlock the essence of the scene.

Staging Solos

Staging solos is challenging. With two or more people involved in a number, the staging options rise exponentially. Unless it is a song like "Singing in the Rain" where the movement is dance-like and easy to plot, staging a solo takes a great deal of sensitivity and willingness to keep things simple and honest. The tough part is keeping it interesting and finding the line between just enough and too much.

The biggest mistake novice directors make is over-staging solos.

Like any other song or scene, the choices come from analyzing the piece and understanding the action, style, objectives, and story. Figure out the behavior that seems natural to the number and start there.

Stylistically, solo staging can vary. In a highly stylized show like *42nd Street*, stock Broadway styles make sense and it is easier to call on that canon of movement to flesh out a solo song. In realistic musicals, and especially contemporary musicals, excessive theatricality often feels false. While still being theatrical, directors and actors have to find what is true about the song and then discover movement that communicates that truth.

Exercise: Finding solo staging through improvisation

Using improvisation is very helpful in staging solos.

Pick a song to work on. The actor starts by standing still. The pianist plays the underscoring and the actor thinks the lines, but does not sing them. The only means of expression is through movement and gesture. Almost like a dance, the actor gestures the lyrics and moves as motivated by the music. Encourage big movement to heighten the emotional content and communicate it physically. Do the entire song with these big gestures and movement.

For the second time through, do the piece without music, allowing only spoken dialogue. Continue the physical exploration. Encourage the actor to overdo the gestures as they speak the words.

Finally, with accompaniment, start the song from a still position. Allowing the exploration to influence movement, tell the actor to move only when absolutely motivated and see how the improvisation influences new movement in the song.

Exercise: Analysis and movement

Break the song down into its component sections, each one defined by a different action. Influenced by the given circumstances, determine the actor's starting position. From that point, identify moments in the scene where the music or intention changes in tone, and determine blocking that manifests those intentions physically. Do it on paper first, and then put it on its feet with actors in rehearsal to test your instincts.

Examples of Solo Staging

Some solos call for big movements and broad staging while others involve just a single movement or none at all. In the original Harold Prince staging of "Send in the Clowns," Glynis Johns didn't move, nor did she need to. Any movement would have diluted the emotional impact of the song. By sitting still, with Frederick on the floor close by her, the audience focused completely on her face, her voice, and the way she did or didn't look at Frederick. Movement would have been distracting.

But in "Something's Comin'" from *West Side Story*, the music screams out for urgent crosses, heartfelt staging, and plenty of gesturing. Found organically, it can be a very powerful number. But if the staging is not motivated by the music, lyrics, and desires of the character, it looks stagey and disingenuous. Look for ways to create big, broad strokes that are motivated and natural.

To return to an earlier example, "I Am What I Am" from *La Cage Aux Folles* begins quietly. There is an inner rage that builds through the song. The first section is done without movement because Alban is stunned. He is hurt, betrayed, and finding his voice in that first section. Then, after the key change, a cross downstage brings the actor closer to the audience, and he can "let it rip" as the "brewing anger" section gives way to the "emotional release" section. His movements become bigger and at the end, he takes off his wig as he always does in his drag numbers. But this time, he rips it off and throws it at Georges as he storms off the stage. The physicality mirrors the emotional content of the song.

Buttons

A **button** can be either a flashy final picture that "buttons" the scene, or a final, organic, and quiet end of a song. In *42nd Street*, every song requires a "pizzazz" button. The button is an indication to the audience to applaud, and it captures the essence of the song in a stage picture that is held during applause.

> **Button:** the "final moment" of a song; it is the final picture and the musical finish.

Buttons are wonderful devices in staging classic musical comedy, but can be employed with equal power in musical drama. The difference is, in musical drama, the button communicates the emotional power of the song in a lingering final image.

For example, in "Far From the Home I Love," when Tevye's daughter finishes singing this emotional song, she looks up at her father and they hug. That button allows for emotional release. The love they both feel is made clear by the quality of the hug. The audience applauds, but as they do, they watch father and daughter share what might be their very last embrace. It is a powerful end to a moving song. When the hug is released, the song is over and the audience knows it's time to continue with the scene.

Act One Finale

Most musicals have act one finale numbers. An act one finale ideally leaves the audience wanting more. There are many types of act one finales.

Rousing Entertainment

The first and most common in early musical comedy is the "rousing entertainment" type. For example, the end of Act One of *Anything Goes* is a huge dance number that whips the audience into a state of rapture. Despite what might have happened up to then, the audience is so excited they can't wait to return for more in the second act. This "bolt of entertainment" is common to musicals written pre-*Oklahoma*.

Fun, then Conflict

A second type of act one finale is the "fun, then conflict" finale found in *Fiddler on the Roof*. It begins as rousing entertainment. The wedding scene and the bottle dance is an immensely entertaining demonstration of virtuosity. Yet when the Russians crash the wedding to warn the Jews, the mood plunges. After the Russians have wreaked havoc and left, Tevye simply tells everyone to clean up. The audience is left with a terrible sense of dread and return to see if they survive or not.

Rising from Adversity

In *Gypsy*, the act one finale is the "rising from adversity" type. Baby June has run off with one of the boys in the act, leaving Mama Rose without her daughter and her star. She shrugs it off with steely resolve, singing the show-stopping number, "Everything's Coming Up Roses." A rousing anthem of possibility when out of context, in the show it is a chilling exercise in unrestrained, irrational optimism.

The audience leaves with a feeling of queasy uneasiness as to what will come next.

The Eleven O'clock Number

Many classic musicals have an eleven o'clock number. Traditionally this was reserved for the star to shine one last time before the show was over and to give everyone a reason to stay until the show's end. In *Gypsy*, it is "Rose's Turn." In *Jesus Christ Superstar*, it is "Gethsemane." Let the star be a star. Don't shy away from the "show-biz" nature of the eleven o'clock number.

Most modern shows with contemporary structures don't have this kind of star-turn number.

The Finale

In the early American musicals, the finale was a big splashy extravaganza after the thin plot lines had been resolved. In Golden Age musicals like those of Rodgers and Hammerstein, they were an emotional moment of resolution, e.g. the King dying in *The King and I*, or Billy ascending to Heaven during "You'll Never Walk Alone" at the end of *Carousel*. Today's shows are a combination of both, but still rely on the crowd-pleasing chorus number to send the audience out happy. "You Can Hear the Beat" from *Hairspray* is a prime example.

The director identifies the function of the finale. In the case of *Carousel*, the staging not only focuses on the interaction between Julie and Billy before he ascends, but creates an innate sense of Americana that tugs at the heartstrings, putting their relationship in a broader context. The setup of the graduation scene creates the pretty picture against which the painful and heartening final moment is played out.

The end of *Hairspray* is not only is a joyous celebration where each character celebrates the culmination of their journey and the freedom they have found, but also encapsulates an entire era of change and a breakthrough in race relations—all this while entertaining the audience.

Sorting out what is important, and then making staging choices that insure proper focus is the key.

Chorus Numbers

When directing big musicals the director has to be both traffic cop and artist. That means keeping the actors out of each other's way and ordering entrances, exits, and stage movements so that it is organized without looking artificial, orderly without looking planned.

Luckily for stage directors, in most big musicals before 1960 the chorus numbers are dances handled by the choreographer. But in scenes where everyone is on the stage, the director has to get them onstage, organize their movement, and then get them offstage.

It is helpful to plan these scenes in advance, using whatever method works to keep track of who is where. As stated earlier, a useful method consists of creating small pieces of paper with each chorus member's name, and then moving those papers around on the ground plan to organize and keep track of each person. (See Chapter 12.) Creating groupings that move simultaneously is another way of organizing the crowd scenes.

The trick in chorus scenes is to make the chorus feel intrinsic to the action of the scene and to make their presence and movement feel motivated and not chaotic.

Techniques for Staging Group Scenes

- Organize the large group into smaller groups of characters that share associations like being in the same family.
- Assign each member of the group a number if you can't remember their names.
- Assign a leader in each group who will be responsible for remembering the movement of their group.
- Change the placement of the groups throughout each number for variety, if appropriate.
- Avoid grouping everyone in the same place or cluster. Fill the stage with smaller groups and vary the group size. Put those that move and look best in front.
- Don't change the stage pictures unless motivated by text or action.
- Number stage areas and use commands such as "in one" to facilitate explanation of movement.
- Stage the movements one group at a time. When you add the next group, have the first group repeat their staged movements and work with them to identify potential traffic issues.
- When you have staged a series of moves, run them and ask the actors where the problems are. Let them try to find solutions.
- Step back and look at the staging. If you spot anything that looks awkward or false, fix it.
- Start small and work your way up to the larger mass movements.
- Vary the timing of the entrances and exits to avoid everyone flooding on or off the stage at the same time.
- Always run the scene several times before moving on to set the work and check for problems.

Staging large group scenes is always nerve-wracking. It will make life much easier to remain calm, prepare in advance, try to know everyone's name, and be willing to adapt, experiment, and change your ideas.

Stock staging

While no move should ever feel like a stock move, there are a few stock movements that always work well.

Forward Embrace: The woman stands in front of the man with his arms wrapped around her shoulders and upper chest area.

Hold Hands, Face Each Other: The two singers hold outstretched hands as they sing facing each other. This can segue with a twirl into a forward embrace.

Swaying Forward Embrace: Same as forward embrace, but adds a sway; ideal for creating sense of playful romance

Twirl In or Out of Embrace: With a spin, moving into or out of an embrace to another position

Chugs: For a razzmatazz number's big moment, hops on both feet moving in a downstage direction in time with the music

Walking Hand In Hand/Arm In Arm: A slow stroll in a duet, usually from upstage to downstage. Be careful of sight lines.

Spin Onto Knee Sit: Spinning into a sit on bent knee

Button Kiss: A final held kiss as the button

PART V:
REHEARSALS CONTINUE

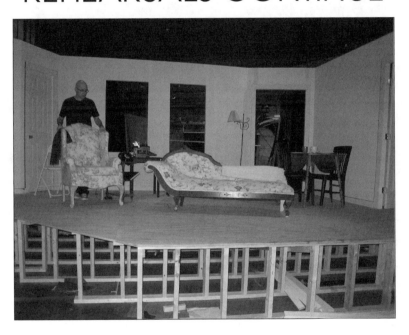

Chapter 16
Listen to your Inner Voice and Direct the Moments

Listen to Your Inner Voice

There are two aspects of directing that are so simple, yet so important, they deserve their own special chapter.

Every human being has an inner voice. Some call it conscience—what allows us to know right from wrong, decide what to eat for dinner, and when to go to sleep at night. In the artistic process, because we are open and receptive to what is happening around us, our inner voice is constantly speaking to us. While watching a scene, when things happen that don't seem right, that inner voice nags at us, intuitively reacting to what is wrong.

This inner voice is divine, offering ideas and inspiration. Being receptive to the inner voice is the key to fully utilizing your imagination.

This divine intervention can take many forms. A scene is going on, and suddenly you see in your mind's eye a different blocking choice. Or the actor speaks a line in one way, and you hear it in another. Suddenly you have a flash of inspiration in the form of a brilliant staging idea. Don't brush away these thoughts. Grab them and act on them.

You can even call on your inner voice for help. When you can't find a solution to a persistent problem, meditate on it. Let your imagination wander to a solution. Brilliant ideas present themselves at unusual times—waiting for a red light to turn green, when you are falling asleep or waking up, in dreams. Be open to this insight and never ignore your inner voice.

Direct the Moments

Nothing is more unsatisfying than a show that glosses over or rushes past emotional moments. Perhaps the most important job of a director is to find and allow for these small detailed moments to happen fully, impacting the actors and the audience.

As stated numerous times in this book, identifying the important moments in the script analytically, and then realizing them directorially, is central to true success of any production.

Every story has its moments of high intensity, emotional depth, and plot points that change the characters or redirect the plot. Finding these moments and directing the actors to experience them is critical.

So many college and amateur productions miss these moments because the director doesn't know how to find them and the actors don't give them the focus required. Look closely as you direct and stop for those moments, talk to the actors about them, explain what impact they should have, and how important they are. Give personal examples of what the moments mean to you, and then explore those moments fully to find as much emotional payoff as possible.

In *The Glass Menagerie*, when Jim compliments Laura, talk to the actress about the emotional impact of that moment. Make sure she has a powerful reaction to his compliment and the audience clearly understands its impact. Make this moment complex and human. Don't overlook this moment or any moment like this where a character's forward action changes.

Direct the details!

Chapter 17
Working with Actors

Once a show is staged, the process for musicals and plays is the same, save for the brush-up dance and musical rehearsals. The following sections deal with the relationship between actors and director and offers advice on how to communicate with and assist actors through the rehearsal process.

Even though it often seems the focus of a director is on everything but the actor, this relationship is both the center of all play direction and its most important element. The way in which a director creates the rehearsal environment, conducts rehearsals, and handles the actors influences the outcome of every project.

General Guidelines

Here are a few general guidelines to follow, with explanations. Directors must :

- Be specific, never vague.
- Know what the actors want, but remain flexible and open to new ideas.
- Be ready to explain ideas.
- Listen to actors.
- Value the input of actors.
- Understand the process of actors.
- Understand the actor's ego.
- Play psychologist on occasion.
- Remain uninvolved with offstage drama.
- Create a rehearsal atmosphere conducive to creativity and risk-taking.

Specificity

What does being specific mean? It means being clear, concise, and confident in what you are saying. You don't have to be right, but you have to be clear.

Being specific enables effective communication. Intuitive ideas are difficult to explain, but lack of specificity confuses actors, leading to a loss of confidence, which creates insurmountable problems. Communication has to be clear and specific.

Questioning the Director

If the actor questions a staging choice, the director has two options:

1. Listen to what the actor has to say and reconsider your choice with an open mind.
2. If absolutely confident in the idea, ask the actor to try it with full commitment.

If after the actor tries it and it works beautifully, but the actor still disagrees with the choice, the director has to decide if the battle is worth fighting. If so, tell the actor to continue with the choice for a while to see how it settles. Promise to revisit it later.

If an actor makes a choice you don't agree with, let him or her know you don't think it works and give an alternative, using "to the point" language to explain the adjustment. Ask the actor to try the adjustment and then decide which choice is best.

Avoid "showing" them what to do. While sometimes it is necessary to **give line readings**, the actor might mimic the director instead of living truthfully in the moment.

> **Giving line readings:** when the director demonstrates how a line should be spoken.

Regardless of the situation, always let an adjustment become the actor's idea. Let the actor vary the adjustment slightly so that your idea becomes the actor's. That is true collaboration and the line will work better if it's the actor who owns it.

Not every idea is specific; some are hunches or vague thoughts. Directors must think through their ideas before presenting them. If, after some thought, the idea is still vague, present it that way, extending an invitation to the actors to help flesh out the idea. This allows for a very valuable collaborative experience.

The bottom line is this: know what you are talking about, have strong reasons for your ideas, communicate clearly, and be honest in your evaluation of the idea's validity.

Listen to Actors

Novice directors often make the mistake of not listening to actors. On the other hand, they also make the mistake of not valuing their own ideas enough and being intimidated by actors.

In professional theatre, actors know they have to listen to the director and defer to their judgment. In university theatre, inexperienced actors don't have enough experience to understand the actor/director relationship and often disrespect the director.

It is the director's job to teach the actor about the relationship with the director, by earning the actor's respect and demanding that respect when necessary. Actors come up with great stuff that, as director, you shouldn't ignore. Listen to the actors and give them freedom to explore.

Every idea that works is a credit to your work as director. There is no reason to ignore or discount the contribution of actors to the process.

Ultimately, directors get blamed for what doesn't work and ignored for what does. It doesn't matter where the good ideas come from. The show's success is paramount.

Be flexible and open to everyone's ideas.

About Actors

Respect the Actor's Process

Directors are impatient; they want results. The actor's process of creating a role can't be rushed. An experienced director knows how to relax and respect that process. While a director's job is to move things along, being patient and trusting the process are essential to gaining the actors' trust.

Actors encounter many obstacles that slow their process. Memorizing lines, getting comfortable with language, and dealing with style take time. Before they can lose themselves in the reality of their character, they have major technical hurdles to overcome. Only then can they reveal themselves in a way that would embarrass normal people. They also have to be open to the director's input, deal with their own insecurities, and those of the other actors. By design, acting is about slowly peeling layers away one by one, and that takes time.

The most successful directors enjoy witnessing the actor's slow and exciting process of creating a character. They agonize with the actors, feel their pain and joy as they navigate the thorny path to a fully realized performance. If a director is able to support and assist an actor in that journey, the relationship between the two can be wonderful and satisfying.

Understanding the Actor's Process

If directors understand the acting process, then they can offer suggestions, and solutions that are useful to the actor.

Study acting. Knowledge of the actor's process is the single most powerful tool a director can bring to the rehearsal process.

Directors don't have to be good actors; they just need a working knowledge of the acting process. Just like a basic knowledge of lighting helps a director talk to the lighting designer, knowledge of acting allows the director to speak the actor's language. A director who understands this process will be able to assess actor problems more accurately and offer the right kind of help.

Actors work differently than directors. Whereas directors focus on people and issues outside of themselves, the actor's focus is inward. There is a very fine line between professional criticism and character assassination in an actor's mind. Actors are very vulnerable, and directors with the best intentions can derail an actor's work with bad advice or insensitivity.

When actors lose confidence because they sense the director doesn't believe in them, the game is over. It is very hard to win back an actor's trust.

A professional actor generally has thicker skin than amateur or student actors, who have trouble separating themselves from their work. Many haven't learned that direction and critical feedback is meant to support and improve their work. Actors who resist feedback hear only "you are bad," instead of "this is what you need to do to make the work better."

The director has to balance the importance of critical feedback with the insecurities of each actor, and find the right time and the right way to address problems. Understanding each actor's psyche is helpful in determining how to deal with each individual actor.

Directors who are sensitive to the needs and vulnerabilities of each actor will have greater success. By building trust slowly through the rehearsal process, even the most insecure actors will begin to listen and accept feedback in a positive way.

Establishing trust is critical. How is trust established? Listen, support ideas, and facilitate the process, offering positive and nurturing advice. The greater the level of trust, the more honest the director can be. As the trust builds, the director will have greater freedom to be critical and honest with the actor.

But what about that actor who resists direction, refusing to listen? My advice is to ignore them. Lavish direction, positive and critical, on the other actors and give nothing to the problem actor. Eventually, problem actors will feel left out, their ego will kick in and they will come to ask for help simply because they want the attention. Once they ask for help, you've got them.

Director or Psychologist?

A director is also a psychologist. Every actor has a unique set of issues. A director, like a psychoanalyst, must quickly assess what makes each actor tick and then use that intuitive knowledge to make judgments about when and in what manner to give direction and feedback.

The director's ego must be set aside when dealing with actors. Because each situation has its own best solution, directors often have to do things they would never do in real life in order to maintain a positive atmosphere in rehearsal.

Remember, the process of directing a play is not about "the director." The director's job is to serve the play and the playwright. Sometimes directors have to swallow their pride and do what is in the best interest of the show, even though they want to wish away the actor creating the problems.

The psychological aspect of directing is tricky and precarious. The director must understand both individual personalities and the group dynamic. Emotional responses are human, but managing the emotions of the group and knowing how and when to intercede is vitally important. It's almost as if by remaining aloof from the emotional dynamic of the group, the director can retain the influence necessary to positively affect the situation to benefit the show.

Good directors are experts in understanding human behavior.

Offstage Drama

It is the nature of actors to create offstage drama. Some of the theatre's greatest achievements were rife with offstage drama. Consider *A Chorus Line*. In their book *On the Line*, Robert Viagas, Baayork Lee, and Thommie Walsh detailed an extremely contentious process that resulted in one of the greatest shows of the American theatre. Not that I advocate offstage drama as a means to an end, but it exists—and in its simple form it doesn't have to detract from the outcome. It is natural for actors to fight, compete, and complain. The director stays outside the drama and tries to remain objective.

Actors will be actors. Don't try to control the offstage drama. As long as it doesn't interfere with or compromise the onstage drama, everything will work itself out. The worst of enemies in rehearsal can become the best of friends once the show has opened. Makes sure the offstage drama stays out of the rehearsal hall and all will be fine.

Novice directors are less secure and prone to getting drawn into the offstage drama. It is very seductive to become entangled with the actors, but it is not helpful. If the offstage drama is affecting the work in rehearsal, then take the reins and demand that the chaos end and that everyone focus on the task at hand.

Creating the Rehearsal Atmosphere

A director creates the atmosphere in the rehearsal room. The ideal atmosphere encourages risk taking, adventure, fun, creativity, and imagination.

A positive rehearsal environment starts with the director's state of mind. If a director is organized, on top of the material, and prepared for the rehearsal, a sense of calm and confidence will pervade the room. This doesn't mean you have to have all the answers to every question. Just don't let the actors see you sweat.

If you are confused or lost, be honest about it. By making it clear from the outset that you are in control, confident about the material, and well-prepared, if you temporarily lose your way, the actors will support you.

On the first day, let the actors know that the rehearsal room is a place to fail miserably in the process of finding success. Demand that they come into rehearsal with specific goals. Glory in their successes and find the humor and humanity in their failures.

Discipline is important. Setting rules and sticking to them gives the actors a sense of security. Let the actors know what you expect and how you run a rehearsal. Take breaks, allow for discussion time, and encourage exploration of ideas with no obligation to produce immediate results.

Dealing With Actors

Difficult Actors

While most actors are easy to work with, there are actors that don't listen and are only interested in their own agendas. Because these actors can upset the balance in the ensemble, the director has to determine the best way to deal with them. Usually a short conversation that validates the actor's contributions and then requests they refrain from whatever behavior is causing problems suffices. But in extreme cases, difficult actors refuse to play nice, and they either have to be fired or dealt with more harshly.

Don't be afraid to deal directly with difficult actors. Allowing disruptive behavior to persist compromises the rehearsal process. Be sensitive, professional, and respectful, but don't be intimidated.

A few guidelines:

- Always start a conversation on a positive note, then get to the point and be honest. Explain exactly what the problem is and how it can be corrected.
- Don't demean the actor. Difficult actors will feel like you are attacking them, so don't attack. Discuss the issues in a supportive but honest way.
- Listen to what they have to say. If they believe you are interested in them, they will be easier to deal with.
- Don't let your anger show. Stay calm and relaxed. This can be very difficult, but losing your temper only makes things worse.
- Don't relent. If, after one discussion, the behavior continues, speak with the actor again. Reiterate the problem and remind the actor of the

initial conversation. Let problem actors know how their behavior is affecting rehearsals and ask them in a professional, relaxed way to make adjustments.

- If an actor is disruptive to the point of endangering the final product, consider replacing the actor sooner rather than later.

Dealing with Divas

Some actors, especially inexperienced ones, have inflated opinions of themselves and their skill level, and are more concerned with "I" than "we." Dealing with divas is an occupational hazard that every director encounters.

Divas thrive in an atmosphere that overvalues their participation. The idea of the "diva" comes from the opera world, where the leading soprano was treated like a queen to ensure a great performance. The idea of a diva morphed into an opera singer that was demanding and difficult, and now applies to any performer that puts his or her own self-interest ahead of the production's. Most divas are insecure, disingenuous, and desperately in need of attention. Understanding what drives a diva is important. *For a director, knowledge is power.*

Create an atmosphere that levels the playing field. Pay equal attention to all, giving the diva enough attention. But make it clear that the play is performed by an ensemble of actors, all equally important. This might initially irritate a diva, but be firm in your commitment to an ensemble approach and most divas will come around.

If you have a "star" in the show, make sure to show that actor the respect that is deserved, but don't go overboard. The goal is to encourage everyone in the show to form a tight ensemble where all are equally important to the final outcome.

Never embarrass a diva in front of others! Divas don't respond well to shaming. Take them aside and talk to them privately. Like any conversation, start with a compliment before getting to the point. Directors must understand the actors, and manipulate them (yes, it's true) in a way that assures a positive outcome. If a diva is unwilling to play nice, then weigh that actor's contribution to the play against the problems being caused. You can always fire them.

If they are big stars you have to find a way to work with them; find out what makes them tick. Be sensitive to what drives them and be straightforward about the needs of the production and the other actors. Instead of allowing feelings of anger and hatred to overwhelm you, sympathize with them and try to understand their feelings of insecurity.

Managing Diverse Personalities

Part of the director's job is to assess the personalities of the cast and to encourage them to harmonize in the creation of a unified work of art. Creating a positive rehearsal environment is the best way to offset potential problems.

Starting at the first rehearsal, assess the different personalities in the cast. An experienced director senses intuitively what each actor needs, how they work, and what insecurities they have. Begin to develop intuitively an understanding of each actor.

Common sense is a great guide for dealing with each actor. Stay focused on the work at hand, but don't lose sight of the subtlety of actor relationships. They can make or break a show.

Setting a few rules, like "Don't direct other actors," at the beginning will help. Stay on your guard, be aware of the dynamic between performers, and don't let things get out of hand. If you sense a problem, it is best to confront it right away. Make this clear to the actors: if they have a problem, come to you immediately.

Actors Who Dislike Each Other

> **From Experience: *Funny Girl***
>
> I was directing a production of *Funny Girl* and the actors playing Fanny and Nick did not like each other. The audience had to believe they were madly in love, but when the two actors were in a room together, their mutual loathing was palpable. I couldn't fire either performer so I had to find a way to make it work. After short conversations with both actors, it became clear that it was the actress playing Fanny who didn't like Nick.
>
> I spoke with Fanny, who was young and inexperienced. It was impossible for her to separate her personal feelings from the world of rehearsals. We talked about her reasons for disliking him; she said she wasn't attracted to him. I convinced her that the needs of the play superseded her own feelings and that she had to find a way for her character to convincingly love him. We decided on using substitution and she agreed to try. Although their feelings were never totally convincing to the trained eye, things improved as she started to connect her success in the role to convincing the audience she loved Nicky.

Actors don't always get along. Real pros convince the audience of whatever they need to, but novice actors need coaching on how to get past their personal feelings. Talk to actors; find out what the problems are, and work with them to solve them.

Actors Who Prefer to Self-direct

Most actors welcome the guidance from their director, but a select few refuse to listen.

It is the director's job to direct the production, and it is the actor's job to collaborate with the director. If an actor is unwilling to enter into that collaboration, then the director must be firm and insist that the actor take direction. The problem is this: by giving the actor the freedom to self-direct in the beginning, the director loses control for the entire rehearsal process. Once gone, that control is difficult to regain. But on the other hand, pressuring this actor to follow direction usually makes them hostile.

If the actor is very good with great instincts, and if the actor works well with the others, sometimes the best tactic is to stay out of that actor's way.

Unfortunately, with a problem actor like this, usually it's the opposite; they have terrible instincts and don't work well with the other actors. Their disrespect can cause other actors to disrespect the director. The director must take the upper hand from the start, let the actor know what is required, and insist that the actor listen to and respect the direction.

If the actor refuses, pick your battles. You won't win on every point. Choose the most important issues and focus on those adjustments. If you let the actor win a point, you might have success on the next issue. Sometimes this doesn't work. If problem actors get their way once, then they may want their way every time. Each situation is different.

If problem actors can't or won't make an adjustment, you have two choices: let them have their way or insist on your way. Ask them to try your idea, assuring them if it makes them uncomfortable you'll relent. When they try it, compliment them for doing it so well, and maybe they will relent.

If an actor simply refuses to follow direction, you also have two choices: accept it and move on, or fire the actor. If an actor is sinking the ship, don't be afraid to recast.

Don't get intimidated and don't compromise on the quality of the show.

Ultimately the show is more important than anything else. Always make the decision that you feel is in the best interest of the show.

Actors Who Direct Other Actors

This is a big problem in community, high school, and college theatre. It also exists in professional theatre. State at the first rehearsal that actors directing other actors won't be tolerated. Make clear there is one director, and invite the actors to speak to you if they are being directed by other actors. Assure them you will listen to and address their concerns.

If the situation arises, talk to the problem actor immediately and ask the actor to stop.

If the actor doesn't stop, make a general announcement and tell the group that there is one director and that nobody else should be giving direction. This will make it much more difficult for the problem actor to continue the disruptive behavior.

Final Thoughts

For most directors, working with actors is the most enjoyable part of the directing process. Observing a brilliant actor working their process and discovering their character is thrilling. I have nothing but the utmost respect and admiration for actors and feel privileged as a director when an actor allows me to be part of their process. Directors are responsible for creating a positive experience for the actor through their own preparation, guidance, and respect. Don't take that obligation lightly.

Chapter 18
Solving Problems

There are a myriad of actor-related issues with which directors grapple. While most actors are collaborative and generous, the occasional problem actor can make the director's work difficult. Most solutions require nothing more than simple common sense. However, there are many exercises that are useful in solving acting problems. A list of common problems and the exercises which address them are shown in figure 18.1. The following are inspired by methods of Michael Chekhov, Sanford Meisner and Stanislavsky, but the variations are my own. Each example is prefaced by a statement of the problem to be solved, followed by an explanation of the exercise.

Exercises for Solving Problems	
Problem	Appropriate Exercise
Actor not understanding entirety of performance	Visualization of a moment
Actor not linking physicality to inner life	Character movement visualization
Actor not finding emotional truth in a moment	Exploring a moment with repetition #1
Responses aren't spontaneous; actors not listening to each other	Exploring a movement with repetition #2;
Subtext improvisation	Run-through and dance brush-up period
Scene is one-dimensional, actors not playing subtext	Subtext iteration with word method
Actors are pushing (trying too hard)	Being real
Actors unexpressive, physically stiff	Soap opera exercise
Actors lack energy	Opera exercise
Actor has no sense of place	Atmosphere
Atmosphere not affecting actor choices	Mass group atmosphere

Figure 18.1
Appropriate exercises for common acting problems

Exercises for Rehearsal

Visualization of a Moment

Problem: Actors are not finding a sense of the entirety of the performance nor the arc of the character's journey.

Notes: Everyone must know the play well and have done preliminary analysis work on their characters. This exercise is not suitable for first rehearsal, but is best employed early in the staging process.

Preparation

1. Actor finds a comfortable position in a chair or on the floor.
2. Actor closes eyes.
3. Actor clears the slate of the vision in mind's eye.

Step One: Warming up the imagination

Explain that you will be making a series of short statements that will conjure a response. In response to each statement, the actor captures the first image that comes to them in their mind's eye, whatever it might be. It can be realistic or abstract. The important thing is not to edit, but as in a daydream state, to let the mind wander to whatever images appear.

Step Two: The first images

1. The actors are relaxed and their eyes are closed.
2. The director speaks the first image, "Red rain."
3. The director says, "Catch the first image and study the detail."
4. There is no expectation as to the nature of the image.
5. Actors let image pop into their mind's eye without questioning it. They can't look for an image; they just have to let it come to them.
6. Each actor describes what he or she sees.
7. They let the first image go and return to a blank slate.
8. Repeat the above steps for "blazingly sunny day."

Step Three: Main exercise content

1. Actors visualize the first moment their character is onstage in the play.
2. Prompt them to study the detail of the exterior, their own bodies, environment, smells, whatever is conjured by their imaginations.
3. Then after looking at the external details, ask them to "pierce the inner life" of the character, to invade the soul of the image and feel its feelings.
4. Instruct them to experience it fully, then let it go.
5. Actors imagine the character's final moment in the play and then repeat the previous steps.

6. Instruct them to experience it fully, then let it go.
7. Prompt actor to imagine their character's climactic moment of the play and repeat steps above.
8. Instruct them to experience it fully, then let it go.
9. Prompt them to go back to the first image, then the second, then the final, and then repeat the sequence at least three times, going from image to image, visualizing and experiencing each quickly.
10. Repeat the movement from first to second to third image several times. This will give the actors a sense of the character's arc; the journey they take and how they change from the beginning to the end.
11. Encourage actors to be open to whatever their imagination shows them and just allow the experience to wash over them.
12. Finally, let the images go and relax. Breathe gently and open the eyes.
13. Discuss the experience and define the arc they discovered. By visualizing the three moments while feeling the feelings of the character at those moments, the actors get a sense of the entirety of the journey of their character as well as a specific sense of who they are and how they relate to those moments.

Character Movement Visualization

Problem: Actor can't find the character's physicality as it links to inner life.

Prompts (given by director)
1. Find a comfortable position, lying on the floor.
2. Close your eyes.
3. Visualize your character in the same position as you are now.
4. Visualize their body and clothing.
5. Visualize the feel of your body in your character's clothing.
6. Relax and breathe.
7. Visualize your character moving their left arm up then down, a small, slowly executed and repeatable movement.
8. The movement has a beginning, middle, and end.
9. As the arm moves in your mind's eye, study the detail of the movement.
10. After each visualization of the movement, relax before repeating it again.
11. Repeat the visualized movement five times with a moment between each repetition.
12. Memorize what you see.
13. Open your eyes, and move your arm up and down, trying to mimic precisely what you saw in your imagination.
14. Allow yourself to feel as if you are in the body of your character as you move your arm.

15. The goal is to recreate as closely as possible the exact movement you saw in your mind's eye.
16. After each movement, evaluate how close you got to what you saw in mind's eye.
17. Do it again, trying to recreate in space what you saw in your imagination more precisely with each repetition.
18. Be sensitive to the awareness of character that bubbles up as you do the exercise.
19. Be open to feeling the world in the skin of the character.
20. Lift and lower the arm several times, pausing between for evaluation.
21. How does your soul resonate? What are your feelings? Do you feel a sense of the character? Relax and breathe before moving on to the next part.
22. Repeat this for the other arm or another small movement.
23. Get off the floor and find a comfortable seated position in a chair.
24. With eyes closed, visualize getting up out of the chair in the same way you visualized lifting and lowering your hand.
25. Repeat the visualization several times, pausing before each, and memorizing what you see.
26. Open your eyes.
27. Recreate the rising from the chair movement you saw in your mind's eye.
28. After each rise, sit again, close your eyes, and evaluate your success.
29. Repeat the rising several times until you get very close to what you visualized.
30. Be sensitive to the awareness that bubbles up as you do the exercise; feel the character coming alive in your body.
31. Be open to experiencing the world as the character.
32. Rise out of the chair many times, pausing between for evaluation. Each time try to get closer.
33. How does your soul resonate? What are you feeling? Do you gain insight into the character?
34. Relax and breathe before moving on.
35. After the fifth rise, remain standing and close your eyes.
36. Imagine your character walking.
37. See your character walking in your mind's eye and study the detail of your character's movement.
38. Watch long enough to get a deep sense of the quality of the walk, its style, pace, rhythm, and balance.
39. Open your eyes.
40. Begin to walk in the room.
41. As you walk try to match your walk with the walk you saw in your mind's eye.

42. Continue to walk, deepening your experience of the character through the experience of matching the character's walk.
43. You can look at others in the room.
44. Don't try to go into a "zoned out" kind of mental state. Stay relaxed and keep it easy.
45. Move as your imagination showed you how your character moves.
46. When you move in the same way, there is a mysterious force at work that sends messages to your body and that deepens your experience of the character.
47. When you find it, something inside of you will click and you will feel the character come alive in you.

Afterwards, talk about the experience with the actors. Allow the actors to share what happened as well as any physical, emotional, or psychological insights they had into their character.

Another very useful Chekhov exercise is psychological gesture. Consult the suggested reading at the end of this chapter for further information.

Exploring a Moment with Repetition, No. 1

Problem: Actors are not finding emotional truth in a moment.

Notes: This is an improvisational exercise that focuses on a moment in the play and is based on the Meisner repetition exercise. The director uses this exercise to unlock something emotional that should be happening in a specific moment but is not. The director should have a sense of what is lacking in the moment and conduct the exercise to lead the actors to find that which is missing.

Steps:

1. Isolate two lines in the section that aren't working. Instruct the actors that they will say their selected lines over and over again, the same two lines back and forth to each other. Do this without the blocking.
2. Explain that there are no expectations and they should not plan their responses; they should simply listen and respond, allowing the emotional life of the interaction to change when they feel motivated.
3. Ask them to begin saying their lines, back and forth, repeating them endlessly. One actor says a line, the other says the next line, then the first actor says their line again, and the second actor responds with the next line again, and so on. Don't let them change the lines.
4. Be careful that they don't say their line before the other has finished which indicates they aren't really listening and responding. You want them to listen to each other and react, with no obligation that the connection move in any particular direction at first.

5. Things will not always start in the right emotional place, and the repetition might get very monotonous and boring, but be patient and encourage them to continue repeating regardless of what is going on. Let them fumble around and find their way.
6. Encourage them to listen if they are not reacting to each other.
7. Allow them to laugh or be silly if that is what they want to do, as long as they stay honest with whatever is happening.
8. If they start laughing, side-coach them to follow the laughter through, and see where it takes them.
9. Ideally, after some time, they will begin to connect emotionally to the situation and each other, and the line readings will begin to deepen and change.
10. Often anger is the first thing they will find; let the anger happen and it will lead to more complex feelings.
11. Be observant, pay close attention to what is happening and side coach as needed.
12. When they find the heart of the moment and it gets intense enough, give them the cue to jump right into the next lines of the scene, maintaining the emotional place they have discovered and allowing it to inform the remainder of the scene. It is important they don't get things under control as they jump into the scene.
13. Notice how the emotional connection influences the rest of the scene.

Exploring a Moment with Repetition, No. 2

Problem: Responses are not spontaneous; actors aren't listening to each other.

Notes: This is a more improvisational version of the last exercise. In this exercise, the actors don't use lines from the script and only one actor has an assigned line. The purpose of this version is to force actors to listen to each other and to experience a deeper emotional level.

Steps:

1. Assign one actor to begin "in the scene" and one to enter into the scene.
2. Assign physical business to the actor "in the scene."
3. Assign a specific objective to the actor entering the scene.
4. Assign a specific line to the actor entering the scene that captures the essence of the relationship or conflict; don't tell the other actor the line. For example, if the actor is angry at the other actor, the line could be "I hate you."
5. The first actor begins the activity. A moment later the second actor enters the scene and says the assigned line.
6. The first actor improvises a response—whatever comes spontaneously—and they begin to repeat the two lines back and forth as in the previous exercise.

7. They say the same lines for the duration of the exercise but they can change their lines if there is a strong motivation to do so.

8. If the improvisation becomes narrative, stop them and begin again.

9. Explain that they should simply listen and respond with no obligation to create a story. They are just isolating a moment in time and finding a core relationship in that moment. Let them fumble around until they find the right direction.

10. Encourage them to confront the conflict that arises without fear or obligation to perform. Ideally, after some time, they will connect and things will start happening.

11. Be observant. When they find the heart of the moment and it gets intense, give them the cue to begin the scene at a predetermined starting place. It is important they don't get things under control as they jump into the scene.

12. Notice how the emotional connection influences the scene.

Example: Act 1, Scene 2, *The Glass Menagerie*

In the confrontation scene between Laura and her mother in scene 2 of *The Glass Menagerie*, Amanda is not feeling the disappointing anger and Laura is not listening. Nothing is happening between them.

Steps:

1. Assign Laura the activity of playing with a glass animal (use something unbreakable).

2. Assign Amanda the objective: to get the animal from Laura.

3. Instruct Amanda to enter the room and begin yelling "Why do you hurt me so?"

4. Don't give Laura a specific response line. Spontaneously the actress playing Laura says, "I love my animals."

5. They start repeating the same two lines back and forth.

6. At first, not much happens. They say the lines and push for a little conflict. Side-coach them to stop acting and start listening. Encourage them to do nothing but just say the lines.

7. The energy starts sagging. Let it go that way.

8. Amanda is clearly getting aggravated with the exercise and starts expressing anger in her line.

9. Laura hears the anger and introduces a tone of defensiveness in her repeated line.

10. Amanda's anger intensifies, and instead of being an actor's irritation with the exercise, it transforms into Amanda's anger at her daughter.

11. Laura starts really protecting the animals, and Amanda starts lunging for them, trying to take them from her.
12. The repeated lines intensify further. The stakes start going up.
13. Suddenly Amanda says, "Put those damn animals down and listen to me." Laura replies, "Leave me alone." The lines have changed naturally.
14. The two new lines are repeated, and there is a very clear and intensifying connection between the actresses.
15. The director tells them to jump into the scene.
16. As they start the scene in the same emotional place, there is a heightened sense of connection between the two and the scene bristles. The connection from the improvisation clearly has influenced the scene.
17. The actors are really working together, listening and reacting to each other. The conflict is clear and there is a sense of danger.

Subtext Iteration with Word Exercise

Problem: Scene is one level, actors are not playing subtext.

Steps:

1. Identify the general subtext of the moment or beat in question.
2. Discuss the subtext so the actors understand it and can put it in their own words.
3. Have actors say their written lines in their own words, expressing what their character is really thinking and feeling at that moment.
4. Each actor chooses one word that captures the essence of his or her character's subtext based on what they decide in the previous step.
5. Using that word, begin the improvisation.
6. Before each actual dialogue line, each actor says his or her chosen single word with emotional intensity, and then immediately says the actual dialogue line, charged with the emotion stirred by the subtext iteration. The other actor responds with subtext word followed by their dialogue.
7. Continue the entire section this way, subtext word followed by written line, word then line. Do this over and over again for as long as needed.
8. Once the subtext comes alive and begins informing the dialogue and charging the connection between actors, begin again, but this time the actors "think" the subtext word before saying the dialogue line instead of saying it out loud.
9. Go through the section this way, thinking the word "loudly," and saying the line aloud. Do this a few times.
10. Finally, run the section normally and see how the exercise has changed the performance of the section.

Variation: The complete thought method

1. Using the same idea as one word subtext iteration, create a sentence of 3–7 words that expresses the subtext in the actor's own words.
2. Use "I want" or "I need" statements if possible.
3. Follow all the steps with the complete sentence instead of the single word.

Being Real

Problem: Actors are pushing (trying too hard).

Notes: Inexperienced actors love to push for emotional depth. The truth is, emotional depth can't be forced; it can only be allowed to happen. To help actors who are "overacting" or "pushing," seat them in chairs facing each other and try the following:

Steps:

If not off-book:

1. With script in hand, the first actor looks down at his or her line and quickly memorizes it.
2. The actor then looks up at the second actor, and with absolutely no "acting" simply says the line to the second actor.
3. The second actor listens, and allows the line to "wash" over him or her.
4. The second actor looks down, memorizes the next line, looks up and says it simply to the first actor.
5. Go back and forth like this until the scene is complete.
6. There is no obligation to act or do anything.
7. The point is to really hear the other line and allow the reaction. Then, look down, read, and memorize the next line and say it, allowing the reaction to influence how they say the new line.

If off-book:

1. With the rule of "no acting" in place, the first actor says the first line.
2. The second actor listens and takes it in, then says his or her first line as first actor listens.
3. Repeat back and forth, just simply listening and reacting.
4. The director coaches the actors to keep it simple
5. If the "acting temperature" starts rising, remind them that you are looking for simple listening and reacting with no obligation to perform, but allow them to follow their inspiration.
6. Watch closely; there will be a moment when the actors start really listening and emotional truth starts brewing. This is what you are looking for. When it happens, just let it happen.
7. Don't allow the actors to start pushing. If they do, start over.

8. It is okay if not much happens at first. Just let them be simple and boring for a while until something real starts happening.
9. With some actors, this might take time. They might have a difficult time "not acting."
10. Be patient and supportive, but insist on simplicity.

Subtext Improvisation

Problem: The scene is not spontaneous or truthful; no one is listening; character relationships are unclear.

Notes: Rehearsal exercises should not stray from the script, but improvisations that don't use actual dialogue may be helpful in some instances.

For off-script improvisations, set up situations that closely mirror the given circumstances of the scene in question. Set up situations that the actors can easily relate to. Define each actor's role in the improvisation, the objective of each, and the obstacle. Set up clear goals for the improvisation.

Steps:

1. For this exercise, each actor will choose an improvised line that summarizes the gist of the character's subtext.
2. The director will set up a loose plot for the improvisation that the actors will follow. But, as in a gibberish exercise, they will be able to say only the selected line, back and forth.
3. If there is a strong motivation to change the line, they can do so, but the scene must not become narrative. The point is to focus in on the subtext of the scene and see where that takes the actors.
4. Keep the improvisation focused on listening and reacting to the stimulus and achieving the set objective. There should be a clear beginning, middle, and end.
5. Ideally, the actors begin the scene, saying their lines, things happen unexpectedly as they move through the pre-set plot, and ultimately they find the end organically.
6. If they begin to wander off point, side-coach them to stay focused on their objective.
7. It's okay to stop, discuss the work, and begin again in order to redirect the improvisation.

Example: Act 1, Scene 2, *The Glass Menagerie*

Using the Amanda/Laura scene from earlier, tell Amanda to come into the room, pull Laura away from the animals, and smash them all. Tell Laura she must protect the animals at all costs. Amanda's lines are: "I'm a failure." Laura's are: "Don't look at me." Amanda enters and says her line. Laura says her line. Amanda circles her as the repetition continues. Amanda becomes very emotional and starts crying. This causes a drop in energy. The director side-coaches her to go after those animals. Amanda's tears are tears of shame and she is suddenly angry, angry at the world for hurting her and she sees those animals as the cause of all her pain. Laura senses Amanda's anger at the animals, and changes her line to "Don't hurt us." Amanda's line suddenly changes to "You are a failure just like me." Laura takes all of her animals in her hand and runs to the corner of the room. Amanda follows, reaching for the animals. Laura runs from her mother, and suddenly Amanda stops and breaks down, unable to move. Laura rushes to her mother and comforts her. Director calls the scene over.

Through this improvisation, the actors have discovered the core sources for their pain and their intense love and caring for each other.

Discuss the outcome of the exercise with the actors to process their discoveries.

Soap Opera Exercise

Problem: Actors are not finding adequate depth of emotion; actors are emotionally and physically stiff and unexpressive.

Notes: Using the melodramatic acting style of soap opera, actors push towards a deeper connection with the emotional truth of a scene. This can be a fun exercise, and often makes the actors laugh and feel silly. Get past that and encourage them to make it truthful.

The actors will perform the scene as if in a soap opera, given the direction to really make it very big and over-the-top but, as they push to that extreme, they must go deeper emotionally to support the "bigness." They will get energized, start breathing deeper and often find deeper emotional resonance.

The important aspect of this exercise is to support the large acting style with deeper emotional connection.

After an improvised run of the scene in this way, go back to running in the right style and see if they have found more emotional depth.

Opera Exercise

Problem: Actors are not energized.

Notes: This is best used in college, community theatre, and other situations with less experienced actors. Aimed at energizing actors and raising the stakes, this exercise is more about fun than a probe of emotional depth.

Actors sing through, in faux opera voices, the entire scene. They don't have to be great singers or singers at all. The primary goal is to emulate the overacting, huge physicality, and emotional strength of the stereotypical opera performer.

Some performers might question the approach or say they are not singers. They will laugh and find it silly. Encourage them to keep going. If nothing else, it loosens them up, gets them to breathe, and can be a lot of fun.

Atmosphere

Problem: Actor has no sense of place.

Notes: In rehearsal, the director should paint a clear picture of the scene's atmosphere. For example, if it is a hopeful atmosphere full of possibilities, talk about hope and what that feels like; how it influences the action. Actors react to the specifics the director provides.

Actors often don't understand that atmosphere is an external force. They try to internalize atmosphere, trying to "act" the atmosphere. But atmosphere "acts" on them. This exercise helps actors understand the nature of atmosphere and how it can influence their performance.

Exercise warm-up

1. Choose a situation, e.g., a coffee shop in a crowded mall.
2. Choose a specific emotional atmosphere, such as "an atmosphere of lively fun and joy."
3. Choose a specific action to occur. Example, while on a computer checking email, the actor learns that he or she has just won the lottery.
4. Put other actors into the improvisation and assign them roles, like waiter, customer, and friend.
5. Have them play out the improvisation with a set beginning point, but with no plans beyond that.
6. Be careful that they don't play the joy itself, but play the action in the atmosphere of joy.
7. Without changing the action, change the place and emotional atmosphere. For example, a funeral home in an atmosphere of sorrow.
8. Repeat the action and allow the atmosphere to change how the actors react to each other in the new atmosphere.
9. Keep changing the atmosphere and place and let them freely improvise, experiencing how atmosphere affects their behavior.

Main exercise

1. Select a section of dialogue from the play
2. Choose a few different atmospheres and read the scene in each atmosphere.

3. Finally, identify the atmosphere of the actual scene.
4. Read or run the scene in the actual atmosphere.
5. Watch closely for behavior changes. How does that atmosphere impact their performances? Do they understand—and react to—the impact of atmosphere as an external force? Is the sense of place palpable? How is it important to the overall scene?

Repeat for other scenes in the play with different atmospheres.

Mass Group Atmosphere

Problem: Atmosphere not exerting appropriate influence over actor choices.

Notes: This exercise is designed to give actors a sense of how atmosphere affects behavior. It is a visualization exercise.

Steps:

1. With actors' eyes closed, describe a large group of people viewed from above. For example, ask the actors to imagine a huge crowd of Japanese businessmen waiting to cross the street at a busy intersection in downtown Tokyo. There are ten thousand people spread across four corners of the intersection and all the traffic lights are red. The traffic lights turn green and the sea of humanity floods into the street with fifteen seconds to get to the other side before the lights turn green and traffic starts moving again.
2. Ask the actor to see the entire scene in their mind's eye. You have painted a picture of an atmosphere of "anticipation" followed by one of "urgency."
3. When the light turns red and people cross, ask the actor to feel the overall sense of the atmosphere within the large group as they rush to the other side of the street. They are not feeling the atmosphere of a single person in the group, but instead, of the group as a whole.
4. Freeze the frame.
5. Ask the actor to transport themselves into the middle of the group, and look at individual faces.
6. Enter the body of one person in the group.
7. Feel the individual's experience of the overall atmosphere.
8. Unfreeze the scene.
9. Stay inside the individual, hurrying to the other side.
10. Then, transport back out from the person and back to viewing the entire large mass of people from above.
11. Feel the sense of atmosphere as it shifts from inside one person to above, observing the mass of people. How does the mass atmosphere produce reaction in one individual member of the group?

12. Create varied examples wherein there is a mass group with a strong atmosphere and repeat.

Suggested Reading

Chekhov, Michael. *To the Actor.* New York: Harper & Row, 2002.

Chapter 19
Stumble-throughs, Work-throughs, and Run-throughs

The primary purpose of a director's interaction with actors is giving direction. What is direction? Beyond explaining blocking, it is the specific information communicated to the actors about their acting choices, or in the case of novice actors, helping them make those choices.

The rehearsal process is broken down into table work and initial discussions of character, blocking, and then work-throughs and run-throughs. Run-throughs allow the director to observe the big picture while paying close attention to detail. Directing is a constant balancing act between the micro- and macrocosm of the play. A schedule of the latter half of this process is shown in figure 19.1 on the next page.

The big picture is a composite of thousands of details. Using intellect, imagination and intuition, the director "directs" each moment based on the sense of how these moments will add up and tell the playwright's story. Inexperienced directors often make the mistake of plowing through the details to get to end results.

With enough experience, directors come to understand that the secret to success is in the details, and that the real work of a director is clarifying the minutia.

Whether it is a dance move in a musical or an acting moment in a scene, working moment by moment on problems is the only sure way to solve them. They rarely work themselves out without input from the director. A moment that isn't working can compromise an entire show. Allow for time in a rehearsal schedule to review the work you've completed. This allows actors to cement the work in their minds and bodies while the director views the work and considers its merits.

Direct the details!

Schedule of blocking, work-throughs, and runs	
For a play	For a musical
1. Block scenes in act one, working each scene as needed.	1. Stage scenes, songs, and choreography in act one.
2. Stumble through act one blocking.	2. Stumble through act one.
3. Work through act one for blocking and acting.	3. Work through act one for staging and acting.
4. Run act one a few times working details as needed.	4. Schedule brush up rehearsals for dances and music as needed.
5. Block scenes in act two.	5. Run act one a few times.
6. Stumble through act two blocking.	6. Stage choreograph act two.
7. Go back and review act one.	7. Stumble through act two.
8. Work through act two blocking and acting.	8. Review act one.
9. Run act two.	9. Work through act two staging.
10. Run entire show. (At least a few days before tech)	10. Schedule brush up rehearsals as needed.
11. Work through entire show.	11. Run act two.
12. Run entire show.	12. Run entire show. (At least a few days before tech)
13. Work through entire show or scenes that need attention alternating with run--throughs, until you are ready to just run. After that point, only work sections as needed. This step begins no later than a few days to a week before tech.	13. Work through entire show.
	14. Brush up dances and songs as needed.
	15. Run entire show.
	16. Work through entire show or songs, dances or scenes that need attention
	17. Run entire show, giving notes and working sections as needed through first tech.

Work-throughs

A work-through allows for the following:

- Correcting blocking problems
- Deepening relationships or addressing relationship issues

- Addressing listening issues
- Deepening a sense of honesty and truth
- Working on pace and rhythm
- Enhancing comedic elements
- Making acting adjustments
- Building stamina and getting a sense of the big picture

How to Work Through a Scene

Once a scene is blocked and on its feet, the next step is to work through the scene beat by beat. This takes patience and discipline. Every director wants to see results and enjoy their accomplishments, but slow and steady is the way to go.

Working a scene beat by beat allows the director to improve upon what is working and to fix what isn't. For example, an actor might feel awkward or actors might not be listening to one another. The director might notice that blocking looks clunky, too busy, or without motivation.

When you get to a moment that isn't working, first determine the problem. If it is a blocking issue, try other choices or let the actors improvise a bit to find better staging. If it is an acting problem, discuss the issue with the actor and give adjustments or employ exercises to solve the problem. Don't go on to the next moment until the problem is solved. A work-through of a short scene can take hours, but it is time well spent.

Plan for working through a scene

1. Run the full scene once, noting where the problems are.
2. Jot down what you want to fix—don't count on your memory.
3. Go back to the beginning and start the scene again.
4. Stop at each point where a fix is needed.
5. Identify the problem to the actors.
6. Communicate what you want to fix and why.
7. If it's a blocking issue, fix the blocking and let the actors walk through the new movement a few times before continuing.
8. If it's an acting issue, give the actors an adjustment.
9. Allow the actors a chance to explore the adjustment and make it their own.
10. Evaluate the impact of the adjustment on the scene and the actors. If it is working, move on. If not, try a different adjustment.
11. If needed, use exercises or improvisations to solve problems, but stay on point. Any exercise should be directly focused on solving a specific problem.
12. Once the goal is achieved, repeat the beat or start from the beginning and run through the scene to the next section to be fixed. Work through the entire scene this way until the majority of the issues are resolved.

13. After you have reached the end, repeat the entire scene without stopping, allowing the actors to feel the flow of the scene and to incorporate the new adjustments.

14. If problems persist, go back and review the problematic moments, fix them, and then repeat the scene again.

15. Some problems will require additional time; some may never be solved. The director learns to identify what can and what can't be fixed.

Working with Actors

Make sure to compliment the actors' progress. Privately, you should realize when your actors have reached their limits, knowing not to push further. Gently pushing them past their limitations has its virtues, but asking them to accomplish what they are clearly not capable of will only make them feel inadequate, leading to insecurity. A potentially adequate performance can be destroyed this way.

Often a problem can't be solved in one attempt. Keep working on the problem. Ideally, over time, the actors will find a solution. Pick your battles wisely, and know when to accept the inevitable.

If the work is embarrassing an actor, stop. Take the actor aside and work privately, away from the eyes and judgments of other cast members.

Directing is tricky. Each actor has a different kind of work ethic, ego, and energy level. Many actors don't like to work through scenes. They just want to be left alone. Others thrive on the detail work, because it allows them time to work on their performances in a careful and thorough way.

The art of directing is also the art of manipulation. Often used negatively, manipulation is used here in a different sense, as in *the seamstress manipulated the pair of scissors*. A director brings together a group of artists, comes to understand their natures and abilities, and then leads them in the process of bringing a playwright's work to life. A director uses subtle manipulation to get desired results from actors. Don't be afraid of this positive manipulation.

Don't worry about being liked. Earn respect by being consistent, challenging the actors, and keeping the play's best interest ahead of your own ego. The director's goal is to create a masterwork—not to win a popularity contest.

The Stumble-through

The first time the actors run blocking for an entire act is what I call a "stumble-through." The purpose of a stumble-through is to solidify the blocking.

For the stumble-through, inform the actors that their primary focus should be on remembering the blocking and not to worry too much about acting. In order to free them in future runs to "act," they must have the chance to focus solely on blocking so it gets "into their bodies."

Let the actors "stumble" around as they recall and execute the blocking. The stage manager checks the blocking against notations in their prompt book, correcting the actors as needed. If there are problems, work out the blocking issues and repeat the scene before moving forward. Get through the entire section this way, focusing solely on blocking issues.

Don't expect much in the stumble-through. If the actors remember most of their blocking and don't fall off the stage, be happy!

Once the stumble-through is behind you, rotate work-throughs with run-throughs. After each work-through period, a run-through without stopping allows actors to apply the accomplishments of the work-through. The director notes what has "stuck" and what still needs work, and then focuses on problem areas in the next work-through.

Running with Notes

In a run-through with notes, the director takes notes during an uninterrupted rehearsal of a large chunk of the show—if not the entire show. Before each run, state goals and review the gains of the last work-through, then let the actors run the show without interruption.

You can run selected scenes, entire acts, or the whole play. The director's responsibility during a run is to take notes about what is and what is not working. It might seem redundant to take notes about what is going well, but *affirming the positives is just as important as pointing out problem areas.*

If the actors have brilliant moments, let them know. Try to balance positive reinforcement with constructive criticism. If the actors only hear about the problems, they may lose confidence.

Work-throughs can happen immediately after staging a scene, and then can alternate with run-throughs. After each run, a work-through can afford the opportunity to delve into the details once again. Work-through rehearsals can continue right up to tech week, but scheduling frequent run-throughs as the opening approaches is important as it gives the actors a chance to build stamina and get a sense of flow.

Each rehearsal process is different. Some shows will require a lot of detail work while others will flow smoothly. For each show, be sensitive to the situation and rehearse as needed to ensure a production that is an amalgam of a thousand perfectly crafted details.

Taking Notes

During run-throughs of either individual scenes or the entire show, the director takes notes about the actors or design issues; writing down specific issues that need to be addressed. Notes can be general or specific. Before tech, notes apply only to actors.

Actor notes

General notes:

- Deal with broad approach to an entire role or scene, relationship or character choices, tone, or other major adjustments that apply to more than one moment
- Observe whether an actor's overall scene objective is not clear
- Address energy, major choices, and prevalent issues that affect the entire cast
- Deal with issues such as manner of walking, dialect, and speech

Specific notes:

- Are tied to a single line or moment
- Deal with pace, volume, action, objective, depth of feeling, truth or lack thereof, blocking adjustments, etc.
- Can be as simple as "don't cross to the couch until two lines later," or "the tactic of flirting is not working there, try teasing instead"
- Should be "specific" and clear and include solutions when possible

Other kinds of notes

- Personal notes—things the director wants to remember, unrelated to actors
- Work notes—areas singled out for work in future rehearsals
- Tech notes—about props, costumes, etc.

If you don't have someone to sit by you and take notes as you dictate them quietly, try taking notes on a computer (if you can type, you don't have to look down from the stage). Or, take notes the old fashioned way, by hand. Writing notes by hand is not ideal because you are forced to look away from the stage and might miss something. If you write your notes by hand, try to develop a short hand that will allow you to spend less time writing and more time watching.

Organize the notes by scene and act. With the start of each new scene or act, write a heading that separates one group of notes from the next.

Giving notes

After the run-through, sit in front of the actors. If you are working with professionals, assume they have their own way of digesting notes, but with students or amateurs, insist on pads and pencils.

Go through each note, addressing it to the actor or actors involved, allowing for any discussion necessary. Make sure the notes are understood. Encourage the actors to ask questions if they are confused. Let them know which notes you marked to be worked so they can plan on staying afterwards.

Find time to work notes that need attention before another run. Even if you are in final runs before tech, it is important to fix something before running again so you don't repeat the same problem.

Follow the "run-fix-run-fix-run" format.

Designer Runs or "Crew Views"

These are runs specifically intended for the crew and designers. Usually about a week before the show begins tech rehearsals—or a day or two before in the case of short rehearsal periods—the designers and crew come to look at the blocking and determine what issues they might have.

Let the actors know that the designers and crew will be talking during the run.

One very important thing to keep in mind: Designers and crew never laugh, rarely seem interested, and never smile at crew views. But don't fret. They are very intent on evaluating their own work in terms of how your direction is going to mesh with their designs. They are not viewing the show like an audience. Don't get upset if you get little or no reaction at a crew view.

At the crew view the director sits next to the lighting designer and talks about cues and atmospheres; pointing out where specific effects, specials, and cues are needed. For example, a director might want a special fire-escape light in *The Glass Menagerie* with a smoky luminescence to give the feel of the dream or memory play. Or for *Cabaret*, a director may request a down-center **special** for many numbers done in the club. Discuss how those specials work as the designer watches the run.

> **Special:** lighting positions used specifically to illuminate one place on the stage in a unique way.

After the crew view, meet with the designers and assess the staging in terms of the set, costumes, and lighting. Discuss problems and solutions. Invariably, something will happen in a crew view that will require either the designer or director to make adjustments. If you really love something you've done, insist that the designer adjust to fit your concept, but be flexible.

To avoid problems, study the ground plans, renderings, and models before beginning staging. Know what you have to work with. If you have any sudden brainstorms that require adjustments in design, indicate that on the rehearsal report and immediately request—and confirm—that the designer will change what you want.

Final Thoughts

The process of staging generally follows this order:

1. Table reading period (for plays)
2. Initial blocking rehearsals
3. Run- and work-throughs by scene
4. First act (then second act) stumble-through
5. Work-through of the show
6. Run-through of the show
7. Alternating work- and run-throughs
8. Several run-throughs with notes
9. Crew View

During the work- and run-through period, put in the time and energy required to bring the show to its potential before technical rehearsals begin. Don't compromise on realizing potential. By the final run-through in the rehearsal hall, the director has done everything humanly and artistically possible to ensure a good show.

The next step in the process is technical rehearsals. Be prepared for everything to go wrong!

In Your DPN

Be sure to record your notes in your director's production notebook. Every director develops their own way of taking notes. The following is a general notation style sheet:

Notation Style Sheet

For general notes:

Actor name—general note content

For specific notes:

Actor name—line or moment referenced: note about that line or moment

For indicating a moment to work on later:

W - Actor name—note

For indicating a repeat note:

R - Actor name—note

There are certain notes that will require rehearsal after the run. Use the *W* to indicate that it is a work note and ask the stage manager to schedule time to run all the work notes after the rehearsal or before the next rehearsal. Using an *R* before the note helps the director keep track of reoccurring issues, which should be addressed with the actor.

Chapter 20
Technical Rehearsals and Adding Elements

Technical Rehearsals

Even in the most congenial of atmospheres, technical rehearsals can unleash the monster in people. The stakes are high, nothing seems like it will ever be ready, designers are scrambling to finish their work, actors are nervous, the director feels like no one cares, and the producer is mired in regret for financing the project in the first place.

From Experience

Stay calm; keep your eye on the prize. The show always comes together. Only one show in my twenty-five years as a director wasn't ready to open, and despite a half-finished set, we did the show anyway. The show must and does go on.

The director is, by decree of the job description, at the center of the storm and can either encourage the storm to become a destructive Category 5 hurricane, or by adopting the right attitude, contain the storm as a mild tropical depression.

Technical rehearsals can be the most thrilling and agonizing of experiences. Seeing the physical reality materialize is a joy. Through incredible patience and a strong will, a director can minimize the stress of tech rehearsals.

The director's first rehearsal on stage is called a **spacing rehearsal**, which rarely happens on a completed set. This rehearsal gives the cast and director the chance to put the show on the "actual" stage. This is usually done on a few unpainted platforms and flats with maybe a staircase. Through the ensuing tech period, the set pieces are finished, slowly but surely; lighting, costumes, sound, and music are added; and the play comes to fruition.

Tech rehearsal allows the crew and designers the time they need to get the technical elements of the production worked out. That doesn't mean the actors should sit around chatting amongst themselves. There is no reason an actor's process can't continue through tech. Actors can familiarize themselves with their physical environment, work on relationships, run lines, and discover the world their character will inhabit.

Preparing for Tech Rehearsal

Prior to the first onstage spacing rehearsal, have the stage manager let the tech director know what you need so the tech director can prioritize as the set is loaded-in. For example, if there are levels on stage that will affect the dances in a musical, let the tech director know the levels are more important than the window treatments or hanging chandeliers. Anything that affects staging needs to be in place for the spacing rehearsal.

Get on stage before the actors arrive and become familiar with the flow, entrances and exits, sightlines, distances between areas, any onstage impediments, and off-stage traffic flow patterns.

Make sure the stage manager has put glow tape backstage, around the edges of the set, and wherever else things protrude or dangerous edges exist.

When the actors arrive, have the stage manager walk them around the set, identify entrances, exits, stairs, levels, and anything that might affect the way they move. Let them explore a bit on their own before starting.

Tech behavior—rules for actors

Discuss the rehearsal rules you wish enforced during tech and have the stage manager inform the cast of these rules. In a professional environment, the actors understand the rules already but some of the guidelines in figure 20.1 are worth stating regardless of the actor's level of experience.

How to best utilize the actors during tech

- Remind them to continue the rehearsal process during the long stretches of down-time in tech, running scenes and lines, thinking about their characters, running through blocking, etc.
- Plan a daily **speed-through**.

> **Speed-through:** a spoken run of the text by the group done as quickly as possible. The purpose of a speed-through is to solidify line memorization. It can be done sitting around the green room or in a corner somewhere. The rapid pace is the key. No acting.

Figure 20.1
Rules implemented
by the director to
govern technical
rehearsals

Technical Rehearsal Rules

1. Arrive on time.

2. Be respectful of the crew.

3. Ask, don't demand.

4. If you have a problem with a crew member, tell the stage manager.

5. Don't touch anything!

6. Don't change anything!

7. Put costumes back on the racks when finished.

8. Wear costumes as instructed.

9. Return props to the prop table.

10. Don't talk onstage during tech work.

11. Don't leave the rehearsal area without informing the stage manager.

12. Bring food for long rehearsals.

13. Eat only in assigned spaces and never in costume.

14. Don't use cell phones during rehearsal.

15. Be prepared to sit around, bring work or a book.

16. Bring pencil and paper.

17. Don't wear white, yellow, or other bright colors.

Tech Rehearsals Offstage

Paper Tech Paper tech rehearsals happen anywhere from a day to a few weeks before the first onstage tech. Designers, tech crew, and the director sit around a table to plan all the scene changes and fly cues in the show. The stage manager records plans for personnel.

Dress Parade At the dress parade rehearsal, the actors try on each costume and appear onstage alone or in groups, moving from scene to scene as the director and designer watch and discuss. Dress parades are not often done anymore, but still can be useful.

First Onstage Spacing Rehearsal

In the first onstage spacing rehearsal, the director and actors work out the blocking on the set, as there are always adjustments to be made. What seemed like good blocking in the rehearsal hall might not work onstage. Use this time to find new solutions. With musicals, the choreographer "spaces" the dances onstage. Because of the kinetic nature of dance, adjusting the dances to the actual space is critical before actually running any dance numbers. Do not run dances without spacing them first, slowly and safely.

Spacing non-musicals onstage

- Run fights. If the show has any fights, work through them before anything else happens onstage. A fight captain is assigned by the fight choreographer. At every rehearsal, before the cast comes to the stage, run fights slowly, under the supervision of the fight captain. Always work through the fights slowly and then pick up their speed. Only when the fight captain feels the actors are ready, can the fights can start to run at full show speed.
- Go through scenes for blocking. Starting at the top, work the entire show, checking that all the blocking choices made in rehearsal look and feel right on the set. Correct any upstaging and work out timing and patterns of movement.
- Consider stage pictures. Not only can stage pictures be things of beauty, they can empower a moment, create an atmosphere, and enhance relationships between characters. Consider the positioning of the actors, particularly your use of levels. Is the dynamic right? Does the picture create a resonance that goes beyond simple placement onstage? Always look for the beauty and the power you can attain with the right stage picture. Don't be afraid to work on stage pictures throughout spacing and technical rehearsals.
- Traffic and offstage patterns. Work out any offstage crosses (especially fast ones), group entrances and exits, and group stage crosses.

Spacing for musicals

- Set the dances onstage first. With the rehearsal accompanist, the choreographer slowly works through each dance and adjusts as needed for safety, pictures, and sight lines.
- Run fights. (See spacing for non-musicals above.)
- Go through scenes for blocking. (See spacing for non-musicals above.)
- Set group stage pictures. Using all levels and areas of the stage, set pictures that are aesthetically pleasing and powerful.
- Work out mass entrances and exits. You have already set the entrances in the rehearsal hall. Now, make sure they work and feel natural in the actual space. You will work on timing and placement. Every entrance and exit should seem natural.
- Work out traffic. For large onstage chorus movements, work out movement patterns.

Tech Rehearsals with the Crew

Generally the Production Stage Manager (PSM) runs all tech rehearsals. In smaller theatres, it might be the stage manager. Allow the PSM to do their job, but if things are not going as planned, speak up.

Tech rehearsals last for a few days to a week or so. The following is a description of the types of onstage tech rehearsals.

Dry tech: lighting, fly, sound—before tech period begins

- Without actors present, the technical crew runs all scene changes, and sound, lighting, and fly cues.
- The lighting designer, ideally working from preplanned cues, shows the director each lighting cue and adjusts as needed. Stage managers stand onstage in place of actors.
- This can be a very long process, but it affords the crew the chance to "rehearse" their part of the show without pressure from actors waiting.
- Stage manager and deck chief determine where actors will be needed for set changes and begin to create **run sheets** from which all cues will be managed.

Dry tech: cue to cue—early in tech period

- Moving from one cue to the next, the technical crew runs all sound, lighting, and fly cues without actors present. The stage manager reviews the cues to ensure everyone knows their job.
- If cues aren't working, adjustments are made.
- The stage manager creates a run sheet for wet tech, noting who is responsible for what and where actors will be needed.

Wet tech—follows dry tech

- The wet tech is the same as a dry tech but with actors present.
- Actors often are called upon to assist with scene changes. Actor responsibilities have already been defined in the dry tech. The stage manager assigns actor tasks as each cue is explained, rehearsed, and run.
- The stage manager revises the run sheets to include specific actor's names.
- Run sheets are handed out and posted as soon as possible thereafter.

Cue to cue with actors—solidifies work in wet tech

- Once all responsibilities have been assigned, each individual cue is run, jumping from one to the next.
- Actors are present but there is no acting during cue to cue.
- Actors are told by the stage manager where to start—generally a few lines before a given cue—they run the lines through the cue, the crew runs the cue, and then the stage manager indicates with a loud "stop"

that the cue was successful and informs everyone where to jump to in the script for review of the next cue.

First dress tech (or first dress rehearsals)—technical run-throughs

- This is a rehearsal with costumes, often supported by full tech, including lights, sound, set changes, props, etc.
- Fast costume changes are rehearsed.
- Pre-set of costumes and backstage choreography of costume changes are worked out.
- Actors start "acting" again.

Subsequent dress techs—occur between first dress tech and final dress

- These rehearsals are full run-throughs with most or all elements present.
- Includes full tech, costumes and possibly make-up, hair, etc.
- Allows for stops to work out problems.
- Director takes notes and works problem areas after run.
- Production meetings: after each run, the PSM, stage manager, director, crew, and designers meet to evaluate the work, report on progress, receive notes from the director and production manager, and make plans for the next day.

Musical Orchestra Rehearsals

The tech process for musicals has special requirements to consider.

During the final week of rehearsals, the musical director will rehearse the orchestra prior to their first meeting with the cast. During these rehearsals, the MD communicates to the players all of the tempi, score changes, and interpretations that have been set during rehearsals with the cast. Producers try to limit the number of orchestra rehearsals because of the expense.

In a union house, the orchestra is limited to a four-hour session, with any extra time being paid in overtime.

Sitzprobes and wandeprobes

The musical orchestra rehearsal process borrows two German terms from opera: *sitzprobe* and *wandeprobe*.

At a **sitzprobe** (in German *sitz* means seated or to sit and *probe* means rehearsal), the actors sit in chairs and sing through the score with the orchestra. The MD stops and starts, working to ensure the orchestra and actors are working well together.

At a **wandeprobe** (in German *wande* means to wander, or walk and *probe* means rehearsal), the actors move through their staging as they rehearse with the orchestra. This approach can be useful in determining where there are sightline issues and to ensure the actors can hear the orchestra and vice versa.

At both of these rehearsals, the sound designer can choose to set levels and balance between the orchestra and singers.

Piano runs

Because the orchestra is expensive, most technical rehearsals and initial dress rehearsals are with piano only. The MD either plays or conducts the pit pianist, if there is one in the orchestra.

Adding in the Elements

Lighting

A set can look drab in work lights, but through the magic of theatrical lighting, that same set becomes a world drenched with atmosphere and beauty. Sets are designed with lights in mind. Good set designers understand how lighting will add richness, color, and texture to their scenic elements.

Lighting serves the following purposes:

- Illumination of the set and addition of dimension to the scenic elements
- Creation of atmosphere
- Establishment of time of day, season, and in some cases, location
- Illumination of actors
- Creation of specific visual pictures within an overall lighting scheme

Lighting is critical to the visual success of a show, and can be successful using eight or eight hundred instruments. How the designer uses those instruments determines the power and beauty of their design. While big Broadway productions might use more than one thousand lighting instruments, a typical college or community theatre production gets by with somewhere between twenty and two hundred.

During early design meetings, the director and lighting and scenic designers collaborate closely as the set design is considered. After that, the lighting designer creates a lighting plot—a schemata of all lighting instruments, defining what kind of instruments will hang where, what gel colors they will have, and at which angle they will hang.

There are many different kinds of lighting instruments. Some focus on small areas, others cover wide areas. There are instruments that are best used to create color washes over large areas, and others used for specials that create one single look used repeatedly in one area of the stage. A short list of basic instruments is shown in figure 20.2 on the next page.

Stage Lighting

Instrument	Description
Spotlights	Lighting instruments that throw a long-distance circular beam from the back of the house to illuminate the faces of actors or specific areas of the set. They are flexible and can be manipulated to follow movement onstage. Their light can be altered through use of color and throw size.
Fresnel spotlights	These are fixed lights hung from a grid whose beam can be adjusted from a spotlight to a floodlight. They have a soft edge and are effectively used in color washes. Named after their inventor, Augustin Fresnel, their lens has concentric rings on the glass.
Parabolics	They are permanently sealed in their housing, with the size of the beam set by their construction. They are used for color washes, back lighting, and the lighting of specific areas.
Pin lights	Used generally for specials, they throw very tight beams.
Ellipsoidals	Usually referred to as "Lekos," which is a brand name, they project directional light whose edge is adjustable through the movement of the lens forward or back. These are great for specials or area lighting. The edges of the light can be adjusted using sliders on the instrument.
Floodlights	The most basic of theatre instruments, these are usually used as work lights or for back lighting or washes. Sometimes referred to as "Parcans."
Striplights	Long groups of lights joined together in one unit used either for color washes or to light set pieces or cycloramas. They are often found in high schools and older auditoriums.
Automated lights	These are lights whose color changes and movement are controlled automatically at the light board. They have been around since the 1970s, but are getting more and more sophisticated.
Barn doors	Fresnels don't have internal beam adjustment capabilities. Barn doors are attached to the light and have small metal pieces on hinges that can bend in and out to adjust the edges of the light.

As the designer works on the lighting plot, the designer considers discussions with the director about time of day, general atmosphere in each scene, specials the director wants, and the rhythm and dynamics of the design. Once the play is in run-throughs, the lighting designer comes into the rehearsal hall and watches the show to get a sense of how to best design the actual cues.

Seeing the run affords the lighting designer insight into the show, its rhythms, and atmospheres. When the lighting designer has a grasp on what is required, the designer goes back to the lighting plot to fine-tune it. At this point, the designer will incorporate any unexpected changes and begin writing cues.

Different lighting designers have different ways of working. Some write cues before tech rehearsals, others write cues during tech rehearsals, using pre-set looks and adapting them to each scene. The latter method can be painstakingly slow, but it does allow the director more control over the final result.

A director who understands the basic tenets of lighting design and can speak its "language" is going to have more influence in the final design. It makes it easier for both parties if there is some common understanding of the basic language. A list of lighting design terms is shown in figure 20.3.

Figure 20.3
Language of light-
ing design

Lighting Design

Term	Definition
Cool colors	blues and greens that create a 'cool' feeling that could be night, winter or isolation
Warm colors	ambers, reds and yellows that create a 'warm' feeling that could be daytime and sunny, summer or coziness
Gobos	inserted metal disks that have patterns cut in them. They are placed inside the instruments and the lights projects throught them, throwing textured light patterns onto the stage.
Lights up	the transition from darkness to the first lighting cue of a scene
Blackout	transition from scene light to darkness
Transition cue	a cue that is used to link two other cues
Wash	a general color choice applied to the full stage
Follow spot	a spotlight that follows the actors as they move around the stage
Counts	the number of seconds it takes for a cue to fully execute or fade. Three count to black, for example, means it would take three seconds to go from full scene lighting to blackout
Special	a lighting cue with a unique characteristic that is applied to a single area once or repeatedly
Cues	each individual lighting look
Bump	change with a zero count, from one cue to another, usually into a blackout
Fade to black	slow fade to darkness

Stage lights are referred to as fixtures or instruments (Abroad, they are referred to as lanterns in the UK; luminaires everywhere else). A lighting package refers to the full combination of mechanisms that create one working theatre light and includes the housing, electrical wiring, reflector, bulb and socket.

The following are some of the areas which the director can and should exert influence.

Decisions on Time of Day and Location Usually time of day and location is clearly indicated in the script, but not always. The director will make these decisions if directing a script that does not indicate time of day, such as classic Greek plays. Even when the time of day is suggested, there often is wiggle room. The designer needs specifics and the director provides them.

Focus Each scene has its own focus requirements. Where does the director want the audience to look? Each lighting cue applies some kind of focus. For example, in *The Glass Menagerie*, when Tom is on the fire escape, the focus is on the fire escape. The rest of the set has some illumination, but the fire escape and Tom are brighter than the rest of the set, pulling focus. The contrast between the area of focus and the rest of the set creates atmosphere.

Using the example above, the design would have a "fire escape" special. There is one grouping of lighting instruments that focus specifically on that spot and are only used for lighting that spot. Because of the multi-scene nature of musicals, specials are used frequently. In *Cabaret*, the Kit Kat Club stage would have a special where the MC or Sally sings solos. The "MC down center special" would be used for those moments. There could be five Kit Kat Club specials (UR, UL, DR, DL, C), each focusing on a different part of the stage, used in the opening to illuminate the Kit Kat girls, then doubling for other scenes, such as Cliff's initial ride on the train in the show's second scene. In houses with limited lighting capacity, clever designers use specials more than once.

Faces Lighting illuminates actors. When working on light cues, make sure you can see the expressions on actors' faces. Faces should never be in the dark.

Atmosphere Atmosphere is subjective. Defining atmosphere is both specific and mysteriously vague. Atmosphere comes from an intuitive sense that isn't always easy to clearly explain. Directors have to find the words that express the vision in their imagination. Clarification of the atmosphere ideas may come through conversations with the lighting designer and then through looking at the ideas onstage and working to find just the right tone for any given moment. After seeing the moment onstage, the director can explain if something isn't working to the lighting designer. Ask the designer to play with the cue until the perfect tone is achieved.

Through the use of cool (blue palette) or warm (amber palette) colors, gobos (inserted metal disks that have patterns cut in them which are projected through the instruments onto the stage to create texture or specific patterns), and intensity, virtually any atmosphere can be created.

Be specific. Discuss atmosphere with the lighting designer. If cues don't feel right, tell the lighting designer why and ask for adjustments to achieve the atmosphere you want. It is a give-and-take process that takes time to perfect. But through collaboration, almost any result is achievable.

Atmospheres change frequently. Through subtle lighting changes, an atmosphere of serenity can become an atmosphere of dread. Using contrasting atmospheres heightens tension.

Rhythm and Dynamics The pace at which light changes occur creates a rhythm. Rhythm is subtle but asserts strong influence. Each show has its own rhythm. Some shows, like many musicals, have fast and furious rhythms with sudden, contrasting lighting changes. A play like *A Long Day's Journey into Night* by Eugene O'Neill has a slow and ponderous rhythm; fast light cues would seem unnatural.

Musicals have their own unique requirements because they are generally multi-scene shows, and as such require different lighting atmospheres for songs and scripted scenes.

Natural lighting is generally used in a dialogue scene. When a song begins, the atmosphere changes. In many classic musicals, spotlights come on and the background lighting becomes darker and more saturated. Spotlights are useful because actors move around the stage in solos and duets, and spotlights follow them while retaining the beautiful general lighting cue that surrounds them.

Using a spotlight also allows the actors to be seen in a dimly lit lighting cue. Many Broadway lighting designs focus a spotlight on each actor for the entire duration of the show so cues can be saturated and atmospheric without worrying about seeing the actors' faces. Because smaller theatres don't have that capacity, the use of spotlights is more selective and primarily reserved for songs.

If the song ends in a button, the lighting design adds its own button. It can be a sudden brightening or a slow fade to natural lighting.

Another aspect of the dynamic is cue-specific. The rate at which a cue fades in or out creates a tone for the moment that exerts strong influence on the feel of that moment. For example, at the end of a big dance number, a fast, zero-count blackout creates a button for the scene that begs for applause. If a scene ends on a quiet note, a five count fade to black has a completely different effect as the audience lingers on the final image until the blackout is complete. A count is equal to one second.

A director and lighting designer collaborate on the rate of the up and down fades. If a transition doesn't feel right, talk to the lighting designer about the rate of the cue to see if there is a different timing that works more effectively.

The lighting design defines, enhances, and magnifies the atmosphere while responding to the overall tone of the show in the way the light cues follow one another.

Costumes

Nothing is more important to an actor's sense of character than the costume he or she wears. Costume designers not only add to the visual look of a show, they influence the actor in subtle and powerful ways. Good costume design enhances the actor's experience of character and period.

Costumes serve the following purposes:

- Identifying period, season, and culture
- Creating for the actor a specific sense of character
- Indication of personality and taste of the character
- Denotation of a character's level of affluence and standing
- Distinguishing between principals and chorus (in musicals)

Whereas set and lighting are external, costumes emanate from the internal world of the character. Of course, costumes identify external influences such as culture and period, but their greatest power is in how they influence the actor's portrayal of a character.

Taking into consideration the set and lighting choices, a costume designer imagines the world of clothing that will comprise their design. After researching the period and discussing each character with the director, the costume designer creates sketches that illustrate the ideas they have discussed. It is helpful to look at the sketches grouped by scenes to imagine how the actors' costumes will interact.

Looking at costumes, consider whether the character would have the outfit in their closet. If not, the costume is not appropriate. Costumes should define and reflect the character's personality, social status, taste, level of affluence, and sense of oneself.

Costumes also take each individual actor's physical characteristics into consideration. Accentuating negative physical characteristics compromises the quality of a design. Actor's bodies need to be taken into consideration when designing their costumes.

The director has many chances to see costume design work in process. When actors go to fittings, the director can sneak a peek. Check the rack, where the costumes hang during the process of being built, fit, and finished. Many costume designers don't look kindly on directors snooping, so ask first.

Often, the first time the director sees all the costumes together is at the first dress; however, it is difficult to make major changes that late in the process. Costumes that are not working can be changed if there is time, but finding ways to avoid last minute crises is important. Look at drawings, go to fittings, do whatever you can to see costumes before they are onstage in dress rehearsal.

The following are some of the areas which the director can and should influence the costume designer.

Decisions as to Time of Day and Location As with lighting designers, communicate information on the time of day and location to the costume designer.

Focus Especially in musicals, the use of color and material can distinguish characters from one another. In big group numbers, the chorus dresses in similar outfits and principals wear colors and styles that stand out from the group, setting them apart, so that the eyes of the audience easily move to the leading players.

Period and Personality Period specificity is critical. Surely, you want the period to be clear in the costume designs. By using a variety of styles from that period, the costumes should capture the personality of the character.

Atmosphere and Character Costumes create atmosphere and character through color, style, and material. Since atmospheres are external, a pleasant and happy atmosphere can be achieved with light colors and fabrics and flowing styles. A dark, heavy atmosphere would employ darker, heavier fabrics and constricting styles.

Even within a single color palette, through style and texture, costumes can define characters. For example, in Garcia Lorca's *The House of Bernarda Alba*, the first scene begins with the entrance of seven women of the household and many female neighbors, all dressed in black. It is summer in Spain following the funeral of Bernarda's husband. The family is in mourning, so everyone is wearing black. Bernarda is very rigid, bound by tradition. Her black costume is stylish because she is wealthy, but prim and tight. Each neighbor's personality is defined through their costume's style and texture. The seven daughters all have very distinct personalities. The youngest rebellious daughter is sex-starved. Her outfit might be more fitted and flattering, with a lower neckline and flowing fabric, while the eldest daughter would wear clothes more akin to her mother's style.

In a comedy like *Anything Goes*, a wacky thirties musical, the palette would be brighter and more saturated with color. Cuts for ladies would be more revealing, and the men's costumes would express their lively personalities.

Talk to the designer about how the costumes can support the atmosphere you want to create.

Dance Musicals In heavy dance musicals, dancers have to move freely. Their costumes have to stretch and be flexible. Ladies' dress design has to take into account the flips and turns that might expose inner thighs. The choreographer should communicate directly with the costume designer to ensure the costumes allow the movement necessary to execute the dances.

Props

Adding props begins in rehearsals but continues through tech. Many props can't be used in rehearsal because they are fragile or not yet ready. It is important to be using rehearsal props from the first staging rehearsal so the actors become comfortable with handling the props and can use them in developing their performances.

Creating props requires research to ensure accuracy. Finding or building props is a time intensive and often expensive process. Great **properties artisans** are incredibly creative. Either by building or buying and altering, their contribution to the overall sense of the show is immeasurable.

Encourage actors to respect props by treating them carefully and always returning them to the prop table following use.

Sound

One of the last elements added is sound. Sound in theatre includes recorded sound effects, recorded music, an orchestra for musicals, and amplification of voices.

Recorded Sound Cues The director provides the sound designer with a list of sound cues that includes specific information about each cue. The sound designer researches and creates the cues and then plays them for the director. Once approved, it is useful to play cues in rehearsal to test how they feel. Often what sounds perfect in a studio seems out of place in rehearsal. Always test the cues to make sure they work before getting to technical rehearsals, when it might be too late to change anything.

Recorded Music Using recorded music for plays is a great way to create or enhance atmosphere. Music is generally played as the audience enters the theatre, during the transition from first blackout into the first scene, between scenes, and during curtain call. Occasionally recorded cues are used as underscoring during a scene.

Follow the same rule as with recorded sound cues; try them out in rehearsal to get a feel for how they impact the scene. You might have to try many different choices before finding the one that does the job.

Choosing Music Choosing music is very tricky but incredibly important. The right music can make or break a show. Music is a powerful creator of emotional atmosphere.

The music played before the show starts sets the mood. If it's a forties comedy, playing Bing Crosby music can set the right tone. If it's a modern show set in New York City about young people, using house music could feel right. The goal is to put the audience in the right frame of mind.

Once the lights go out, a cue for new music that is emotionally specific begins the first scene. While the pre-show music can be general in mood, this first cue must be specific to the emotional atmosphere to be created as the lights come on. Using well-known music can be effective if the song makes a tangibly clear comment on what is to come. Listen to a lot of different music and try things out in rehearsal until just the right cue is found.

Transitional cue music between scenes serves to both end one scene and launch a new one. This kind of music cue ideally begins in the mood of the scene that just ended and transitions the audience into the emotional atmosphere of the new scene.

Depending on the situation, you might have a composer creating music for the show, or you will look through the extensive catalogue of existing recorded music.

Keep in mind royalty issues if you use recorded music. Generally, the music is covered if the theatre has a BMI or ASCAP blanket royalty agreement. Check with the theatre manager to see what is allowed.

Amplifying Voices Large houses and musicals with large orchestras require the actor's voices to be amplified with a microphone. Using body microphones that send a signal to a receiver in the back of the house, the sound of the actors' voices are amplified through house speakers.

The object of vocal amplification is make voices loud enough for the audience to hear but to sound natural. Unless it's a rock musical where loudness is part of the experience, the audience should not be aware of the amplification. Using a live orchestra makes amplified voices a necessity.

Keep in mind that body microphones don't replace projection. They only "amplify" what is already there; mics don't create vocal energy if there is none to begin with. Handling amplified voices requires a professional to set up the system and make all the necessary adjustments to ensure good quality. Anyone can run the sound board during a show as long as they are thoroughly familiar with the show and know when to turn the mics on and off. Sound is tricky and mysterious and bad sound can ruin a great show. Don't skimp on finding a qualified person to set the system up.

PART VI:
OPENING THE SHOW

Chapter 21
Final Dress to
Opening Night

The elements have been added, tech is ready, and opening is imminent.

Depending on the organization, the show will either open or begin a preview period during which the director and artistic team continue to work and make changes, influenced by audience response. In summer stock, the final dress might be the only uninterrupted run of a show before opening. In most situations, there is more time.

The Lead-up to Opening Night

Final Dress

The final dress is the last run of a show before it is viewed by an audience. All design and technical elements are in place and the actors give a fully realized performance as if there were an audience. Many directors invite small audiences to the final dress to provide the actors a chance to work with audience reaction.

On the day of the final dress, talk to the actors. Inform them the run will not stop for any reason, and counsel them on what to do if things go awry. Make it clear; a full non-stop run is the goal.

Once the dress rehearsal run begins, no matter what disasters might occur, *do not stop* unless an actor's life is in danger! The company needs the experience of running the show without stopping. Tell them to figure out what to do if problems arise.

The director's job during final dress is to relax, breathe, and take notes. By this point, whatever is still achievable will be clear, and the unachievable will be equally clear.

Although notes after the final dress rehearsal are the last opportunity to influence the actors before opening, they can have great impact. For example, if you have been consistently giving one actor the same note for days and there has been no progress, weigh the value of giving the same note again against the lack of confidence it might instill. If the note will not achieve anything, don't give the note! Give notes that will get results. Focus on generating excitement about opening.

Preparing Actors for the Audience Inexperienced actors are often thrown by audience response. They don't expect the reactions and don't understand how to integrate the audience into their performance. Live theatre is an interaction between actors and audience. As actors gain experience, they learn how to integrate the audience into their performances and use the energy of the audience to ignite their creativity.

There are things directors can do to prepare actors for the audience. During the rehearsal period, if the director laughs, the actors get used to the laughter and begin to work with it. However, audience laughter is unpredictable. It can come when least expected. Talk to the actors about **holding** for laughs and applause.

Inviting a small, live audience to the final dress can prepare the actors for the first real audience. Many directors use these invited audiences as a means to gauge potential audience reaction and give the actors experience before opening night.

Final Dress: a Working Rehearsal The tech crew and designers consider the final dress a working rehearsal. The crew uses the dress to refine their running cues, and designers note things that still need work. After the dress, the artistic and production staffs have their final production meeting to address any last minute issues and create a priority list of notes in case time is tight.

The director feels the stress of all the details that are not working as well as those that might never work. Oftentimes, all the director sees at this point is the flaws. This is normal. But for every flaw, there are a hundred assets that the audience will see.

The best advice is to let go and trust that everyone's hard work will pay off, but remain observant. There is always work left to be done.

Setting the Show

After the final dress, once final staging details have been addressed, the show is "set." At this point, nothing in the show can change without both the permission of the director and a rehearsal with the stage manager and actors involved.

While this is not a hard and fast rule, it comes from Broadway and regional theatre where the director would leave the show after opening night. The production stage manager takes over the responsibilities of the show, ensuring the director's staging and vision are preserved throughout the run.

In certain situations, such as in college or high school theatre, the director might continue to tweak the show after opening as part of the educational process. In professional situations, however, actors are not allowed to make any changes unless approved by the production stage manager. In fact, they can be fired for doing so. Encourage the actors to observe the rules and to make no changes without permission and rehearsal. It is important they learn this professional way of working.

While staging doesn't change, actors can continue to deepen moments in the show and discover new moments. In long runs, actors can continue their process within the framework set by the director. The show, like fine wine, gets richer and more powerful with time.

Previews

On all Broadway shows and most LORT regional shows, there is a period of preview performances after the final dress. Tickets are sold to these performances, but the show continues to evolve.

During previews, the director and actors continue to make changes and rehearse scenes, especially in the case of a new play or musical. Shows change in front of an audience. A line that the director thought was very funny might fall flat in previews. The director and actors can work on that line to find the laugh by trying different approaches.

If it's a new show, the playwright, composer, and lyricist refine the material. Often, in Broadway previews of new shows, scenes are rewritten, songs are added and cut, and performers can be replaced. Rehearsals are held daily to incorporate the new pages of text and other changes, and then those changes are performed in the show that evening. It is a nerve-wracking process, but it is integral to the development of new shows.

The goal, of course, is to create the best show possible. The audience is an important force in the development of creative works, and their influence is the key to the process. Previews allow for that influence to occur, so that on opening night everyone is delivering the best possible production.

Opening Night

Opening night is the culmination of weeks, months, or even years of hard work, dedication, and perseverance. A great deal is on the line for everyone involved, and by its very nature it is terrifying and electrifying at the same time.

From Experience

When I was younger, I worked as a flight attendant. I remember the feeling, as passengers entered the airplane, of being in control. I helped them place their luggage overhead, communicated safety information, solved seating problems, and got the plane ready for departure. But once the flight was ready to depart and the door to the plane was closed, I was no longer in control. I remember the "whooshing" sound of the door closing caused a slight sense of panic inside me. Anything could happen on the plane after the doors closed and there was absolutely nothing I could do about it. We could encounter turbulence, land in the wrong city, or even crash, and I was powerless to affect any change in the course of events. I experience exactly the same feelings as the lights go out, the curtain rises and the play begins.

It is very difficult for the director to let go of control and let the plane fly. Save for taking notes during the opening performance, the director's job is complete. Better to savor the fruits of your labors than to agonize over what might happen. It is exciting to see the work play in front of a live audience.

Opening night energy is special. Actors reach heights previously unseen. Every director has a moment where he or she thinks, "Why didn't they ever do that in rehearsal?" Even that persistent problem that you had given up on might solve itself on opening night.

On the other hand, the agony of being a director is clearly seeing the alarmingly apparent flaws and wondering if anyone else is aware of them. Take heart, the flaws that seem so obvious to the director are usually invisible to the audience.

Directors learn a great deal as they watch their own work. By separating yourself from the show and viewing it objectively, assessing what did and didn't work, your next effort will benefit. *Choose to be the kind of director that learns from but is not defeated by his or her mistakes.*

Directors have different ways of dealing with opening nights. One director I assisted, as a young intern, couldn't watch his own show. He had me watch the opening night performance and run out between scenes to give him updates on how it was going as he paced in the lobby. Other directors (like me) love to see their work on opening night. Why do all that work and not enjoy the final product? It will never be perfect, but is art ever perfect?

Enjoy opening night. You've earned it.

Before the Show

It's hard to forget your high school theatre director giving a pep talk before opening night. My teacher always cried. We all were overwhelmed with emotion and full of gratitude for her deep belief in us. For the cast, opening nights were our chance to make her proud.

In professional theatre, a few words of support to each actor go a long way. If it's a college or semi-professional show, a pep talk can't hurt. Remind the cast of important notes you have given and thank them for their hard work. The goal is to instill confidence, heighten energy, and to let them know you support them and care about their work.

Check in with the designers. Thank them for their work. The same goes for the stage manager and crew. Be present, but don't get in the way. Let everyone do their job.

During the Show

Watch the show. Try to enjoy it. Take notes if you want. There's not much else you can do. Observe the audience, gauge their reactions, and learn what you can.

After the Show

Some directors give notes after opening night. It is a matter of personal preference and depends on the situation. With inexperienced actors, feedback after the experience of the first audience is helpful. Keep the feedback easy, specific, and supportive.

The actors are in great spirits on opening night, and if you are hard on them, it could be perceived as being insensitive and they could rebel.

From Experience

You can pull actors aside and give personal notes but be careful and thoughtful. Years ago I was directing a musical. I had trouble with the leading lady throughout rehearsals. She was having problems with her performance and I had trouble helping her. On opening night, I finally realized what was wrong. I pulled her aside at the party, expecting her to be as delighted as I that I had found a solution. I asked her to come to a brief rehearsal the following day to discuss my revelation and consider a small adjustment to her performance.

What began as an innocent attempt to improve the show ended as a huge fiasco. She cried all night, the entire cast turned against me for being so insensitive, and when she did come to rehearsal, we couldn't really accomplish anything. I was angry at the actress for not trusting me and turning the cast against me. She felt betrayed by me, and completely lost confidence. For years I couldn't understand her behavior, but now I realize now it was all a matter of bad timing. Had I waited until morning and found a better way to share my ideas with her, the whole thing might never have happened.

Although you can never know how someone will react, think before you act, especially on opening night.

The Reviews

Everyone loves a good review. But if you believe the good ones, you can't dismiss the bad ones. If you are going to read your reviews, read the bad ones closely to see if there is anything you can learn from the opinion (and that's all it is) of the reviewer. Even if you don't agree, don't dismiss the review outright. Criticism can be useful if you know how to use it.

A bad review can damage the attitude and performance of some actors, pros and amateurs alike. Many a fun opening night party has been ended prematurely after reading a bad early morning review.

While nothing more than the opinion of one person, reviews are read by thousands. This fact can't be ignored. Directors can soft-peddle reviews but the damage to the show, the cast, and the company can be devastating.

The best way to handle a bad review is to speak to the actors, listen to their concerns, and be sensitive to their hurt feelings. Assure them that the performance is perfect in your eyes, and the show will go on as directed. If they let the reviews hurt their work then everybody is hurt, including the paying audience.

When some actors are reviewed well while others not so well, check in with the badly reviewed actors. Make sure they are okay, reassure them, cajole them, do whatever it takes to convince them that the review is not true and they are doing a great job.

Watch out for the actor that gets reviewed well and begins to change how they relate with others. Nip that behavior in the bud. It can tear a cast apart if one actor is singled out as being the genius of the cast.

Finally, gauge how the review impacts the show. If anything shows signs of change, address this quickly. Don't let a reviewer become a director. Maintain control and ensure consistency.

After Opening Night

Document the Show There are strict copyright laws governing video reproduction, but recording the show for archival purposes is permitted. In an equity production, the cast members must agree to the taping. If you can, tape the show or sections of the show, and keep all the pictures taken of the show.

Save the Reviews As painful as some reviews might be, save both good and bad. If nothing else, it's fun to look back at them.

Final Thoughts

While I have offered a road map to help guide the director from choosing a play to staging opening night, every director is always learning and being surprised by this mysterious craft. Directing is part art, part psychology, part human being management, a large part hard work, and a good dose of humility.

The only way to become a good director is to direct; anywhere and any way you can. Don't reject opportunities to work in small spaces with minimal budgets. That is the best way to learn how to be creative. Seek out opportunities. If you can't find someone that is hiring, find a few colleagues and create your own opportunities.

Assisting established directors is also a great way to learn. Most successful directors always use assistants, some paid, some unpaid. Identify whose work you like and write an email to them. You'd be surprised how many are willing to take you on.

Studying in a good theatre department is a good way to get started. College studies offer the chance to work on many plays in forgiving environments. The student actors are always eager to perform. If you are in college, take full advantage of all the perks associated with that situation. Direct constantly. After school, look for good internship opportunities at major regional theatres. Most have directing internships. Apply.

Ultimately, all you need is a space to perform, actors, an audience, and a script. Designers bring a great dimension to simple projects, but even they are not necessary. A few well-chosen lighting instruments, a couch from storage, and a few props are enough.

Ideally you will come to enjoy all of the benefits of working in professional theatre, but to earn that right, work simply, create your opportunities, and direct shows!

It is a great career, one whose rewards far outweigh the costs. I wish you well on your adventure to be creative, productive, and collaborative.

Appendix 1
Genre and Playing Style

> **Genre:** a category of artistic composition, as in music or literature, characterized by similarities in form, style, or subject matter.
>
> **Style:** a manner of doing something; a way of painting, acting, writing, composing, building that is characteristic of a particular period, place, person, or movement.

As a director approaches a play, identifying the genre of the play is key to understanding the style in which that play will be performed. In theatrical production, each genre has both its own rules of playing style and its own directorial approach.

Styles

A list of popular playing styles is shown in figure A1.1 on page 239.

Genres

Plays fall into two general categories: tragedy and comedy. A tragedy is a drama that has an unhappy ending; in a comedy, there is a happy ending in which the characters triumph over adversity. There can be funny moments in tragedy and dramatic moments in comedy.

Beyond those two broad categories is a large group of theatrical genres. The following is a list of several of those genres and their inherent "rules" that will guide directors to develop playing style.

Realistic Domestic Drama

Example: *A Doll's House* by Henrik Ibsen

Definition: Starting with the realism movement of the late-nineteenth century and the plays of Ibsen, the domestic drama deals with everyday life of everyday people. Plays usually focus on a family situation and are placed in domestic settings like a home.

Playing Style: The domestic drama is generally played realistically. Find the moment-to-moment truth. The style should feel spontaneous as the story unravels and the characters find their worlds shifting. Though the tempo is the tempo of daily life, theatrical tempo moves forward.

Dangers: Pay close attention to pace. Like any drama, pacing can't be hurried, but in each moment, there needs to be a fabric of intensity. Tensions between characters must be enhanced so the underlying drama of the relationships per se is compelling to the audience. Avoid melodramatic playing style and avoid a pace too slow to keep the audience interested.

Romantic Comedy

Example: *Barefoot in the Park* by Neil Simon; *Romantic Comedy* by Bernard Slade.

Modern Examples: *You've Got Mail* (film), *When Harry Met Sally* (film).

Definition: A comedy where the main conflict focuses on a developing, existing, or deteriorating romantic relationship.

Playing Style: Played realistically with breezy pace and spontaneous, fresh style. Depending on the period of the play, physical style and manners can vary from play to play.

Dangers: Overplaying. Comedy is not farce. Comedic style must be based in truth, and unravel in a spontaneous manner. Pace is critical to sustain believability and audience interest. Must be romantic chemistry between the lovers.

Comedy of Manners

Example: *The Importance of Being Earnest*, by Oscar Wilde.

Definition: A comedy that satirizes the behavior of a particular social group, such as the upper class in England. Much of the comedy comes from the silliness, absurdity, and tension caused by strict adherence to behavioral standards of the period.

Playing Style: With great zest, physical precision, emotional truth, and broad comic approach. Characters have strong subtextual influence. What goes on inside each character is constrained by the behavioral limitations of the time.

The comedy comes from:

1. The struggle between what characters want to say and what convention allows them to say.
2. What characters want to do and what convention allows them to do.

The limitations come both from society standards and each character's own personal understanding of that standard.

Dangers: Not doing enough homework. If the director does not have a thorough understanding of the manners of the particular period, then they are unable to define the playing style. Because these plays are dependent on playing style in order for the comedy to be expressed, if the playing style is inaccurate, the play loses its sting.

Figure A1.1
Common
theatrical styles

Style	Description	Look at
Absurdist	Irrational, illogical, and disconnected from realism in every way. Driven by a specific world created by the dramatist, usually steeped in chaos with no certain progression of plot.	*Rhinoceros*, a film with Gene Wilder and Zero Mostel based on the Ionesco play; any YouTube video of work by Open Theatre, Mabou Mines.
Expressionist	Non-realistic, distorted, bizarre in-your-face style that is unapologetic. Fourth wall is usually broken and theatricality is more important than truth in each moment. However universal truths are explored.	*Brazil* (film), *Nosferatu* (film), and most film noir such as *Citizen Kane*.
Melodramatic	The playing style is over-the-top, with big gestures. Characters are drawn from known types such as the hero, the damsel in distress, the caring parent, and the evil bad guy.	These websites for traditional melodrama: http://www.americanmelodrama.com/ http://www.melodrama.net/
Naturalistic	Life is portrayed in very specific detail, drawn from what is real about the moment to moment existence in everyday life. Shows the gritty truth.	*Look Back in Anger*, film starring James Dean; *GlenGarry Glen Ross*, film based on the play by David Mamet; *A Taste of Honey*, film based on stage play by Shelagh Delaney.
Postmodernist	Can take many forms, but usually involves multi-media, lack of realistic fully-drawn character creation, absence of traditional dramatic conventions. Elinor Fuchs wrote that in postmodern theatre, we witness the "death of character and the eradication of the plot."	Ozono's production of *Fuerze Brutta*, films of Andy Warhol.
Realistic	Characters are played in a manner that reflects everyday life, with setting and staging that feels honest and spontaneous. Rejects beauty in favor of sincerity and a simple, non-idealized treatment of life. Despite rejection of beauty, realism finds the beauty in the ordinary.	*Ordinary People*, film starring Mary Tyler Moore and Donald Sutherland, film of the play *A Doll's House*, starring Claire Bloom.
Comedy of manners	Characters are played in a way that reflects the social mannerisms of the time, often making fun of those mannerisms or using the limitations of those manners to create conflict, comedy and relationship.	Many of the Merchant-Ivory films, *Pride and Prejudice, The Importance of Being Earnest*.
Broad farce	Characters are played in an over-the-top way that emphasizes physical comedy, sight gags, fast pace.	The Three Stooges, The Marx Brothers

Dark Comedy

Example: *The House of Blue Leaves*, by John Guare; the plays of Joe Orton

Definition: A comedy that uses grim or bleak situations and satiric humor, often disturbing and thought-provoking; can be farcical.

Playing Style: Very earnestly. Playing style can be farcical or comedic, depending on the particular script. Characters should fully believe in their situations and relish the dark elements. Can include elements of expressionist style.

Dangers: Overacting; squeezing the comedy.

Farce

Example: *Lend Me a Tenor*, by Ken Ludwig; *A Little Hotel on the Side* by Georges Feydeau and Maurice Desvallierès.

Definition: A comedy that uses fast pace, sight gags, improbable situations, and crude characterizations. Evolved from short comic interludes inserted into religious plays. Known for slamming doors and double-takes.

Playing Style: Loud, fast and furious, and played with absolute conviction. The characters can't know the situations are funny.

Dangers: Lack of sincere conviction, slow pace.

Tragicomedy

Example: *Endgame*, by Samuel Beckett.

Modern Examples: *American Beauty* (film), *Life is Beautiful* (film), *Stranger than Fiction* (film)

Definition: A drama that includes elements of tragedy and comedy, usually with an unhappy ending.

Playing Style: Realistic, truthful, with emphasis on spontaneity.

Dangers: Embracing the tragic elements at the expense of the comic. For the greatest effect, the comedy must be as funny as possible to heighten the fall into tragedy.

Tragedy

Example: *Hedda Gabler*, by Henrik Ibsen.

Modern Examples: *Midnight Cowboy* (film), *One Flew over the Cuckoo's Nest* (film), *Titanic* (film).

Definition: A play with an unhappy ending, usually involving the downfall of the protagonist.

Playing Style: Realistic and truthful.

Dangers: Avoid melodrama. Director must seek out every possibility of hope and possibility to enhance the impact of the ultimate tragic end.

Epic Theatre

Example: *Angels in America*, by Tony Kushner; *Mother Courage and Her Children*, by Bertolt Brecht

Viewing Suggestions: *Angels in America*, HBO Films

Definition: A long play that includes multiple events over long periods of time. Often has many characters and several plots and sub-plots.

Playing Style: Depends on the specific play, period, etc.

Dangers: Slow pace; coherence of the main and sub-plots.

Political Theatre

Example: *The Normal Heart*, by Larry Kramer

Definition: Drama that explores political events with a specific point of view. Can be epic or realistic depending on the subject matter and playing style.

Playing Style: Often uses in-your-face, unapologetic style. Naturalistic approach.

Dangers: Becoming polemic, favoring ideas over realistic portrayals and honesty.

Morality Play

Example: *Everyman*, fifteenth-century morality play, no author known

Definition: Common in medieval Europe; uses symbolic characters to teach moral lessons.

Playing Style: Depends on period, but generally with a whole heart and utter conviction. Simple.

Dangers: Losing the humanity in the characters.

Kitchen Sink Realism

Example: *Look Back in Anger*, by John Osborne

Definition: Term used for the British movement in the 1950s and '60s in which realistic social situations were depicted using characters and locations common to the middle class. Like the domestic drama, an intensely realistic play that focuses on life's minutia.

Playing Style: Naturalistic. Use of rough dialects, slang, tough naturalistic style.

Dangers: Overacting; pushing for truth.

Restoration Comedy

Example: *The Way of the World*, by William Congreve

Viewing Suggestions: *The Country Wife* (1977 film), Various made-for-TV versions of Moliere's plays.

Definition: A style of comedy that flourished in post-restoration London in the mid-17th century. Has complicated plots full of wit, cynicism and bawdiness. Rules of 'Comedy of Manners' apply.

Playing Style: Very broad and physically stylized, with sensitive awareness of the subtext, which drives the constrained behavior.

Dangers: Not being specific with physical movement or behavior, not understanding the style, under-researching the period.

Theatre of the Absurd

Example: *Waiting for Godot*, by Samuel Beckett; *The Chairs*, by Eugene Ionesco.

Viewing Suggestions: *Beckett on Film* series available at Amazon.com, Film of Ionesco's *Rhinoceros* starring Gene Wilder, any video of productions by Mabou Mines, the Open Theatre. Search YouTube for a variety of materials.

Definition: A theatrical movement that began in the early twentieth century and flourished by mid-century, marked by non-realistic plots, situations and settings. Plays deal with situations utterly inconsistent with reality, and can be very funny, but also very tragic. Often makes strong comments on modern society and man's inhumanity.

Playing Style: Expressionistic, postmodernist, or sometimes naturalistic or realistic. Each specific play assumes its own playing style. The director analyzes and studies each script, allowing intuition to dictate the playing style. Generally, style will be broad but truthful, with strong physical choices and an absolute belief in the unusual circumstances. Analysis and research are the keys to directing in this genre. The director must identify the meaning of the playwright's words and then find the most powerful means of expressing that meaning. Through free exploration in rehearsal, the company finds a playing style that suits the material.

Dangers: Like the material itself, there is no anchor, no set of rules specific to this style, so to try to apply any existing rule is a danger. The only real danger is not believing in the given circumstances and not relating in an honest way with the other actors.

Commedia dell'Arte

Example: *A Servant of Two Masters*, by Carlo Goldoni

Viewing Suggestions: *Carlo Goldoni*, the movie. http://www.goldonithemovie.com/

Definition: Genre popularized by touring troupes in Italy during the sixteenth and seventeenth centuries, characterized by use of masks and stock characters that improvised around set story lines.

Playing Style: Very broad, using physical slapstick and specific physicality to define the stock characters.

Dangers: Losing believability; not understanding the specifics of the style.

Melodrama

Example: *Sweeney Todd*, various authors

Definition: Good vs. evil style popular at the turn of the twentieth century that used exaggerated plots and characters to appeal to the emotions of the audience. Modern melodrama, which found genesis in Hollywood films like *Mildred Pierce*, is the basis for many films and TV shows.

Playing Style: Melodramatic; very broad, over-the-top style that flies in the face of most modern acting methodologies; modern melodrama is very focused on the depth of emotional life of the characters and situations, portraying strong emotional reactions. Because the style is broad, the connection to the inner truth must be deep and solid.

Dangers: Not going deep enough, creating caricatures instead of characters.

Documentary Theatre

Example: *The Laramie Project*, by Moises Kaufman and members of the Tectonic Theatre Project.

Viewing Suggestions: TV version of *The Laramie Project*.

Definition: Uses actual events as source material for script, usually using specific quotes to form dialogue.

Playing Style: Naturalistic with a slightly heightened intensity.

Dangers: Not doing enough research to capture the essence of the real people being portrayed; trying to create characterizations that are not specific, instead of recreating real people.

Solo Theatre

Example: *Fires in the Mirror*, by Anne Deveare-Smith, *A Search for Signs of Intelligent Life in the Universe*, by Lily Tomlin and Jane Wagner

Viewing Suggestions: The video version of *A Search for Signs of Intelligent Life in the Universe*, available on Amazon.com.

Definition: A play acted wholly by one person playing all of the parts.

Playing Style: Can be a subgenre, as in the case of *Fires in the Mirror*, which is documentary theatre. Define the genre of the actual material to ascertain the playing style.

Dangers: Lack of variety in characterizations.

Historical Drama

Example: *St. Joan*, by George Bernard Shaw

Viewing Suggestions: *The Lion in Winter* starring Katherine Hepburn and Peter O'Toole

Definition: A drama that examines a specific incident in history.

Playing Style: Determined by the period, usually played realistically.

Dangers: Not enough research leading to lack of realistic detail; favoring accuracy over storytelling.

Musical Comedy

Example: *Oklahoma*, by Rodgers and Hammerstein

Viewing Suggestions: *Hairspray* (film), *Dreamgirls* (film), original versions of *Oklahoma* (film), *Carousel* (film) and *The King and I* (film).

Definition: Theater that combines music, songs, spoken dialogue and sometimes dance in the telling of a comic or light-hearted story.

Playing Style: Depends on the specific piece, period, and musical style. Generally the style of the piece is inspired by the style of the music and book. Modern musicals are generally played realistically, but in musical comedy, there is a whole-heartedness that leads to broad characterization.

Dangers: Not being able to create truthful characters or realize a specific style; having inadequately skilled singers or dancers.

Musical Drama

Example: *Rent*, by Jonathan Larson; *Parade*, with book by Alfred Uhry and music and lyrics by Jason Robert Brown.

Viewing Suggestions: *Rent* (film), *Jesus Christ Superstar* (film); *Fiddler on the Roof* (film); *Cabaret* (film).

Definition: Drama that combines music, songs, spoken dialogue and sometimes dance in the telling of a serious or dramatic story.

Playing Style: Realistic.

Dangers: Not creating believable characters; not being able to create a world onstage in which singing makes sense.

Opera

Example: *Carmen*, music by Georges Bizet; libretto by Henri Meilhac and Ludovic Halévy.

Definition: Musical drama wherein all or most of the dialogue is sung.

Playing Style: Realistically, with a certain grandeur and intensity. Different operas require different playing styles. Subgenres include comic opera, singspiel (where some of the dialogue is spoken) and grand opera.

Dangers: Bad singers! Overacting, or no acting.

Improvisation

Example: Shows by Second City, Upright Citizens' Brigade

Viewing Suggestions: Saturday Night Live (more sketch comedy), Boys in the Hall, Second City Television.

Definition: Theatrical form in which all dialogue is improvised, or made up on the spot.

Playing Style: Improv has its own unique style, but it is generally realistic but a bit over the top, depending on the show and sketch.

Dangers Inability to be spontaneous enough or quick on your feet.

Appendix 2
Script Analysis Case Study—
The Glass Menagerie by
Tennessee Williams

This case study follows a formalist analysis format, grounded in the Aristotelian elements. This is a rigorous and detailed format that offers the director the deepest insights into the play. I have used Williams' *The Glass Menagerie* because it is a perfect play and universally known. If you have not read the play, I recommend doing so before reading this chapter.

Each section explains what to define, then analyzes that element of the play and most importantly, gives examples of how to use the information when directing a play. The analysis sections are what the director determines from reading the play. How the questions are answered defines the director's psychological and visual concepts. The analysis is not meant as an intellectual exercise, but a way for the director to understand and develop a point of view that leads to concept development.

I. Spectacle

1. **Define the play's genre**
   Psychological realism

2. **Given circumstances**
   i. Time

   What to define: Time of play's writing, time in which play is set, the time that passes during the play.

   Analysis: *The Glass Menagerie* is a memory play. The prologue and epilogue take place in 1945, and the main action takes place in 1937.

   How to use this information: Tom views his family through the refracted lens of memory, which distorts truth. The approach to directing the "memory" is influenced by the subjective way Tom remembers his past, eight years before. In addition, design choices are driven by the era in which the play is set and the atmosphere of Tom's memories.

ii. Place, or Physical Environment

What to define: Exactly where are they—immediate location, city, state, country? How does the physical environment influence the characters and contribute to the overall meaning of the play?

Analysis: The play is set in the Wingfields' tenement apartment in urban St. Louis, Missouri in the United States.

How to use this information: The apartment is critical to our understanding of the dynamic in Amanda's personality that enables her to express graciousness despite being stuck in a run-down tenement. This is vital to discussions with designers who need to capture in the setting Amanda's "hope" and strong desire to retain the glories of her past. If the curtain goes up and the audience feels gloom and doom then there is nowhere to go. The despair at the end of the play should be avoided for as long as possible. If the designers create an atmosphere of possibilities, the tragedy of the play will be enhanced when those possibilities are not realized.

iii. Society

What to define: Class structure, social groups that impact the play.

Analysis: Amanda came from the aristocratic class, but because of a bad marriage, sank into poverty of the struggling workers' class.

How to use this information: Disappointment is intrinsically tied to Amanda's resentment and shame. Tom is a factory worker, which in itself is not shameful, but given the dreams Amanda has for her children his job is a great disappointment. Tom and Laura are the victims of their mother's shame. Every time Amanda tells the story of her gentlemen callers, the past comes alive for her like a poison. She escapes through her memories. The only thing that gives Amanda comfort is to remember her glorious past as part of the aristocracy.

iv. Economics

What to define: The large-scale monetary systems and small-scale financial transactions that the characters engage in.

Analysis: Amanda is engaged in selling magazines as her primary source of income. She relies on Tom to bring home income from working in the shoe factory to make ends meet. She tries to prepare

Laura for a career as a secretary but fails miserably. They are at the mercy of financial insecurity and this creates an external bond that forces Tom to stay in the house. He knows that they cannot survive without him, which leads to his intense inner turmoil.

How to use this information: Much of the conflict of the play finds expression in the economics of the Wingfield household. The actors can use the knowledge to develop their characters. The extreme anxiety caused by financial ruin defines the emotional level of many of the scenes. Each character has their own special relationship to these economic realities. Tom must work in a job he hates to put food on his mother's table; Amanda relies on Tom for that sustenance; Laura is desperately ashamed because she is unable to contribute.

v. Intellect and Culture

What to define: Enlightenment and excellence of taste acquired by intellectual and aesthetic training.

Analysis: The refinement of Amanda's past is in direct contrast to her present circumstances. The only culture or entertainment is the dance hall across the street—a low class dive where crude people go to have fun—the music Laura plays on the Victrola, the magazine stories sold by Amanda, and the movies Tom goes to see.

How to use this information: The fact that Amanda can so clearly recall with all her senses the refinement of the past makes her present all the more disappointing. Amanda's children escape into movies, glass animals, and music, while her only escape is into the memories of her refined and hopeful past. If the actors understand why they make the choices they do, they can discover a great deal about the nature of their characters and make potent choices in performance.

vi. Spirituality

What to define: the religious or spiritual aspects of the play

Analysis: There is no strong religious aspect to the play. Amanda does refer to her client being a "Christian martyr", but that is more a tactic meant to flatter her client than it is a true invocation of her religious beliefs.

How to use this information: Amanda invokes religion to manipulate her client, but not because she has a deep-rooted belief in Christianity as a way of life. This tells us a great deal about Amanda. She is a woman who is clever and does whatever is necessary to get what she wants.

She uses guilt and flattery to exert control over others, particularly her children.

vii. The World of the Play

What to define: The cumulative effect of all the given circumstances plus social standards they embody creates the world of the play. This also includes the point of view of the characters and how they exist within that world, the atmosphere, and what is normal in their world.

Analysis: *The Glass Menagerie* is a memory play. The world of the play is heavily influenced by the way Tom recalls this difficult period in his life. Time has a way of shading reality, giving it texture tied to the subjective viewpoint of the one remembering. Tom's memories of his home in St. Louis are romanticized. Williams' creation of the character of Laura was inspired by his sister Rose, who suffered years of mental illness in an asylum. Williams felt responsible and never resolved his feelings for her. The world of *The Glass Menagerie* is a world where worn furniture, cheap wallpaper, and decaying identities can be beautifully tragic. In Amanda's world, as remembered by Tom, there is hope. In this world of hope, everyone that inhabits this apartment is longing for something; they are all seeking to escape their reality to find the promise of their future or to regain grandeur from the past.

This is a world oppressed by what is missing or just out of reach; the father who left, for example. His portrait hangs on the wall as a constant reminder of his abandonment. The lights from the dance hall, where people go for a night out, flicker through the apartment, reminding us of what lies just outside the door.

Love has been warped by disappointment. Their world is a pressure cooker of rage, a prison from which the inmates yearn for escape, but to which they are hopelessly bound. Finally, there is shame. Amanda's shame that she married the wrong man and can't adequately support her family; Laura's shame at her limp and her lack of prospects; Tom's shame at his own inability to leave his world behind, and the regret that is his constant companion these eight years later.

How to use this information: Talk to the designers about creating a sense of charm and gentility in a weary, worn apartment; of finding hope in the despair. Talk about the atmosphere of hope to the actors. The intense desire for things to get better will create conflict. Remember, tragedy is intensified if the possibility of success exists.

II. Character

3. Identify and define the characters

i. Protagonist

Tom. He drives the action of the play and it is told from his point of view.

ii. Antagonist

Amanda. She is the obstacle keeping Tom from leaving. Her determination to see Laura taken care of makes Tom feel guilty and unable to leave. She drives Laura to the dinner and makes sure they are left alone.

iii. Other Characters

Laura and Jim. Laura is unable to function in the world so Amanda makes it her mission to find a man to take care of her. Jim is a friend of Tom's and possibly the man to take care of Laura, but Jim is engaged to be married.

iv. Relationships and Conflicts

Tom vs. Amanda: Tom is Amanda's son

Amanda vs. Laura: Laura is Amanda's daughter

Amanda vs. fear for her children's survival

Laura vs. her past/low self-image

Laura had a crush on Jim in high school

Tom and Jim are co-workers

Laura and Jim were classmates in high school

4. Character analysis

Example: Amanda

i. Given Circumstances

She lives in a rundown apartment in St. Louis with her two children. Her husband left years before and never writes. She sells magazines to eke out a living. She is in her late forties to early fifties, petite, shows the signs of once being attractive. She has a meager income and must scrape to get by. She is partially supported by Tom's income. She once was a southern belle from a good family in the upper class, but has fallen on very hard times. She has nothing.

ii. Objective

To protect her children

iii. Qualities

She is manipulative and clever, unrelenting in her desires to protect her children. She lives in the past, revels in former glory as a means of coping with the reality of her disappointing life.

iv. Conflicts

Amanda vs. Laura; she is at odds with Laura's inability to make a life for herself and her unwillingness to commit to Amanda's ideas of what would be good for her.

Amanda vs. Tom; Tom wants to leave but Amanda sees Tom as her only salvation in saving Laura. Amanda also wants desperately to protect Tom from what she sees as his greatest enemy—the legacy of his deadbeat father and the Wingfield men's desire to run away.

Amanda vs. her past: Amanda's dreams of being a well-heeled, well-taken-care-of member of the landed gentry never materialized. Instead, she married the wrong man and lost her hope. She lives in the past to cope with the present.

v. Conflict of Objectives; Obstacles for Amanda

Laura's fear

Tom's wanderlust

Her husband's abandonment

Their poverty

Jim's engagement

vi. Willpower

Amanda is persistent, unflagging in her energy and determination; her will is intense!

vii. Values

What does she value? Protecting her children, working hard, being reliable, telling the truth, wealth, beauty, refinement.

What does she dislike? Not valuing hard work, shirking responsibilities to your family, running away, poverty, laziness, aimlessness, ugliness.

viii. Personality

She is flighty, high-energy, and controlling. She likes to dominate every situation she is in and loves to be the center of attention. Her manner is genteel, in an old-southern-belle kind of way, but inside she is tough, hard and unforgiving. She fears growing old; she fears that her children will endure the same life of disappointments that she has.

ix. Appearance

Strong yet frail, 40–50 years old, faded beauty, easy elegance, always well-put together but of another era.

x. Thoughts and Feelings

Amanda believes the world is against her; she is resentful towards her husband, disappointed in Tom, concerned about Laura. She dislikes her magazine job and hates the women she calls on the phone. She thinks of herself only in terms of the success of her children. She is desperately disappointed at the way her life turned out. She needs hope, she needs glory.

xi. Behavior

She is constantly plotting ways to achieve success for her children. She is cordial on the phone because selling subscriptions is more important than her pride. She is always trying to control her children, demanding them to live up to her standards, but operates out of a desire to protect them. Living in the past is her way of finding some glory in her dismal life. She is like a desperate bird. When Jim is invited to the house, she goes to extremes to snare Jim for Laura. She wears her best dress not only to look good for Jim and to charm him, but because she wants him to think highly of Laura's family. She will literally do anything to save her children.

xii. Complexity

Amanda is aware of the desperate situation she is in, but unaware of how her behavior affects her children; she is unaware that she is bizarre in any way. She is driven by her fear and worry, and that, along with her past history of being a flirt and a coquette, causes her to behave as she does.

III. Plot

5. Action Points

Create an outline of action points; define the internal and external action in each plot point, the given circumstances of each scene. For the sake of brevity only the first two scenes will be outlined below.

Scene One

i. Given Circumstances

The Wingfield's apartment in St. Louis, and the fire escape, 1945, then 1937.

ii. External Actions

- Tom begins on the fire escape, speaking in 1945.
- He explains that this is a memory play.
- He speaks of society and historical context.
- He describes his role and the role of the other characters in the play and speaks of his father, who left the family years before.
- He explains the father's absence
- He enters the apartment and joins Laura, his sister, and Amanda, his mother, at the dinner table.
- Amanda insists that Tom chew his food
- Amanda does not allow Laura to rise from the table because she must keep herself "fresh" for gentlemen callers
- Amanda scolds Tom for not chewing his food properly
- Amanda tells her story of the seventeen gentlemen callers that pursued her on Blue Mountain when she was young.
- Laura urges Tom to listen, and he does, asking questions that he surely asks her every time she recounts these tales.
- Amanda continues with her story, recounting different men and the one that died carrying her picture.
- Laura mentions that she has had no men calling on her because she is not popular like her mother.
- Laura states that her mother is worried that she will end up an old maid.

iii. Internal Actions

- Tom directly addresses the audience and tells us that this is a memory play.
- He makes clear that the story is told from his point of view.
- The characters behave as Tom recalls them behaving, and not as they necessarily behaved. This is critical information for all of the

actors. The way Tom interacts with the others is far more emotional than they way he recalls them in the opening monologue. The longing and sadness under the surface rises and is expressed throughout Tom's interaction with the family.

- Tom resents his father's leaving and is perhaps jealous that he was able to escape
- There is a sense of longing and sadness inside Tom
- Tom moves from present day to memory, and becomes part of the story he is remembering
- Tom obediently joins Amanda and Laura at the table
- Amanda is frustrated with Tom's table manners and urges him to chew his food
- Tom is agonized by his mother's controlling behavior
- Amanda relives her former glory as she recounts stories of the past.
- Tom wants to run, but Laura insists that he listen. Laura wants to respect her mother.
- Laura explains that she doesn't have gentlemen callers because she is not as beautiful as Amanda once was, which makes Tom groan.
- Laura tries to calm Tom by rationalizing Amanda's behaviors and fears for Laura
- There is an atmosphere of tension, of entrapment, that is palpable in this scene

Scene Two

iv. Given Circumstances

The Wingfields' apartment, a few days later.

v. External Actions

- Laura is polishing her menagerie animals as Amanda enters.
- Laura pretends to be studying a picture of a typewriter keyboard when she hears Amanda. Amanda takes the picture and tears it up, and recounts the story of her visit to Rubicam's business school.
- Amanda explains that she knows Laura only attended for a few days and then quit, lying to her mother every day since.
- Laura admits to leaving school and spending her days walking on the streets, going to the zoo and the occasional movie.
- Amanda insists that Laura's only hope is to marry and asks Laura if there has ever been someone she has liked.
- Laura tells Amanda about Jim, who mistook the word "pleurosis"

for blue roses when Laura explained to him why she'd been out of school for several weeks.

- Laura explains that Jim is probably married already because he was promised in the final weeks of school.
- Amanda reassures Laura that she will find the right man but Laura insists, because she is crippled, that she has no chance of finding a man.
- Amanda reprimands her for using the word "crippled," and insists that she "cultivate charm."

vi. Internal Actions

- Laura is taking care of her animals and at peace.
- Her means of coping, the animals, the music, are exposed.
- In a life with little joy, she finds her solace in glass animals that, like her, are fragile and desperately in need of care and love.
- Into that quiet moment comes an enraged Amanda, full of the anger of someone who has unselfishly given of herself, and has been deceived.
- Amanda feels betrayed by Laura, and she is hurt.
- Her actions are driven, however, not by these feelings of anger, but instead, by the desperation driven by her inability to take care of and protect her daughter. (If an actress only sees the anger, and ignores the love which Tom clearly recalls, then the Amanda becomes two-dimensional.)
- Amanda sees a bleak future for Laura and being a woman who has barely survived her own fate, she is driven to insure that Laura will know some degree of happiness and protection.
- Amanda is aware that she won't live forever, and without her, she doubts Laura can survive.
- This is what drives her anger, and in the final moments of the scene, her reassuring behavior and warmth.

6. **Backstory**

i. Outline the Backstory

- *Amanda's husband and Tom and Laura's father was a telephone salesman that "fell in love with long distance" and has been gone for sixteen years.*

  Director's Notes: Talk to the actress playing Amanda about why she keeps her husband's photo in the living room. The discussion will clarify her feelings about her husband and her resentment towards him. Talk to the actors playing Tom and Amanda about seeing their father's picture day in and day out and how they feel about their mother's insistence on leaving it there as a constant and painful reminder. Talk to designers about how they will illuminate that photo—what presence will it have on the set?

- *Amanda comes from aristocracy in the south and was a very lovely and popular young woman who had long lines of gentlemen callers. She married the wrong man.*

  Director's Notes: In order to emotionally capture her longing, the actress must understand Amanda's past. If she can imagine "what might have been", then she can play the pain of "what is."

- *Tom and Laura went to high school with Jim, who was a football star and star of the high school musical which Laura saw several times. Laura had a crush on Jim in high school.*

  Director's Notes: This gives emotional and psychological impact to Jim's impending visit. Laura is scared to death to see the object of her affection once again and wants to run and hide. She is ultimately able to connect with Jim and gain confidence from their experience together after dinner, giving her a hope that Amanda doesn't share as Jim exits.

- *Jim was a popular and talented singer, debater, class leader and athlete in high school. There was an article written about him in the yearbook.*

  Director's Notes: He was a star who has fallen on tough times. Like so many high school stars, Jim loses his status, but not his charisma. He reinvents himself, and unlike the Wingfield children, is fearless in his determination to succeed.

- *Laura dropped out of high school after she did not pass her final exams.*

  Director's Notes: Unlike Jim, Laura is unable to reinvent herself. She is stuck.

- *Laura was ill with pleurosis in high school and Jim, who was in choir with her, called her "blue roses" because he misunderstood her explanation of her illness.*

  Director's Notes: The embarrassment Laura feels is key to the scene with Jim and her performance in act two. By understanding their former relationship the actors can get very specific with subtext in their scene.

- *Laura wore a brace on her leg during high school and is crippled with one leg longer than the other. Walking in front of the choir to her place caused her great embarrassment.*

Director's Notes: This fact is very important because Laura and Jim remember those moments so differently.

- *Amanda worked in a department store to save money to pay for Laura to go to Rubicam's Business College.*

  Director's Notes: Amanda sacrificed again and again for her daughter, but Laura still dropped out. This intensifies Amanda's anger at Laura, and Laura's sense of shame.

- *Tom did not pay the electric bill. He used the money to join the Merchant Seamen.*

  Director's Notes: Clarifies Tom's priorities.

- *Laura has been collecting glass animals for thirteen years.*

  Director's Notes: If the actress understands the motivation to play with the animals, she can make the relationship with the animals believable and heartbreaking.

- *Jim met Betty, his girlfriend and fiancée, on a boat.*

  Director's Notes: The existence of the fiancée, the fact they met on a boat (a means of transportation and therefore escape, romantic atmosphere) is the painful revelation that might have shattered Laura's world if her experience with Jim hadn't awakened in her a newfound strength of spirit.

ii. How the Backstory Information is Revealed

Each backstory element is revealed in a particular way. In some cases, the backstory of one character is questioned by the others. Tom's questioning of Amanda's stories throws into doubt the veracity of her claims. Jim tells Laura about Betty only after their romantic interlude; a tragic turn after a hopeful connection. By identifying the way each backstory point is delivered, the director can intensify the drama.

7. Dramatic action structure

Identify the major moments in the play.

i. Inciting Action

When Amanda confronts Laura in scene two, her fears for Laura's future, Laura's impossible retreat from life, and Amanda's desire to find Laura a husband are revealed. It is these three aspects that lead to the invitation to Jim and the ultimate disappointment Laura and Amanda suffer at the play's end.

ii. Main Climax

Tom's climax is the argument with Amanda at the end of scene three. Tom breaks one of Laura's animals, which is a metaphor for breaking from his mother's grip.

The climax of the play is when Jim crashes into the glass animals and breaks the unicorn. It is not only a moment of high intensity at the peak of Laura's hopes, but it dashes any chance that Jim will be the one to rescue Laura and give her the life that Amanda wants for her daughter.

iii. Falling Action

There are two possible falling actions. The first is when Laura hands Jim the unicorn, which is symbolic of her acceptance that she will never find love, or in Tom's final monologue, when he tells us he left shortly after the dinner, and reveals that although he left them he has never been able to let go of the love and concern he felt for Laura. He never truly escaped.

8. **Identify the major and minor conflicts and obstacles**

There are two ways to look at the main conflict: Tom vs. Amanda or the Wingfields vs. despondency. Directing a play has as much to do with creating the ebb and flow, the rhythm, as it does with directing actors. In any great production, there is a sense of movement, shifts between relaxation and tension. These shifts are what keep the play interesting and compelling. In order to achieve this, we need landmarks to work towards.

The director defines the major conflict as a source of inspiration. If we choose Tom vs. Amanda, that information feeds us as we direct the actors in their scenes. We zoom in on Tom and Amanda's personal battles as the center focus of the play.

If we choose the Wingfields vs. despondency, then the battle between each character and their hopeless fight to overcome their bleak circumstances becomes our central focus. Each decision would lead to a very different production.

IV. Ideas

9. **Identify ideas in the play.**

i. Ideas in the Words

- **Title**: The Glass Menagerie: the title suggests a fragile world in which characters, like glass, are transparent and break easily.

- **Allusions**: The movie theatre and the dance hall as places of escape, Amanda's husband and Tom and Laura's father who abandoned them, Amanda's home where she received her gentlemen callers and enjoyed the life she was destined to lose, the factory where Tom works, the magazine that Amanda sells, the school that Laura dropped out of.
- **Imagery**: Examples are found everywhere as the characters use images freely to express themselves.
- **Symbolism**: The fire escape, literally, a place to get out of the fire that is the hell of their life in the small apartment; the dance hall as a lure for something better; the glass animals, a symbol of Laura's fragility, the picture of the father, and Laura's music.
- **Prologues and Epilogues**: Tom introduces and concludes the piece with monologues told eight years prior to this action. This contextualizes time and place and introduces the idea of the memory.

ii. Ideas in the Plot

- **Conflict**: The central conflict of ideas exists in the struggle within Amanda to accept her present given the hopes and expectations of her past.
  How to use: Talk to the designers about creating the dreariness and the prison-like atmosphere of the apartment, but don't ignore the idea of hope! Amanda would splash hopefulness everywhere, in color choices and in the accessories. Her past can be a constant presence in their dreary present, through costuming choices, and through the emotional place the actress goes when recounting the past.
- **The Main Idea**: "When aspirations exist in a world where reality cannot be confronted and accepted, realizing those aspirations becomes impossible."
  How to use: Bring this statement to the first design meeting, share it with the actors, and refer back to it constantly. Let everyone know how you view the play and the direction you wish to go with the play. The main idea is a seed that can grow inside the actors as they approach their roles and inspires the designers.
- **Climax**: When the unicorn is shattered, so is Laura and Amanda's hope for a better life. The animals, Amanda's past and Tom's movies are the ways they escape reality. Their insistence on avoiding reality dooms them from the start. The moment when hope

reaches a crescendo is "shattered" by the destruction of the uni-corn and Jim's revealing his engagement.

How to use: Talk to the actors in the scene about the impact on the crashing unicorn, what it means to them personally. Direct the scene to crescendo and then explode. Make sure that the broken unicorn has different meanings to Jim and Laura and allow their own points of view to be expressed.

- **The Super-Objective**: "To be free:" Tom wishes to be free of the burden of his family, Laura from the burden of her fear and in-security, and Amanda from the burden of insuring her children's survival, and of her disappointment.

  How to use: Every decision you make should go back to the main idea and super-objective. Explore how each character contributes to the super-objective. What does freedom mean for each char-acter, how badly to they want it, what are the obstacles to their freedom, do they ultimately achieve the freedom and at what cost? In every moment, how can the idea of freedom tie into the characters' objectives?

- **Action Summary**: Tom Wingfield remembers the final days spent with his family. Amanda Wingfield, desperate to insure the welfare of her children, convinces Tom to invite a gentleman caller to come to dinner in the hopes that he will marry Laura and save her. He is engaged and, although they have a powerful conversation that forever changes Laura, he leaves and Amanda is devastated.

  How to use: Keep the storytelling clear and moving forward. A director tells the story in a clear and compelling way.

10. Themes

- **Themes**: The inability to accept reality, the power of memory to alter the truth, escape, love, survival, abandonment, disappointment.

  How to use: If we know what the recurring motifs are, then we can emphasize those moments of dramatic action where themes are ex-pressed. Share the themes with everyone. Actors, designers and the director will personally relate to different themes. Find ways to ex-press the themes that Williams has presented in all aspects of the production.

V. Rhythm

11. Atmosphere

- **Pace:** From scene to scene the pace varies greatly. Characters tend to have their own pace. For example, Laura's pace is slower than that of Tom while Amanda's is faster than everyone.

  How to use: For each scene, determine the pace by looking at the plot of the scene, how much information is revealed, the length of lines, and your general intuition about the "feel" of the scene.

  In scene five, the scene begins at a fast pace, with Amanda nagging Tom. He retreats to the fire escape, his place of escape, and the pace slows as he recalls the neighborhood where he grew up, and the dance hall. He talks about how the kids that frequented the dance hall had no adventure in their lives, but he hints at adventure to come with the advent of the war. This is also a foreshadowing of the battle just moments away between Tom and Amanda. In an uncharacteristically warm moment, Tom and Amanda share their dreams on the fire escape, ended by Tom's announcement that Jim will come to dinner.

  With the introduction of this exciting information, the pace quickens. Amanda is suddenly overwhelmed by the impending dinner. From there, the pace builds until Tom leaves, followed by another relaxation in the pace as Laura and Amanda make wishes on the moon.

  As the director, it is your job to literally direct the pace.

  You set the pace by talking to the actors about the scene and what you want in terms of pace. You give them the reasons for the stakes going up, and direct the highs and lows.

- **Tempo:** This is something you have to pay attention to but not something you can affect, because it is drawn from the playwright, who dictates tempo.

  How to use: When dialogue is crowded with information, tempo needs to be slower. You want to tell the story in a clear and understandable way. When there isn't much in the way of information, the tempo can go faster. In *The Glass Menagerie* the tempo varies, but is somewhat consistent. Ideas and information are delivered evenly throughout, with the variations being emotional instead of informational. The intensely emotional outburst by Tom has a rapid tempo, but the scene between Jim and Laura has a leisurely tempo that increases in pace as we get closer to the shattering of the unicorn.

- **Rhythm**: There is an ever-changing rhythm in the play. Each scene has its own ups and downs. The changing rhythm in the play gives us clues as to how to direct each scene.
  How to use: Look at the rising and falling of the intensity in each beat. As things heat up, move the pace along. But in the quieter moments, allow the actors a more relaxed pace. This will create the play's internal rhythms.

  In the example of scene five, you can look at all of the beats on the fire escape. How does the tension change, what is the rhythm inherent in the movement towards the moment when Tom tells Amanda about Jim? Once told, in Amanda's ensuing beats there are moments when pure joy is contrasted with moments of terror at the thought of not being ready and all that needs to be done.

  Each of those beats should be directed to give this section the right rhythm. It would be very boring to play all the moments as pure joy, or pure terror, but if you can find the constant back and forth between those two, then you will find a rhythm that creates dramatic tension and gives the actors very specific places to go emotionally.

- **Mood/Atmosphere**: There is a distinct atmosphere of hopefulness embedded in an external atmosphere of faded possibility and disappointment. Don't confuse what Williams sees as dreary furnishings and location for hopelessness. It is the desire to see hope in hopelessness that drives Amanda to capture whatever essence of beauty and grace that she can in her environment.
  How to use: Tell your designers, **no gloom**! Yes, of course, the furnishings and wallpaper should be worn, but Amanda does what she can to brighten things up. When the curtain rises, the audience should sense the hope in the air, not the desperation; let that be revealed through the performances of the actors. The actors should fight for what they desire instead of relenting. They never stop fighting.

- **Polarity**: In *The Glass Menagerie* the play begins on a note of hope and ends on the note of despair.

- **Style**: Defined as psychological realism, or memory play, the style of performance is realistic, within the nonrealistic embellishments of memory. Playing style can be slightly broader, and there should be a clear difference between Tom recounting his past on the balcony, and the way he behaves when he is in 1937.

VI. Dialogue

12. Analyze the dialogue

- **Style of the Dialogue**: *Realistic*. Sometimes Amanda sounds formal, and Jim certainly uses formal language at the dinner table. The language tends to shy away from the colloquial and naturalistic.
- **Dialect**: Amanda speaks with a soft southern dialect. This connects her to a genteel upbringing in the gracious south. The actress can adopt a dialect that drips with the graciousness of her upbringing and that can exaggerate, for the fractured memory's sake, the tone of her past.
- **Grammar and Structure**: Characters use lyrical, colorful language full of images. For example, Tom says of his father, "He was a telephone man who fell in love with long distance; he gave up his job with the telephone company and skipped the light fantastic out of town." There is an abundance of this kind of language in the characters. Because this is a memory play, this lyrical language and use of images feels natural to characters who are bringing alive a memory.
- **Qualities of Dialogue**: Amanda says of Bates Cutrere "[He] was one of my bright and particular beaux!" There is a heightened, dreamlike quality to Amanda's use of words. When Tom expresses his anger in scene three, he uses words like "celotex" and "fluorescent" to express the coldness of the factory. As the monologue continues, the words get harsher; dynamite, blow up, and then he compares his mother to a witch on her broomstick, using "Blue Mountain" and "seventeen gentlemen callers" as a knife to wound his mother and her distorted memories.

The way characters express themselves is a key to their inner life. Amanda's descriptions and phrasing is the key to understanding the fragile nature of her character and the distorted glaze of memory through which she recalls her past. Tom's use of memories particularly dear to his mother, in order to wound her deeply, illustrates the depth of his frustration and contempt for all that she stands for.

Make sure the actors understand the qualities of the dialogue so they can find deep insight into what drives them and how they are defined through use of language.

i. Subtext

In *The Glass Menagerie*, the subtext is not often concealed. In Act 1, scene 1, Tom is very forward, expressing exactly what is on his mind in his dialogue around the dinner table as Amanda nags him. The degree to which a character either expresses or conceals subtext is a direct key to that character's nature.

If a character is truthful and direct, then the actor needs to find that quality. But if untruthful, then the actor has to know exactly what the character is really thinking, then behave to cover those thoughts and make choices as to how to be expressive.

Appendix 3
Sample Rehearsal
Schedules

Rehearsal Schedule

Sample Schedule: College theatre musical

Using character names instead of actor names
Conflicts in italics are only for the working version and should be deleted when given to the company
Note that rehearsal locations are given

Song names are in italics
Cast names are in bold, Rehearsal type in bold
Stop times are not in italics (too confusing)

Tuesday, January 6, Crites Studio		
5:30pm	Full Cast Meeting, Designers presentation and introductions	*First musical rehearsals: note*
6:30	**Music Rehearsal, Full Cast**	*each musical number and who*
	June is Bustin' Out All Over	*is called for each. By scheduling*
	Act One Finale	*Mr. Snow at the end, it allows*
	A Real Nice Clambake	*everyone else to leave early.*
	Finale Ultimo (Jigger excused)	*Create a schedule that maximiz-*
9pm	*Geraniums in the Winder*: **Mr. Snow**	*es use of each actor and gives*
9:30pm	Stop	*them time off when they are not*
		needed.

Wednesday, January 7, Crites Studio		
5:30pm	**Music Rehearsals continue**	*Note what kind of rehearsals*
	Mister Snow Reprise: **Girls only**	*will occur and then a break-*
6pm	*Mister Snow Reprise*: **Girls and Mr. Snow**	*down of time and cast called.*
6:30	*What's the Use of Wonderin'*: **Julie, Girls**	*Notice that girls are excused at*
7:30	*When the Children Are Asleep*: **Carrie, Mr. Snow**	*7:30, then Mr. Snow, and then*
8:15	*Mister Snow*: **Carrie, Julie**	*Carrie. Organize for efficiency*
9pm	*If I Loved You*: **Julie**	*to respect actors' time.*
9:30pm	Stop	

January 8th, all other musical numbers are rehearsed

Friday, January 9, Crites Studio		
Conflicts: Billy can't arrive until 12:45pm		*Note conflicts for reference.*
12pm	**Music Rehearsals Continue**	*Include reviews. Once all music*
	Music: *You'll Never Walk Alone*: **Julie, Nettie**	*is learned, schedule a full read*
12:45	Music: *If I Loved You Reprise, Soliloquy*: **Billy**	*and sing-through of the entire*
1-2pm	Cast Photos by appointment	*show. Leave enough time to get*
2pm	Music: *Solos and Duets review*: **All principals**	*through the entire piece with a*
3pm	Music: *Read and sing through*: **Full Company**	*break. When all principals are*
5:30pm	Stop	*called, you don't need to list*
		individual characters.

Figure A3.1
A guide to the creation of a rehearsal schedule using a grid. The guide illustrates major components of the schedule and how to organize.

Saturday, January 10, Crites Studio & Dance Studio

Dance Studio		*After read-through, staging and dance rehearsals begin. Note where rehearsals occur in title and in groupings below. Always try to schedule dance and staging rehearsals concurrently using different cast members, to maximize rehearsal time. This is contingent on having two spaces. Note kind of rehearsal, content and who is called. Be specific about section of scene to be staged.*
1-5pm	Dance Staging: *Ballet*, **Principal Dancers**	
Crites Studio		
12pm	Staging: *Act One, Scene Two (opening dialogue)* **Carrie, Julie, Billy, Mrs. Mullins**	
1:30pm	Staging: *Continue Act One, Scene Two (Mr. Snow song)* **Carrie, Julie**	
3pm	Staging: *Continue Act One, Scene Two (Billy returns)* **Billy, Carrie, Julie**	
3:30pm	Staging: *Continue Act One, Scene Two (After Carrie's Exit To end of scene)* **Billy, Julie, Policeman, Mr. Bascombe**	
5:30	Stop	

Monday, January 12, Arnold Hall, Dance Studio
Staging and dance night example

Dance studio		
6-9pm	Dance Staging: *Blow High, Blow Low*, **All Men except Billy**	
Arnold Hall		
5:30pm	Staging: *Act One, Scene three at Julie's entrance* **Girls, Carrie, Nettie, Julie, Mr. Snow**	
6:30pm	Staging: *Continue Act One, Scene three* **Carrie, Mr. Snow, Julie**	
7pm	Staging: *Continue Act One, Scene three, When the Children Are Asleep* **Carrie, Mr. Snow**	
8pm	Review: *Mr. Snow and If I Loved You* **Carrie, Julie, Billy only**	
9pm	Stop	

Wednesday, January 14, Arnold Hall and Dance Studio

Conflicts: Julie and ladies, can't arrive until 6pm		
Dance Studio		*First review should be scheduled no later than 3 days into staging. Consistent review time will assure well-prepared actors. In this example, there is a dance review while principals review scenes, and then everyone comes together to stage new content and run everything staged to date.*
5:30pm	Dance Review: *Blow High, Blow Low*, **Men**	
Arnold Hall		
Review all to date		
6pm	*Act One, Scene Two* **Billy, Julie, Carrie, Policeman, Bascombe, Mullins**	
6:45	Staging: *Finale, Act One* **Full cast**	
Then . .	Review: *Run all scenes Act one* **Full Cast**	
9:30pm	Stop	
	Staging continues, with frequent reviews scheduled	

Tuesday, January 20, Arnold Hall		
5:30pm	*REVIEW Act One*, **Full Company**	*Once the entire act is staged and choreographed, schedule a full run with all elements. Leave plenty of time for stumbling, re-do's and notes after.*
9:30pm	Stop	

Wednesday, January 21, Crites Studio		
5:30-9	Staging *Act One Review*, **Principals ONLY!!** **Chorus night off**	*Immediately following the full cast review, schedule a principals-only scene work review, giving the chorus the night off. This allows for focused work with principals without the distraction of the chorus.*

Thursday, January 22, Arnold Hall		
5:30	Music Review *Act Two*	*Immediate following the principal-only review, bring everyone back for a final run of the act leaving time at the end for review of details as needed. Always schedule a music review when starting a new act.*
then . .	Run *Act one*, **Full Cast**	
then	Review *Act One stuff as needed*, **Full Cast**	
9:30	Stop	

Repeat same schedule strategy for Act Two. Schedule a review of Act One during the Act Two staging period.

Monday-Friday, February 2-5, Arnold Hall		*(repeat for the next several rehearsals)*
5pm	Dance and staging: **TBA Cast**	*After Act Two has been staged and reviewed, begin run-throughs with TBA work time before each run for dance, scene work and musical rehearsals.*
7pm	Run through: **Full Cast**	
9:30pm	Notes	
10pm	Stop	

Friday, February 6, Arnold Hall		
5pm	Final clean up day: **Full Cast TBA**	*Schedule long rehearsal with TBA cast to address all remaining issues in a long work-through rehearsal.*
10pm	Stop	

Saturday, February 7, Arnold Hall		
12pm	Final run in rehearsal hall: **Full Cast**	*Before moving on stage, schedule a final run with no stops, followed by notes. Leave time after to work notes as needed.*
3pm	Notes, work as needed	
5pm	Stop	

Monday, February 9, Onstage		
5pm	Dance spacing rehearsal onstage: **full company**	*Musical spacing rehearsals require extra time for dances. If you can, schedule an entire night just to space the dances. If it is not a heavy dance show, then do dance and scene staging concurrently.*
11pm	Stop	

Tuesday, February 10, Onstage		
5pm	Spacing rehearsal: **full company**	*Second night on stage used for a work through of the show, spacing scenes and running the dances spaced previously.*
11pm	Stop	

Wednesday, February 11		
12-4pm	Orchestra rehearsal	*The tech process and scheduling is the same for a non-musical. Leave plenty of time. Incorporate orchestra rehearsals in schedule and make sure Musical Director is not needed at another rehearsal at the same time.*
5pm	Actor call for tech (bring a book and wear dark clothes)	
12am	Stop	

Saturday, February 14th		
Happy Valentine's Day		
10am	Sound check	*Little notes like "Happy Valentine's Day" helps soften the blow when rehearsals fall on holidays. The sitzprobe is the first rehearsal with orchestra. If there is amplified sound, schedule sound check first. Leave time to tech costume changes. In this example, the two acts are broken up by a dinner break. Leave ½ hour to get into new costume. Limit time between morning start and evening stop to 12 hours.*
10:30	Call for Sitzprobe	
1pm	Lunch break	
2pm	Call for first dress, get into first costume or first fast change costume	
2:30	Rehearsal fast changes	
3:30	Begin dress, Act One (with orchestra)	
6pm	Dinner Break	
7pm	Call for Act two, get into first Act Two costume	
7:30	Dress rehearsal, Act Two (with orchestra)	
10pm	Stop	

Sunday, February 15		
11:30	Call for Dress Rehearsal, add make-up and hair	*Note when orchestra will accompany. Note additions of make-up and hair, and always leave time for notes. The use of "then" indicates that notes will happen for as long as needed followed by the dinner break when notes are finished, with a guarantee of going no longer than one hour. Incorporate sound check calls.*
12:30	All actors wearing mics called for sound check	
1pm	Dress Rehearsal (with orchestra)	
4pm	Notes	
5pm	Dinner Break	
6pm	Call for Final Dress	
7pm	Sound check	
7:15	Final Dress (with orchestra)	
9:45	Notes	
11pm	Stop	
Monday, February 16 OPENING NIGHT!		
5pm	Actor call TBA for scene work	*Schedule a TBA for last minute clean up. Indicate time house opens and sound check.*
6pm	Call for Opening Night	
7:30	Sound Check	
7:40	House opens	
8pm	Opening night performance begins	

Rehearsal Schedule

Sample Schedule: Community theatre non-musical

Conflicts in italics are only for the working version and should be deleted when given to the company
Cast names are in bold, *Stop times are in italics*

Wednesday, October 1		
5:30	Introductions of Company: **Full Company Called**	List all calls, determine the time for each. Start from the beginning and move call by call to the end, assigning times and durations to each.
5:45	Designer presentations: Costume and Set designs	
6:15	Introduction of rehearsal rules by stage manager	
6:30	Read through	
9pm	Discussion	
10pm	*Stop*	

Table Read Period

Thursday, October 2		
Conflicts: John Paul Gattis		Note conflicts and availability issues, then schedule around them if you can. For table period, limit work to table readings of acts or scenes, note actors called in bold so their names are easy to see.
Availability limitations: Sally Garrett, can't arrive until 7pm		
	Miguel Sims, available until 8pm	
5:30	Read Act One/discuss - **All Act One Actors**	
7:30	Read Act Two/discuss - **All Act Two Actors** - *Sims leaves 8pm*	
10:00pm	*Stop*	

Friday, October 3	
Conflicts: None	
5:30	Directed read-through, Act One, Scenes 1-3: **Gattis, Sims, Garrett, Johnson, Maxwell**
7pm	Directed read-through, Act One, Scenes 4-6: **Gattis, Sims, Garrett, Marshall, Jones**
8:30	Directed read-through, Act One, Scenes 7-8: **Gattis, Jones**
10pm	*Stop*

Saturday, October 4	
Conflicts: None	
Availability limitations: Garrett leaves 2pm	
12-2	Read through Act One: **Gattis, Sims, Garrett, Johnson, Maxwell, Marshall, Jones**
2pm	Directed read-through, Act Two, Scenes 1-2: **Marshall, Jones**
4pm	Directed read-through, Act Two, Scenes 3-4: **Gattis, Jones, Johnson, Sims**
6pm	*Stop*

Rehearsal schedule continues with staging calls until work-through period begins

Tuesday, October 7		
Conflicts: Jim Marshall (out all night)		For each call, note type of rehearsal (staging), then content (Scene 1), then cast called in **bold**. Since Jim
6pm	Staging, Act One, Scene 1: **Gattis, Sims, Garrett**	
7:30	Staging, Act One, Scene 2: **Gattis, Simes, Jones**	

Figure A3.2
A guide to the creation of a rehearsal schedule using a grid. The guide illustrates major component of the schedule and how to organize.

Wednesday, October 8

Conflicts: none		Include many reviews. Once a chunk is staged, review it. Actors forget. Keep it fresh through repetition. This rehearsal starts with review and continues with new staging.
6pm	Review Scene: Act One, Scene One: **Gattis, Sims, Garrett**	
6:30	Review Scene: Act One, Scene Two: **Gattis, Sims, Jones**	
7pm	Review Scene: Act One, Scene Three: **Jones, Maxwell**	
7:30	Staging, Act one, Scenes 4-6: **Gattis, Sims, Garret, Marshall**	
10pm	Stop	

Work-through and stumble through reviews

Friday, October 10

Conflicts: none		Once an act is staged, begin work-throughs followed by stumble-throughs. Leave plenty of time for work-throughs. Work-throughs can take hours and even days. Schedule plenty of time to work each scene.
Availability limitations: Maxwell arrives 7pm		
6pm	Work Scenes, Act One, Scene 7-8: **Gattis, Jones**	
7pm	Work Scenes: Act One, Scene 1-2: **Gattis, Sims, Garrett, Jones**	
8pm	Work Scenes: Act One, Scene Three: **Jones, Maxwell**	
9pm	Work Scenes: Act One, Scenes 4-6: **Gattis, Sims, Garret, Marshall, Jones**	
10pm	Stop	

Saturday, October 11

Conflicts: None		For a stumble-through, schedule time equivalent to 1.5 times the length of expected running time. Once you stumble through the act, you can move on to staging the next act.
12-2	Stumble-through Act One: **Full Cast in Act One**	
2pm	Staging, Act Two, Scenes 1-2: **Marshall, Jones**	
4pm	Staging, Act Two, Scene 3-4: **Gattis, Jones, Johnson, Sims**	
6pm	Stop	

Wednesday, October 15

Conflicts: None		Ask cast to limit conflicts once you are in run-throughs. After first run-through of the whole show, start listing TBA calls that allow flexibility to focus on what needs work. All actors TBA.
6pm	Run-through entire show: **Full company**	
9pm	TBA scene work: **TBA actors**	
10pm	Stop	

Friday, October 17

Conflicts: None		After run-through of entire show, schedule slow work-through over two nights or one long day, then run the show. Alternate work-throughs with run-throughs. If actors are not in early scenes, call them when they will be expected to start working.
6pm	Slow work through Act One: **Gattis, Sims, Garrett, Jones**	
8pm	Add: **Maxwell**	
8:30	Add: **Marshall**	
10pm	Stop	

Saturday, October 18

Conflicts: None		Crew view is usually the week before tech. In this rehearsal, the first part of a long day is
12-3	Slow work through Act Two: **All actors in Act Two**	
2:30	Break	

3pm	Crew View - - Run Entire show: **Full Cast, Designers & crew**	working act two, followed by the full run viewed by the designers and crew. Make sure to give adequate break time for actors to relax and prepare.
5pm	Notes	
6pm	Stop	

Sunday, October 19

Day off for actors	Note days off. If there is potential involvement for actors, like volunteering to help with load-in, note on schedule.
Set Load-in, Actors welcome to come and help!	

Tuesday, October 21

Conflicts: Maxwell unable to attend		First day on set is the spacing rehearsal. Allow plenty of time. Occurs only when set basics are ready on stage. Insist everyone be there.
5pm	Spacing rehearsal onstage: **full company except Maxwell**	
11pm	Stop	

Wednesday, October 22

5pm	Tech: **Full company (bring a book, no white or bright colors)**	Tech rehearsal has no specific calls. Call everyone and prepare them to sit around a lot. Leave plenty of time. Warn against wearing bright colors for lighting.
11pm	Stop	

Friday, October 24

5pm	Actor TBA call for scene work	Once in dress rehearsals, the tech crew will need onstage time for touch-up work. Use this time for scene brush-ups before rehearsal begins. Note the "call for first dress" is the time the actors are expected to arrive and get into make-up and costume.
6pm	Call for First dress	
8pm	First dress, then notes as needed	
12am	Stop	

Saturday, October 25

10am	Call for final dress	Depending on the day of the week, afternoon runs can be called on opening night day. Leave plenty of break time before evening call. Always note opening night call and curtain time.
12pm	Final dress then notes	
4pm	stop	
7pm	Call for Opening Night	
8pm	Opening night	

List of Performance Dates

Sunday, October 25, 3pm	List all performances at the end of the schedule with dates and times. Note strike as well.
Wednesday, October 28, 8pm	
Thursday, October 29, 8pm	
Friday, October 30, 8pm	
Saturday, October 31, 2pm & 8pm	
Sunday, November 1, 3pm and Strike afterwards	

Rehearsal Schedule

Sample Schedule: Equity summer stock

Tuesday, June 30			
10am		Company meeting and designer presentation	Full company
10:30	Music	Interns *Ed Sullivan, Healthy Normal American Boy, Penn Station to Sweet Apple, Kids reprise, One Last Kiss* Then *Telephone Hour, Lot of Livin',* Then Teen girls *We Love You Conrad*	Full company
1pm	Lunch		
2pm	Music	*Lovely to Be a Woman*	Kim
2:30	Music	*One Boy*	Kim, 2 girls, Rosie
3pm	Music	*Telephone Hour music and staging*	Teens
5:30	Music	*Spanish Rose, English Teacher and reprise*	Rosie
6:30pm	Stop		

Wednesday, July 1			
10am	Music	*Lovely to Be a Woman*	Kim
10:45	Staging	Act One, Scene 3	Macafees, Ursula
11:30	Staging	Act One, Scene 7	Macafee family, all women teens and adults
12:30	Staging	*One Boy*	Kim, Ursula, Deborah Sue, Hugo
1:15pm	Lunch		

Figure A3.3

A guide to the creation of a rehearsal schedule using a grid. The guide illustrates major components of the schedule and how to organize.

Appendix 4
Master Schedule of
Director's Deadlines

Action	Date	Action	Date
Select play		Finalize designs	
Apply for license		Begin to advertise	
Create budget		Hold rehearsals	
Read play		Build set and create props	
Analyze play		Build costumes	
Develop concept		Present show to crew	
Recruit production team		Prepare stage	
Begin design meetings		Spacing rehearsals	
Create casting notice		Technical rehearsals	
Hold auditions and cast		Final dress	
Give out scripts		Opening night	
Schedule rehearsals			

Figure A4.1
A master schedule of director's deadlines.

Appendix 5
Contracts

Equity Contracts

The production manager of the company will usually handle contracting. Equity has specific guidelines and procedures to follow and issues their own contracts to the producer. There are set rates of pay that have been negotiated between Actor's Equity and each company based on general Equity guidelines, and the actor will probably be aware of those rates before auditions. Equity sets minimum weekly salaries and each company must pay at least that minimum amount, but can offer more. Negotiations can go back and forth, especially if an agent is involved. Pre-stipulated contractual agreements detailing housing, per diem, company car, transportation, rehearsal and performance schedules must be adhered to and add to the cost of each performer.

Once an actor signs, they have the option of giving two weeks' notice should they decide to withdraw from the production. The company has the same two-week out clause. Always have a backup plan in case you lose a performer.

There are a wide variety of contracts available with equity. Here are a few;

LORT Contract: League of Resident Theatres generally refers to larger regional theatres with one or more theatre spaces. LORT Theatres are ranked by tiers, LORT 1 being the largest and LORT 4 being at the bottom of the ranking. LORT houses can have agreements that allow them to mix equity and non-equity actors in their casts, but stipulate numbers based on a formula.

SPT Contract: Small Professional Theatre contract. This kind of contract covers smaller regional companies and has as many variations as there are theatre companies. Each company negotiates its own special contract with equity based on their financial ability.

CORST and COST: The Council of Resident Stock Theatres and the Council of Stock Theatres governs summer stock companies.

TYA Contract: Theatre for Young Audiences contract that covers all equity children's resident and touring children's theatre companies.

Dinner Theatre Contract: Contract that covers equity members working in Equity dinner theatre companies.

Guest Artist Contract: Reserved solely for university and not-for-profit, non-equity, and community theatres, this allows these companies to hire one or two equity members as guest artists for a particular show. The guest artist contract stipulates a minimum salary and benefit schedule. Companies cannot hire guest artists on a regular basis. If they do so, equity will pressure them to negotiate a full contract.

There are also special contracts negotiated with individual producers such as Disney or for geographic areas such as the CAT: Chicago Area Theatres.

A full listing of equity rulebooks can be found at: http://www.actorsequity.org/library/library.asp?cat=3

Non-Equity Contracting

Because there are no rules aside from general contract law that applies to contracts between non-Equity companies and non-Equity performers, these contracts can be all over the map. As an employer, you want to make sure your contract includes the following:

- Terms of employment, including base rate of pay for rehearsals and performances
- Dates of employment and date of arrival
- Travel stipulations: who will pay, who will book, penalties for non-appearance
- Number of performances per week and any extra pay for extra performances
- Length of rehearsal process and daily rehearsal hours
- Days off
- Comps provided
- Extra duties assigned, such as load-in, strike, and shop duties
- Role assigned for the production
- In-town transportation issues; such as "No company car will be provided. Local transportation is the responsibility of the actor."
- Per Diem rate, if any
- Meals provided, if any
- Housing provided—where, shared, or single—and what the actor must provide, such as towels and bed linens
- Penalty for breaking contract
- Out clause if actor decides to quit during the run or before the contract begins, including required time of notice
- Anything the actor must provide, such as shoes
- Notice of where and how legal issues will be disputed
- Release of liability (check with insurance company)
- Anything else that you want in writing.

Have a lawyer review your contracts. These are legal binding documents and should be taken very seriously.

Community Theatre and College Productions

A contract isn't normally signed for these venues, however, you might want to create a letter of agreement stipulating expectations, comp policy, etc.

Figure A5.1
A sample
non-Equity
contract

Non-Equity Contract

Company logo or name	**Agreement for Services of Independent Contractor**
	This letter of agreement made June 21, 2012 on and between **The Unidentified Theatre, Inc.**, 1025 Access Blvd., Some City, FL 34000 and PERFORMER is for services as a cast member for **The Unidentified Theatre** in exchange for the below stated compensation. **The Unidentified Theatre, Inc.** employs actor to render his/her services, and the actor accepts such employment subject to all the provisions below.

Compensation/Benefits
- **The Unidentified Theatre, Inc.** agrees to pay PERFORMER $425 per week for rehearsals and performances of SHOW NAME
- **Performer** will receive $200 flat fee for rehearsals and $35 fee per performance for any children's shows;
- Housing will be offered, double room;
- A travel stipend will be reimbursed to the actor for the costs directly associated with traveling to the theatre, upon presentation of receipts. This stipend will be paid with the final paycheck at the conclusion of the contract period and is limited to $200. If the actor does not complete their contract, travel stipend will be forfeited.

Actor shall report to **The Unidentified Theatre** on (START DATE). Contract period is through (END DATE). Roles offered as follows: ROLE in (Show Name)

Provisions:
Contract is for up to 9 performances per week (week defined as Monday through Sunday). Additional fee of $50 per show for main stage shows, will be paid for 10th show performed between Monday and Sunday. **The Unidentified Theatre** reserves the right to cancel performances. In the case that performances should be cancelled and be reduced to fewer than 5 in one week, the actor will be paid one half of regular weekly salary. Applicable taxes will be withheld from all paychecks; Room and Board are not considered part of the actor's salary.
Actors are responsible for any expenses they accrue regarding phone usage. A phone is supplied in each apartment, but do not allow for long distance usage except through use of a phone card. Any payment not made prior to leaving will be deducted from final paychecks. All schedules will be sent, in advance, to the cast member but are subject to change.
Pay does not increase for weeks when cast member is rehearsing one show and performing another. Pay is per week and includes first weeks of rehearsals.
Actors will receive two complimentary tickets to any preview performance. Requests must be submitted to the Company Manager.
Cast member must supply one pair of character shoes, tap shoes if requested, and regular shoes as required. Any specialty shoes will be provided.
All cast members must supply their own undergarments (Socks, leotards, hose, underwear, t-shirts, etc.) which they are responsible for laundering.
You will be called upon to do public appearances and other promotional events at no extra compensation.
If you plan to leave town during days off, you are required to return no later than noon of a day on which an evening show is scheduled and the evening before any matinee. Missing a performance will be cause for immediate dismissal.
No pets allowed in apartments.

Termination
The Unidentified Theatre, may, with or without cause, terminate this agreement at any time. Actors are required to notify the Production manager one month prior to first day of work if they plan to terminate this contract. If any actor breaks their contract, they will be responsible for costs associated with their replacement.

Miscellaneous
This written contract contains the sole and entire contract between **The Unidentified Theatre** and PERFORMER. The parties acknowledge and agree that neither of them has made any representations inducing the execution and delivery hereof except Such representations as are specifically set forth herein and each of the parties hereto acknowledges that he has relied on his own judgment in entering into same. Should **The Unidentified Theatre** cease operations for any reason, this contract becomes null and void, and employee will not be compensated for any performances not played. This contract represents the final agreement between **The Unidentified Theatre** and employee and supersedes any verbal or written agreements made prior to signing this contract.

Legal Fees
In the event of any litigation between **The Unidentified Theatre** and PERFORMER concerning the parties' rights under this contract, the prevailing party shall be entitled to recover its expenses of litigation, Attorney's fees, and costs. It is further agreed that no waiver or modification of this contract shall be valid unless agreed to by both parties, in writing, agreed to and signed by both parties. Any disputes of the contract will be handled in the Florida State judicial system.

Glossary

action point A single element of action that advances the plot to the next action point

adjustment A change in choice or tactic. For example, if the actor does a monologue with one strong choice, give them a different choice and see if they can adjust.

antagonist The character or thing that gets in the protagonist's way, and creates the central conflict of the play

atmospheres A palpable, pervasive tone or mood that is external in nature, and thus felt and seen by the audience, albeit influential on the internal life of the characters

backstory Anything referred to in the play about events that occurred in the characters' past

blocking The choreography of the play established by the director and actors

breakeven number The percentage of the gross potential revenue needed to cover expenses

business Activities performed by actors using props

button The "final moment" of a song; it is the final picture and the musical finish

cheat out Looking outward towards the audience in a proscenium setting, even when it feels slightly unnatural to do so

climax The moment when the conflict in the play reaches its highest intensity

coaching When the director or musical director works with an actor specifically on interpretation of music, not vocal technique

cold reading A reading from the script furnished to the auditioning actor by the director, to read either alone or with another actor

concept statement A description of how the focus statement will be realized in terms of both the play as a whole and each character

concept A plan or intention; an idea or mental picture of a group or class of objects formed by combining all their aspects

cross To move from one area of the stage to another

DPN Abbreviation for Director's Production Notebook: primary reference book that includes the director's notes, analysis, rehearsal schedule, blocking, and cast contact information. Accompanies the director throughout the entire production process

dressers Backstage personnel that assist the actors in their costume changes and organize the costumes throughout the show

dropping action A rapid and sudden change in intensity from high to low in the action of a play

dynamic The nature of the relationship between two or more characters expressed physically by their placement or dramatically by their relationship

exposition Dialogue that reveals backstory, spoken by characters or indicated in the playwright's notes

external actions The blocking, movement, and location of characters on the stage. Stanislavski referred to this as "First Plan."

falling action The moment when the conflict in the play is resolved, and what occurs after

fabric swatch Sample of the fabric that will be used in the costume

focus statement A sentence describing what the director wishes to emphasize in the production

French scenes A section of dialogue that begins with an entrance or exit of a character and ends with the next entrance or exit

giving line readings When the director demonstrates how a line should be spoken by acting it out

holding (for laughs) When an actor pauses the action while the audience reacts with laughter to **something funny**

inciting incident The event that sparks the rest of the action in the play

inspirational research Research that is abstract in nature whose purpose is to stimulate ideas in the director's imagination

internal actions What happens in the character's mental, spiritual and emotional life

interpreting Making musical decisions about tempo and style dynamics based on discussions with the director, and then communicating those decisions to the performers in coaching sessions

minimalist Simple, low budget, minimal set and prop elements, enhanced use of lighting

monologue A reading selected and prepared by the actor to be read at an audition

multimedia Characterized by the use of a variety of media

naturalistic Imitating real life in a way that heightens the sense of realism

organic Truthful, believable, and coming naturally from the given circumstances of the moment and relationship between the actors. If something is organic, it feels human and honest.

pre-set The status of the stage before the curtain goes up; includes where the dressers place costumes and the stage manager places props and furniture

production manager The primary manager of all things related to the running of the production; takes over the production when the director leaves; responsible for maintaining the integrity of the production; in smaller houses, the stage manager handles this responsibility.

prompt book The script with all lighting, set, fly, sound and change cues notated to be used by the stage manager who calls those cues during the show

properties artisans Designers or craftspeople who create the set

protagonist The main character who drives the plot

public domain Plays are protected by copyrights, which have a legal life of 50–100 years. Once that time has elapsed, the rights pass into the public domain, allowing anyone to produce the works without paying a royalty.

public performance A play is considered public when it is performed "at a place open to the public or at any place where a substantial number of persons outside of a normal circle of a family and its social acquaintances is gathered."

realistic Creating a real, lifelike feel

recitative A musical declamation of the kind usual in the narrative and dialogue parts of opera and oratorio, sung in the rhythm of ordinary speech with many words on the same note or in a pattern of notes not dependent on interesting melody

representational visual images Pictures used to reflect specific visual information about a period, character or setting; used by the designers and directors to facilitate communication of ideas

run sheets Created by the Production Stage Manager, they are lists of every cue in the show and who executes them.

score All of the music written by the composer and lyricist for the production

sides Cuttings from the play of two- to three-person scenes

sightlines The view each audience member has of the stage

sitzprobe A rehearsal at which actors sit in chairs and sing through the score with the orchestra

spacing rehearsal The first actor rehearsal on stage where the director and choreographer adjust all the staging created in the rehearsal hall to the actual set onstage

special Lighting positions used specifically to illuminate one place on the stage in a unique way

speed-through A spoken run of the text by the group done as quickly as possible. The purpose of a speed-through is to solidify line memorization. It can be done sitting around the green room or in a corner somewhere. The rapid pace is the key.

splashy Very over-the-top, colorful, and exuberant, like a Las Vegas show

stage picture The totality of what the audience sees from their seats. Ideal stage pictures are unified, artistic and reflective of the inner life of the play in every moment.

style A theme running throughout the use of props, lighting, and set design; the behavior of the actors based on specific behaviors associated with a particular period

substitution An acting technique, developed by Stanislavsky, in which an actor uses a memory of something in their life to help them find the emotional truth of a moment onstage

tech rehearsal Onstage rehearsals where all technical elements of the production are added and rehearsed

technical director (TD) The manager of all things technical

theme An idea that recurs in or pervades a work of art or literature

through line The core elements of the story being told

underscoring Music played under the dialogue in a scene to provide emotional texture to the scene

unit set A stationery set that can accommodate many different settings; different scenes are created by lighting, moving furniture, or playing in different areas

upstaging When the positioning of one actor forces another actor to turn upstage in order to engage in conversation

vision The ability to think about or plan the future with imagination or wisdom

wanderprobe Rehearsal where the actors move through their staging as they rehearse with the orchestra. This approach can be useful in determining where there are sightline issues and to ensure the actors can hear the orchestra and vice versa.